THE **VOICE** OF THE **MARTYRS**

extreme devotion

VOM
BOOKS

Original edition produced with the assistance of The Livingstone Corporation. Project staff includes Mary Ann Lackland, Dave Veerman, Paige Drygas, Ashley Taylor, Greg Longbons, Katie Gieser, Carol Ochs, Jill Swanson, Rosalie Krusemark. Design by Mark Wainwright.

Cover design by Genesis Group

ISBN 978-0-88264-214-7

Printed in the United States of America

To those who chose death over denial,
who chose faith over fear, and
who chose to be a witness rather than walk away.

For all those of whom this world was not worthy.

HEBREWS 11:38

Introduction

The believers mentioned in this book are not victims; they are victors. Their stories stretch across history, from Jesus' own disciples to modern-day martyrs. The persecutors are of all stripes, from Romans to Romanians, mobsters to Muslims, and Confucians to Communists. But each of these believers is an example to us, an example of extreme devotion to Christ. The believers whose stories you will find inside these pages found a desire even deeper than the basic human will for self-preservation: the desire to serve Christ and be His witnesses.

* * * * *

When we set out to compile this book, we were entering a new era in America. The events of September 11, 2001, changed the face of the free world and hurled us all into a time of questioning—a time when many looked to the church for answers—a time when the church looked to God and His sovereignty for strength.

It is our ultimate goal that this book be used to expand our thinking and influence our actions when we ourselves face tremendous difficulties. For example, how do we respond to those who do evil to us? How did Christ respond? How did Christians in the past respond? What should our attitude be toward people of other faiths if they violently oppose us? Is it right to risk everything to share God's love with those who may kill us for doing so?

This book will not answer all these questions, but it is guaranteed to challenge your faith. As you read these stories of Christians who have suffered unspeakable atrocities for the cause of Christ, look beyond the tragedy and the hardships to discover the jewels that lie just beneath the surface.

Focus on the faith contained in the testimonies of these courageous brothers and sisters. Recognize that the same Spirit who dwells, or dwelt, in them also dwells in you, and *believe* that you have that same measure of faith available to you in any extreme circumstance.

As you read through these accounts you will also gain a true appreciation of a radical side of faith by gaining an understanding of the theology of suffering.

The first part in understanding this theology is in realizing that these stories are *not* hopeless accounts of torment. Nor are these believers "super" Christians. Certainly they are outstanding in their courage, tenacious beyond human reason, and devoted to Christ in a way that is sometimes difficult to understand. But in reality they are ordinary Christians (like us) who face extraordinary situations.

So what seemingly mysterious ingredient drives them to such "extreme devotion"?

Simply stated, their faith in Jesus as Lord, which resulted in their suffering.

Faith alone is enough. Suffering by human hands can be unbearable. But when combined for the kingdom of Christ with faith, suffering strengthens the heart of the Christian who is open and willing to lose himself in order to gain more of Christ.

The martyrs in this book all share a common passion for God. It is this passion that prevailed over their fears of the severe consequences of being caught sharing God's love with others.

Perhaps part of their passion came from knowing the high price of what they possessed. When faith costs us something, it becomes infinitely more valuable. It is this very aspect of human nature that serves to strengthen Christians who live under repressive governments that don't allow religious freedom.

St. Augustine once stated, "The cause, not the suffering, makes a genuine martyr."

According to the original Greek, the word "martyr" actually means "witness." The martyrs in this book were able to personally testify to the truth and power of Jesus Christ and believed that they should take that witness to others, regardless of the cost.

In his play *Murder in the Cathedral*, T. S. Eliot describes a martyr as one "who has become an *instrument* of God, who has lost his will in the will of God, not lost it but found it, for he has found freedom in *submission* to God. The martyr no longer desires anything for himself, not even the glory of martyrdom."

Being a witness puts you in the line of fire. Pastor E. V. Hill once told the story of a woman who came to him and said, "Pastor Hill, pray for me. The devil has been after me." Pastor Hill told her, "The devil hasn't been after you. You haven't done enough for the devil to be after you." The goal for all Christians should be to "do enough" for Christ's kingdom that we draw the devil's attention.

When some form of suffering does come to you for your Christian witness, our hope is that you, like those in this book, experience the glory and beauty of *Extreme Devotion*.

The *Extreme Devotion* Writing Team
The Voice of the Martyrs

eXtreme question

TURKEY: ERCAN SENGUL

When Ercan Sengul committed his life to Christ in the Muslim nation of Turkey, some saw it as turning his back on his heritage and nation. When he said that he would do anything for God, he had meant it then. But what about now?

Day 1

Ercan sat in a dark, dank prison cell surrounded by cellmates. He had been arrested by local police who said that he'd "insulted Islam" by distributing books for a Christian publisher.

Ercan cried out to God, begging to be rescued. He knew that he'd done nothing wrong and didn't deserve to be there. "You said you'd do anything for Me," God whispered to Ercan's heart. "Did you mean it?"

Broken before God, Ercan wept and worshiped. He told God in his heart, *I really meant it.* Ercan began to preach three hours each day in prison. He learned that God allowed him to be imprisoned to give him a new mission field! Ercan was in prison for thirty days until witnesses admitted that police had pressured them to sign statements, and the judge found no evidence of any crime.

The arrest has furthered Ercan's witness. Since his release, many who shared his cell have visited his church, asking about the God who gave him peace while locked in prison. Ercan still joyfully gives out Christian books, knowing he could be arrested again.

Pray also for me, that whenever I open my mouth, words may be given me so that I will fearlessly make known the mystery of the gospel, for which I am an ambassador in chains.

Ephesians 6:19,20

Most Christians would admit that suffering is not exactly what we have in mind when we say we want to be used by God. Sure, we want to live out our faith—but not to the point of persecution. We resent being overlooked for promotions at work or excluded from social events. We feel slighted. Cheated. Ripped off. However, we must be willing to prayerfully seek God in the midst of our desperation. The moment we do, we find prayer changes our perspective. We begin to see opportunities for growth. We receive hope. We find promise amid pain. Eventually we begin to discover our current situation, however unfair and undeserved, may be part of God's plan after all. When we pray for God's perspective on persecution, we find the courage to be obedient at all costs.

eXtreme unity

MAURITANIA: TIMOTHY

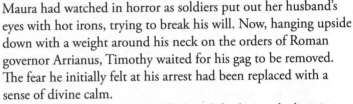

"Tell him, Timothy, please!" shouted Maura, pleading with her husband. "Tell the governor where the Scriptures are hidden and be free! I cannot bear to watch any more of this." Timothy and Maura, residents of the Roman province of Mauritania, had been married only a few short weeks before their arrest.

Day 2

Maura had watched in horror as soldiers put out her husband's eyes with hot irons, trying to break his will. Now, hanging upside down with a weight around his neck on the orders of Roman governor Arrianus, Timothy waited for his gag to be removed. The fear he initially felt at his arrest had been replaced with a sense of divine calm.

My purpose is that they may be encouraged in heart and united in love.

Colossians 2:2

Instead of renouncing his faith and disclosing the location of his church's copies of the Scriptures, as the soldiers expected, Timothy scolded his young wife. "Do not let your love for me come before your love for Christ," he urged Maura, affirming his willingness and determination to die for his Savior. Seeing her husband's courage, Maura's own resolve was strengthened.

Arrianus, already in a rage at Timothy's refusal, set out to break Maura's newfound courage. He sentenced her to the harshest tortures of the Roman world. Yet she would not break. She refused to deny Christ.

After each had endured unspeakable suffering, Timothy and Maura were crucified, side by side.

Jesus did not entrust His ministry to independent believers; He established a spiritual family. He used words like "brother" and "sister" to convey that He did not expect His disciples to be in this alone. Paul continued Christ's mission by instructing new believers to gather together for fellowship and corporate worship. Christians need each other—especially in times of trial. When one believer falters, fellow believers rally in support and encouragement. This is why the New Testament regards living by example as a duty of the Christian faith. One person's example of faith and courage can inspire and unite others to follow suit. Conversely, when one believer cracks under the pressure of persecution, it is easier for others to give in as well. History holds high the camaraderie of Christian community—especially during persecution.

eXtreme readiness

CHINA: PASTOR LI DEXIAN

Just as Pastor Li Dexian began his sermon, the doors of the house church burst open. Armed officers of the Chinese Public Security Bureau poured into the room, threatening everyone present and grabbing Li to arrest him.

Day 3

Dear friends, do not be surprised at the painful trial you are suffering, as though something strange were happening to you.

1 Peter 4:12

"Wait, please allow me to grab my bag." As always, the pastor's tone with the officers was polite yet firm.

The officers were surprised at the request. "What's in there?" they demanded, grabbing the black zippered bag Li held and ripping it open.

The bag contained a blanket and a spare change of clothes, Li told them, because he had been expecting to be arrested that day.

Pastor Li had been arrested many times. Twice police had beaten him to the point that he vomited blood, and one time Li's face was beaten with his own Bible. Li was warned that police were watching the village where he held his Tuesday meetings. He knew if he showed up to preach, he would be imprisoned. Today, Chinese citizens can be sent to labor camps for up to three years without a formal trial.

The risks were great, but Li's bag was packed. More than having a bag packed, though, he had his mind and heart prepared. He was willing to pay any cost to preach the gospel. He was convinced God would care for him—even in prison.

Readiness is a sign of commitment. Commitment that is unprepared to sacrifice is merely compromise in disguise. For example, consider the marriage commitment. It costs one's selfishness and deals a heavy blow to one's sense of independence. However, the result is a stronger marriage. Relationships that are not ready to sacrifice for the sake of commitment do not last. Compromise takes a steady toll and weakens our desire and ability to be committed. In the same way, the believer's commitment to Christ must exact a price in order to maintain its value. We must prepare for the test of our commitment by daily affirming that Christianity is worth it. It's worth spending our time in daily prayer. It's worth gathering for worship at church. It's worth enduring hardship and trial, abuse, and even arrest for the privilege of maintaining our commitment without compromise.

eXtreme light

"I lost all my friends at school. Now that I've begun to 'walk my talk,' they make fun of me." Rachel's journal entries showed her disappointment that the very people to whom she wanted to show Christ's love turned away from her. But she wouldn't give in.

Day 4

In the same way, let your light shine before men, that they may see your good deeds and praise your Father in heaven.

Matthew 5:16

"I am not going to apologize for speaking the name of Jesus. I will take it. If my friends have to become my enemies for me to be with my best friend, Jesus, then that's fine with me. I always knew being a Christian means having enemies, but I never thought that my 'friends' were going to be those enemies."

Rachel was a student at Columbine High School on the day two students opened fire in the school. One gunman asked her if she still believed in God. She looked him in the eye and said yes, she still believed. He asked her why, but he didn't let her answer before killing her.

Rachel Scott passed her test, and because she did, her light reached beyond her school to around the world. Long before the test came, Rachel expressed her willingness to give her all for Christ. The words from her journal, written exactly one year before her death, tell about her commitment: "I am not going to hide the light that God has put into me. If I have to sacrifice everything, I will."

Faith is the invisible expression of our personal relationship with Christ. The Bible characterizes people's faith as a light—a diffusion of hope that affects everyone around them. Jesus chose this illustration because of light's inability to be restrained. For example, as the average child discovers, reading by flashlight under the covers is hardly effective in terms of disguising late night activity! Light simply shines by its very nature, despite our attempts to restrain it. Likewise, tension arises in believers' lives when they must choose to fully express their faith or attempt to muffle it some way. With the reliability of the daily sunrise, those who have affirmed their decision once and for all find shining their light to be second nature.

There is *Hope!*

"Now the God
of hope
fill you with all joy
and peace
in believing,
that ye may
abound in hope,
through the power
of the Holy Ghost."
—*Romans 15:13 KJV*

PACIFIC GARDEN MISSION
Transforming lives since 1877

Prayer

Makes a Difference!

PRAY for the hungry,
homeless, hurting men,
women, and children
turning to Pacific Garden
Mission for help and hope.

PRAY that hearts will
open to the Good News
of Jesus Christ, and the
power of God's love will
take hold in their lives.

PRAY for those who
have graduated from our
programs, that they would
continue to walk closely
with Christ.

PACIFIC ✝ MISSION
GARDEN
Transforming lives since 1877

PO Box 7436 | Chicago, IL 60680-7436
Tel: 312.492.9410 | www.PGM.org

PGM is a 501(c)(3) non-profit organization entirely
supported by friends of the ministry.

eXtreme prayer

CHINA: SISTER WONG

When the Public Security Bureau officer entered the Chinese prison cell, Sister Wong backed away. This heartless man had arrested and persecuted many Christians, and only days earlier had beaten her as he interrogated her.

Day 5

"Please, Sister Wong, my sister is very ill. She has lost all feeling in her legs. Will you come and pray for her?" Was this the same man who had confiscated hundreds of Bibles and Christian books from her? Now he was asking for prayer? Truly God must have gotten his attention.

Days earlier, as the officer had questioned and abused Sister Wong, he received a phone call that his mother had been hit by a car. When he told his mother what he'd been doing, she told him that his harassment of Christians caused her accident. The officer deemed the warning mere superstition.

The Lord told him, "Go to the house of Judas on Straight Street and ask for a man from Tarsus named Saul, for he is praying."

Acts 9:11

The next day, he resumed questioning Sister Wong but got another message that his brother had been injured in an accident. The brother also blamed the officer's attacks on Christians for the family's misfortune.

But when his sister became ill, he asked Sister Wong for prayer. Sister Wong saw the opportunity she'd been praying for: the chance to witness to her persecutors. God healed the sister, and through Sister Wong's actions, He changed the officer's heart. The officer returned all the Bibles that were confiscated and now supports the church.

Most people are drawn to prayer—especially in times of hurt and pain. Barriers against religion are dismantled piece by piece when someone requests or receives prayer. Rare is the person who will refuse a no-strings-attached offer of prayer. "I'm praying for you" can be the most powerful words a believer speaks to a nonbeliever. Why? Prayer is God's agent of change. It gets results. Sometimes it changes circumstances. Most often it changes those who are touched by prayer. The Bible says that immediately before the conversion of Saul of Tarsus, who persecuted Christians, he was praying. Who knows the role prayer will play in the conversion of the "Sauls" throughout the world who are presently bent on Christianity's destruction?

eXtreme "guilt"

MADAGASCAR: RANAVALONA I

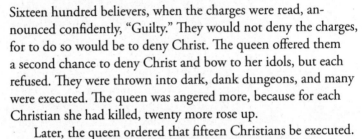

Ranavalona I, the queen of Madagascar, hated the Christians in her kingdom. Her complaints against them were many: they despised her idols, they were constantly praying, they always went to church, and their women were chaste. She sent officers to gather all those suspected of being Christians to bring them to trial.

Day 6

Always be prepared to give an answer to everyone who asks you to give the reason for the hope that you have.

1 Peter 3:15

Sixteen hundred believers, when the charges were read, announced confidently, "Guilty." They would not deny the charges, for to do so would be to deny Christ. The queen offered them a second chance to deny Christ and bow to her idols, but each refused. They were thrown into dark, dank dungeons, and many were executed. The queen was angered more, because for each Christian she had killed, twenty more rose up.

Later, the queen ordered that fifteen Christians be executed. They were to be thrown over a cliff into a rocky ravine 150 feet below. The queen's idols were taken to the top of the cliff, and each Christian was lowered slightly over the edge, tied with ropes.

"Will you worship your Christ or the queen's gods?" the soldiers asked each Christian hanging over the precipice.

Each Christian answered simply, "Christ." The ropes were cut, and they plunged to the rocks. Some sang as they fell to their deaths. One young girl was spared and declared insane. She later founded a large church.

In most countries, defendants are presumed innocent until they are proven guilty. The underlying principle is that there must be a substantial amount of evidence to convict a person of a crime. Expressing one's faith in Christ is often a government offense in many countries where the roles of the justice system are reversed. Believers are guilty until proved otherwise. One would have to reject Christ in order to be innocent in a human, earthly courtroom. However in heaven's courtroom, the guilty verdict is actually a victory. "Extreme guilt" means providing so much evidence of one's faith in Christ that there is no way to be acquitted of the charge! The familiar adage is worth repeating: If you were on trial for being a Christian today, would there be enough evidence to convict you?

Day 7

We have learned that suffering is not the worst thing in the world—disobedience to God is the worst.

A Vietnamese Christian pastor imprisoned for his faith

eXtreme scars

JERUSALEM: THOMAS

He'd heard the rumors. In fact, Thomas had heard it directly from other disciples who had seen the Master alive. At least that's what they had *said*. "When I see His hands and put my fingers into the nail holes, when I put my hand into the hole in His side made by that Roman spear, then I'll believe He is risen," Thomas had said.

Day 8

You, however, know all about my teaching, my way of life, my purpose, faith, patience, love, endurance, persecutions, sufferings—what kinds of things happened to me . . . the persecutions I endured.

2 Timothy 3:10

It wasn't a miracle that Thomas wanted. It wasn't some great sign or wonder. He merely wanted to see the scars on Jesus' body, the symbols of His suffering. Though Jesus had conquered death and lived in a glorified body, He still had scars—reminders of the price He paid for our redemption.

Eight days later Jesus appeared again. How foolish Thomas must have felt when he came face to face with the Master. How silly his grandiose statement must have seemed when the other disciples reminded him of it. However, Jesus did not harshly rebuke Thomas. Looking Thomas in the eye, Jesus offered His hands, encouraging him to touch the scars and to believe.

Christ's scars remained after His resurrection as a reminder of His still-suffering body. For though He conquered death, His body on earth still suffers. And He can identify with those around the world who bear scars because of their faith in Christ.

Scars are our teachers—vivid reminders of painful lessons. They're often ugly to look at and not often pointed out for others to notice. Likewise, the scar of persecution in the church is not often the topic of conversation at many Christian gatherings. We consider it unnerving, a mystery. However, its purpose is to teach us. Persecution plays an important part in God's marvelous plan for the entire world to hear and respond to the gospel. Jesus bore His scars publicly. In fact, He encouraged Thomas to touch them in order to teach him. His scars are our teachers, reminding us of the price that was paid for our salvation. We must continue to learn from, not ignore, the price the persecuted church has paid.

eXtreme choice

ENGLAND: JOHN LAMBERT

Day 9

"Will you choose to live or die? What do you say?"

The questioner was Henry VIII, the king of England, who had unrestrained power in the land. The "criminal" who stood before him, charged with heresy, was John Lambert, a Greek and Latin tutor.

Lambert audaciously challenged his pastor for delivering a sermon that didn't agree with Scripture. Lambert was brought before the archbishop of Canterbury and later before King Henry. Quoting from the Scriptures and explaining the original Greek, Lambert presented his case to an assembly of bishops, lawyers, justices, and peers. The two sides argued strenuously back and forth until Henry, bored with it, presented Lambert with a final choice: "After all the reasons and instructions of these knowledgeable men, are you now satisfied? Will you choose to live or die? What do you say?"

Lambert took a deep breath and answered confidently, "I commend my soul to the hands of God, but my body I give to your clemency."

"You must die," Henry answered scornfully, "for I will not be a patron to heretics." Convicted of heresy, Lambert was burned at the stake. Lambert was unbowed in his slow, torturous death. He lifted up his hands in worship, declaring, "None but Christ! None but Christ!"

> Choose for yourselves this day whom you will serve . . . But as for me and my household, we will serve the LORD.
>
> **Joshua 24:15**

In the modern age of possibilities, our right to choose has grown nearly insatiable. Two hundred television channels are a "basic" right, tantamount to freedom itself. We want options. Variety. Assortment. Even mundane decisions are delivered daily to our doorstep: what to wear, eat, drive, or do. However, our choices are no longer utilitarian—they are virtually limitless. In contrast, when life's greater questions come to us, we have only one answer to give: "None but Christ." Is there another way to heaven? None but Christ—He is the Way. Is there another priority in life that deserves one's full devotion? None but Christ—He is supreme. Can someone else satisfy the longing of the human heart? None but Christ can satisfy. Truth has no alternative, you see. When life's greater questions come, and they will, are you prepared to testify that of all the possibilities, "none but Christ" will satisfy?

eXtreme betrayal

In Communist Romania, churches were closed and pastors arrested as part of a seven-year drive to "eliminate the nations of all superstition."

Day 10

Forgive us our debts, as we also have forgiven our debtors.

Matthew 6:12

So when Brother Vasile and his wife began holding more church meetings in their little home, they knew it would not escape the attention of the government forever. Every evening Vasile prayed, "God, if you know of some prisoner who needs my help, send me back to jail." His wife shuddered while she mumbled a reluctant "amen."

Then they learned that one of the church members' homes had been raided and copies of Vasile's sermons had been confiscated. They also learned that the assistant pastor, their friend and coworker, became an informant and had denounced Vasile.

It was 1:00 a.m. when the police raided the little apartment and placed Vasile under arrest. As they handcuffed him, Vasile said, "I won't leave here peacefully unless you allow me a few minutes to embrace my wife." The police reluctantly agreed. They would have their way soon enough.

The couple held each other, prayed, and sang with such emotion that even the captain was moved. Finally they escorted Vasile out to a police van with his wife tearfully running after them. Vasile turned and called out his last words before disappearing for many years, "Give all my love to our son and the pastor who denounced me."

Extreme betrayal requires extreme forgiveness. If our enemies come against us with such ferocity, should we not be just as generous with our act of forgiveness? When our enemy stoops low enough to denounce us, ought we not reach higher to find the willingness to forgive? Jesus taught us that forgiving evil is for our own good. Deep betrayal can cause us to close our hearts to our own experience of forgiveness. If you find yourself being stingy in the forgiveness department, you will experience a meager sense of release from your own sins. Being betrayed is bad enough. Becoming bitter is a defeat you cannot afford. To whom do you need to offer extravagant forgiveness today?

eXtreme gift

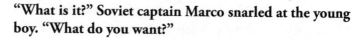

"What is it?" Soviet captain Marco snarled at the young boy. "What do you want?"

The boy, only twelve, swallowed his fear as he stood before the Communist officer. "Captain, you are the man who put my parents in prison. Today is my mother's birthday, and I always buy her a flower for her birthday.

"Since my mother taught me to love my enemies and to reward evil with good, I have brought the flower instead for the mother of your children. Please take it home to your wife tonight, and tell her about my love and the love of Christ."

Captain Marco, who had watched unmoved as Christians had been unmercifully beaten and tortured, was stunned at the act of love of this boy. His tears fell as he slowly walked around the desk and grabbed the boy in a fatherly embrace. Marco's heart was changed by the gift of Christ's love. He could no longer arrest and torture Christians, and soon he himself was arrested.

Only months after the boy's visit to his office, Marco slumped in a filthy prison cell surrounded by some of the same Christians he had previously arrested and tortured. He tearfully told his cellmates of the young boy and the simple gift of a flower. He considered it an honor to share a cell with those he had previously hunted and attacked.

Day 11

But love your enemies, do good to them.

Luke 6:35

Generosity is second nature to the believer. Jesus taught that others would recognize real believers by their demonstration of love. And not just for those who love us in return. Oftentimes, generosity toward strangers and even enemies is the best application of Jesus' teachings. Witnesses to our acts, if not the recipients themselves, are befuddled at the sight. Imagine a wounded Christian worker who prays for the boss who unjustly fired him. Picture the impact of grieving parents who give the gift of forgiveness to a drunk driver. The world doesn't understand generosity. However, it is affected by it all the same. We find we are never more like God Himself as when we give generously to others. God gave His only Son to demonstrate His love for the world and purchase our salvation. What could you give today that might open someone's heart to God's kingdom?

eXtreme difficulties

PAKISTAN: SALEEMA AND RAHEELA

Day 12

I pray that you may be active in sharing your faith, so that you will have a full understanding of every good thing we have in Christ.

Philemon 6

"If you promise to carry your cross, it will be a life full of thorns, mountains, and difficulties," the Pakistani teenager said in a firm voice. Saleema, a Christian who lives in Muslim-dominated Pakistan, shared her faith with a schoolmate, Raheela, who later accepted Christ.

Raheela's incensed family charged Saleema with "converting a Muslim," a charge that can carry the death penalty in Pakistan. Saleema and her pastor were arrested, and her parents were questioned and beaten by police. Saleema was abused while in police custody, but she would not deny her faith. In fact, she softly sang Christian songs in jail, hoping to draw others to Christ.

Raheela fled her home, but her family hunted her down. When they offered her a final chance to recant her faith and return to Mohammed, she refused. For her "crime," her own family executed Raheela.

Saleema went through lengthy court hearings. Raheela's family blamed her for their daughter's death. Eventually the charges were dropped. But Saleema's life will never be the same. She was forced to move to another part of Pakistan for fear of radical Muslims killing her. Yet the thorns, mountains, and difficulties have not dimmed her faith. In fact, she is preparing to serve as a missionary. She says, "No matter how big the mountain, Jesus will help you overcome!"

Missionaries are often mischaracterized as a sort of special forces—a unique troop in God's army of faith which acts on our behalf. The truth is, every believer is called to be a missionary. Some of God's most valuable work may take place around the kitchen table, having coffee in a next-door neighbor's house. The heart of our mission remains the same wherever our mission may take us. We are bound to share the gospel of Christ. For some, sharing their faith with their closest friends would be a personal feat of heroic proportions. For others, sharing their faith in radically different cultures may form their mission field. The location of our mission is not what is important. It is our motivation that counts. To what extreme are you willing to go to share the Good News of Christ?

eXtreme costs

INDIA: PASTOR KANTHESWAR DIGAL

Day 13

Let us, then, go to him outside the camp, bearing the disgrace he bore. For here we do not have an enduring city, but we are looking for the city that is to come.

Hebrews 13:13,14

"I am a strong believer in Christ," Pastor Digal said as he looked at the eighteen men surrounding him. **"You may kill me but I will never become Hindu."**

It was September 20, 2008, and Pastor Digal was traveling by bus back to his home village in Orissa state, India. A month before, hundreds of Hindu extremists—armed with sticks, axes, and knives—swept through multiple Christian villages in Orissa and five other Indian states, burning homes, destroying churches, and beating Christians. More than 100 Christians died during the month-long rampage and nearly 70,000 Orissa Christians, including Digal and his family, were forced from their homes.

Thinking the violence had subsided, Pastor Digal returned home to check on his family's property and livestock. He was nearing his village when eighteen Hindu radicals stopped him. The radicals dragged Pastor Digal off the crowded, dusty bus. They demanded his conversion to Hinduism. When he refused they tied his hands and legs and beat him, ignoring the sickening crunch of bone as his legs shattered. They stripped him of his clothes leaving nothing but a shirt. They burned his face and tortured him in unspeakable ways. Then they dumped his limp body into a creek where it floated for days.

"My father dedicated his life for my village, for people who still did not know Christ," says Rajendra, Pastor Digal's son. "I think for my village, my father also was killed. And by the sacrifice of his own life, they may know Jesus Christ and accept Him as their only Lord and personal Savior."

As Christians we must be willing to pay a price, even if we are never required to do so. This is the lesson of Abraham's life. He was willing to sacrifice Isaac, through whom the blessing was going to come. Being willing to sacrifice for our commitment to Christ makes us stronger. The idea of sacrifice clarifies our goals and solidifies our character. Commitments that cost us something change our family, our neighborhood, and our world for Christ. We learn how strong we really can be. Although we don't wish to lose what we hold dear, we strive to remain undeterred in our devotion, despite any circumstances.

Day 14

Lord, make me an instrument of thy peace.

Where there is hatred, let me sow love;

Where there is injury, pardon;

Where there is doubt, faith;

Where there is despair, hope;

Where there is darkness, light;

Where there is sadness, joy.

O Divine Master, grant that I may not so

Much seek to be consoled, as to console;

To be understood, as to understand;

To be loved, as to love.

For it is in giving that we receive.

It is in pardoning that we are pardoned.

It is in dying that we are born to eternal life.

St. Francis of Assisi

eXtreme smile

SIBERIA: PAULUS

It was getting late, and the Soviet officer had beaten and tortured Paulus for many hours. "We are not going to torture you anymore," he said, grinning cruelly when the Christian looked up. "We will send you instead to Siberia, where the snow never melts. It is a place of great suffering. You and your family will fit in well."

Day 15

Paulus, instead of being depressed, smiled. "The whole earth belongs to my Father, captain. Wherever you send me I will be on my Father's earth."

The captain looked at him sharply. "We will take away all you own."

"You will need a high ladder, captain, for my treasures are stored up in heaven." Paulus still wore a beautiful smile.

"We will put a bullet between your eyes," shouted the captain, now angry.

> Who shall separate us from the love of Christ? Shall trouble or hardship or persecution or famine or nakedness or danger or sword?
>
> **Romans 8:35**

"If you take away my life in this world, my real life of joy and beauty will begin," answered Paulus. "I am not afraid of being killed."

The captain grabbed Paulus by his tattered prison shirt and screamed into his face, "We will not kill you! We will keep you locked alone in a cell and allow no one to come see you!"

"You cannot do that, captain," said Paulus, still smiling. "I have a Friend who can pass through locked doors and iron bars. No one can separate me from the love of Christ."

Despite an uncertain future, we can be sure of one thing: Christ will face it with us. Whether we are going through a private trial or a public grieving, we are never alone. In contrast, every human companion will fail us at some point. There will be places in life's journey where they cannot walk with us—the water will be too deep and their understanding would be murky at best. Only Jesus has the ability to pass through the "iron bars" on our suffering hearts and share these difficult times. Although, in His wisdom, He may not choose to deliver us from our circumstances, His sure presence will see us through them. Smile, knowing you have a Friend from whom you can never be separated.

eXtreme sacrifice

They huddled inside the room while hearing the screams of fellow Christians being butchered outside. Pastor Hendrick Pattiwael and his wife were helping to lead the Indonesian youth camp, and they felt responsible for the young people in their care.

Day 16

The camp had been a joyous time of spiritual growth and worship. Then they were attacked.

When the radical Muslim mob surrounded the building where they hid, Pastor Pattiwael went outside. Distracting the bloodthirsty mob's attention away from his wife and the young people, the pastor was attacked while the others escaped.

"Jesus, help me," were his final words.

His wife next saw him lying in a coffin. Ugly wounds crisscrossed his torso and arms. In shock and anger, Mrs. Pattiwael cried out to God. "How could You let this happen? Why didn't You protect my husband?"

Therefore, I urge you, brothers, in view of God's mercy, to offer your bodies as living sacrifices, holy and pleasing to God—this is your spiritual act of worship.

Romans 12:1

But the Holy Spirit reminded her of her husband's words only days before the attack. "If you love Jesus, but you love me or your family more, you are unworthy of Christ's kingdom." He told her that he was ready to die for Christ's kingdom.

Remembering those words, she refused to become bitter. She still works with her church in Indonesia. The advice that she would give Christians in free nations is simply this: "Seek God more earnestly, so that you can stand in the midst of more trouble."

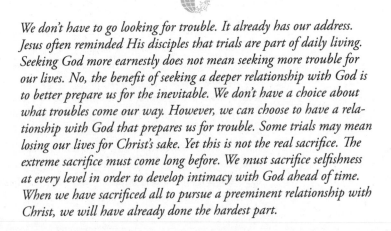

We don't have to go looking for trouble. It already has our address. Jesus often reminded His disciples that trials are part of daily living. Seeking God more earnestly does not mean seeking more trouble for our lives. No, the benefit of seeking a deeper relationship with God is to better prepare us for the inevitable. We don't have a choice about what troubles come our way. However, we can choose to have a relationship with God that prepares us for trouble. Some trials may mean losing our lives for Christ's sake. Yet this is not the real sacrifice. The extreme sacrifice must come long before. We must sacrifice selfishness at every level in order to develop intimacy with God ahead of time. When we have sacrificed all to pursue a preeminent relationship with Christ, we will have already done the hardest part.

eXtreme pain

"Say it with us," the soldiers screamed, kicking and punching the boys' faces and abdomens. "Allah is God, and Mohammed is his prophet. Say it!"

Day 17

However, if you suffer as a Christian, do not be ashamed, but praise God that you bear that name.

1 Peter 4:16

The four young Sudanese boys cried and screamed out for their mothers but they refused to repeat the words that would mean saving their lives yet renouncing their Christianity. Their red blood began to flow across their black skin, but they would not give up their faith in Christ.

The older teenage boys looked on in horror. They had seen their Southern Sudanese families murdered by sword-wielding Islamic fighters. Now they watched as their four young friends and relatives—the youngest only five years old—were beaten to death.

Already the soldiers had forced each older boy to lie over hot coals and ordered them to repeat the Muslim creed and join the Islamic faith. None of the boys would say the words despite the excruciating pain.

There were fourteen boys and thirteen girls abducted in the raid that day. The girls have never been located and were likely sold as slaves or concubines in Northern Sudan. All the boys were tortured, but none relented.

The next night the older boys escaped, still bearing the scars of the previous nights. Not one renounced his faith.

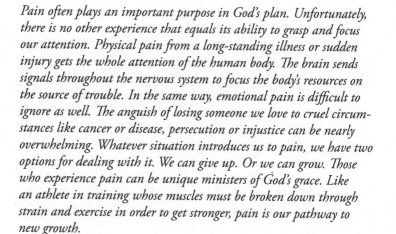

Pain often plays an important purpose in God's plan. Unfortunately, there is no other experience that equals its ability to grasp and focus our attention. Physical pain from a long-standing illness or sudden injury gets the whole attention of the human body. The brain sends signals throughout the nervous system to focus the body's resources on the source of trouble. In the same way, emotional pain is difficult to ignore as well. The anguish of losing someone we love to cruel circumstances like cancer or disease, persecution or injustice can be nearly overwhelming. Whatever situation introduces us to pain, we have two options for dealing with it. We can give up. Or we can grow. Those who experience pain can be unique ministers of God's grace. Like an athlete in training whose muscles must be broken down through strain and exercise in order to get stronger, pain is our pathway to new growth.

eXtreme opposition

ROMANIA: RICHARD WURMBRAND

"I admire Communists." The words seemed strange coming from a pastor who had spent fourteen years in Communist prisons, but Richard Wurmbrand was sincere when he said them.

"Many Communists were willing to die to defend their 'Utopia.' They were more committed to their cause than some I met in churches."

Day 18

You have heard that it was said, "Love your neighbor and hate your enemy." But I tell you: Love your enemies and pray for those who persecute you.

Matthew 5:43,44

In every enemy Pastor Wurmbrand saw a potential friend and a potential Christian. By loving his opponents, he not only saw many come to know Christ but also increased his opportunities to witness.

"When they called me a 'dirty Jew' and told everyone not to read my books, people immediately went out to see what this 'dirty Jew' had to say," he chuckled. "I welcome anyone who has offense against me. Others are not always interested in what you have to say. You need to challenge them to the truth before you share your beliefs. To do this you must understand where they are coming from and be able to speak intelligently. But we must also remember to always speak in love."

Pastor Wurmbrand's words were not some high-minded ideal that he didn't exemplify. He and his wife, Sabina, welcomed into their home a Nazi officer who had worked at the very concentration camp where all of Sabina's family had been exterminated. When the officer saw their forgiveness and love for him, he was won into the kingdom.

Jesus taught us that others would recognize our faith by our love—especially when it comes to dealing with the opposition. How we treat our enemies is equally important as how we treat those in our own Christian family. In fact, our response to criticism often makes a greater statement for Christianity than any other example. When believers put this powerful principle of the Christian faith into practice, they distinguish themselves from the rest of the world. The natural reaction to opposition is to refute it or respond in kind. Instead, believers strive to understand their enemies, not undermine them. Opposition, when put into this perspective, is welcomed as an opportunity to exercise faith and obey Christ's commands.

eXtreme voyage

THE *TITANIC:* DR. ROBERT BATEMAN

Day 19

Dr. Robert Bateman gently helped his sister-in-law into the lifeboat. "Don't be nervous, Annie. This will test our faith. I must stay and help the others. If we never meet again on this earth, we will meet again in heaven." Bateman handed his handkerchief to the woman as the boat dropped toward the dark, icy water below. "Put that around your throat, Annie. You'll catch cold."

Dr. Bateman then gathered about fifty men at the stern of the ship and told them to prepare for death. Earlier that day, he had conducted the only religious service on the large ship, a service that ended with his favorite hymn, "Nearer My God to. Thee."

Robert Bateman had founded the Central City Mission in Jacksonville, Florida, a spiritual lighthouse in a city regularly full of drunken sailors. He had been called "the man who distributes more human sunshine than any other in Jacksonville." Bateman went to England to study Christian social work and was returning to the United States to put into practice what he had learned.

However, late on the night of April 14, 1912, Bateman's ship struck an iceberg. Bateman led the men with him on the stern of the ship in the Lord's Prayer. As the band played "Nearer My God to Thee," the great ship *Titanic* slid under the waves.

Many are the plans in a man's heart, but it is the LORD's purpose that prevails.

Proverbs 19:21

It is said that one sure way to make God laugh is to tell Him our plans! When we trust in Christ, we are embarking on the greatest adventure of our lives. In order to make the journey worthwhile, we must surrender ourselves to His command—the "captain of our salvation." He orchestrates our life's journey as he sees fit, navigating through our whims and wants toward greater goals. At times, even the worst of times, His map seems antiquated and we wonder if He has lost His way. Jagged rocks jut out from the murky depths. The moonless night envelops us in its darkness. How tempted we become at that moment to resume control of our life's plans. The voyage is a venture in faith, however, if it is anything at all. God's plans for our lives steer us in directions we might never choose for ourselves. Yet He knows best.

eXtreme step of faith

EGYPT: A CHRISTIAN YOUTH LEADER

Day 20

Now faith is being
sure of what we
hope for and
certain of what
we do not see.

Hebrews 11:1

"Here is the plan," said the young Christian leader to the youth group. "At 8:30 you must begin to distribute the meeting invitations at the university. You must give them all out quickly before the secret police come and ask what you are doing. If you cannot give them to someone, just leave them lying somewhere. God will get them into the right hands."

"You want us to pass out invitations *before* we have permission?" Images of being arrested by the Egyptian police flashed through the minds of the anxious young men and women gathered around their leader.

"Exactly! Look, we have to exercise a little faith. We'll take the first step, and the rest is in God's hands."

In Egypt, Christian gatherings are closely monitored and cannot be held without government approval. Shortly after 8:30, the youth leader called the police to request permission to hold a Christian gathering.

"You must fill out the proper forms, and we will notify you in a month or so."

"I am sorry, sir, but we have already begun giving out invitations for the meeting," the Christian answered anxiously.

"Why did you give invitations before you had approval? You know we must approve such meetings. Well, I guess since invitations have already been given out I will approve the meeting this time."

Putting our faith into action is all about taking the first step on an uncertain journey. As others who have made this journey will tell us, it's not the actual going that is difficult. It is "going without knowing" that is a bit unnerving. There are no maps on a journey of faith. We navigate by the starlight of God's provision. It's an off-road adventure that leads us to places we cannot see from the main highway of life. It took great faith for these believers to send out invitations to a meeting that they weren't sure would be permitted. God honored their step of faith by blessing them with three hundred new converts that night. Are you ready to step out in faith?

Day 21

During the last war we were taught that,
in order to obtain our objective, we had to be
willing to be expendable . . . We know that there
is only one answer when our country demands
that we share in the price of freedom—yet when
the Lord Jesus asks us to pay the price for world
evangelization, we often answer without a word.
We cannot go. We say it costs too much . . .
Missionaries constantly face expendability.

NATE SAINT, A MISSIONARY MARTYRED IN THE
ECUADORIAN JUNGLE IN 1956

eXtreme decree

LAOS: CHRISTIANS

The ominous red seal at the bottom of the page bore the insignia of the district Communist office for that area of Laos. For local Christians, the words were even more ominous.

Day 22

Peter and the other apostles replied: "We must obey God rather than men!"

Acts 5:29

"If any person, any tribe, any family is deceived to believe in other religions, such as Christianity or others, they must return to the religion in which they [formerly] believed," the document stated. "It is forbidden to propagate that religion. On the contrary, those believers will have to move and live in the new areas. If there is any village or family who believes in another religion . . . party committee members must collect the statistics and make a list of those groups of people . . . and send it to the Office of the Front for Construction. We would like to know especially how many believe in Jesus and are Christians in the district." The document, dated July 18, 1996, was signed by the "Standing Committee of the Front for Construction."

More recently Laotian Christians have been forced, often at gunpoint, to sign a document renouncing their conversion to Christianity. For the atheistic government, it seems that any religion is more acceptable than the worship of Jesus Christ. Despite the government's efforts, the church in Laos is growing as Christians continue to boldly share their faith.

When human authority contradicts God's commands, a line is drawn; a choice must be made. Either we will resign to human authority or align ourselves with God's commands and risk the consequences. While peace is our ultimate aim, we cannot reorder our priorities around human demands. For example, the US Supreme Court has declared official prayers to be an illegal activity on school grounds. However, they cannot really take prayer away from students and faculty who wish to exercise communion with their God. Others may decree a similar or worse religious restraint. However, God overrides their authority, as He alone is king over the human heart. We can confidently choose to obey God rather than human authority as an act of our will.

eXtreme smuggler

CHINA: WATCHMAN NEE

Watchman Nee, the Chinese church leader, had only six hours. He must lead the guard in front of his prison cell to Christ so that his letter of encouragement to Christians outside the prison could be delivered.

Day 23

To this end I labor, struggling with all his energy, which so powerfully works in me.

Colossians 1:29

Chairman Mao's government was infuriated by the spread of Christianity in China. In order to stop the spread of this "foreign cult," they had forced out or killed all foreign missionaries and had sent thousands of Chinese church leaders to prison or to "reeducation through labor" camps. But the church still grew.

When the police discovered that Nee's beautiful, powerful letters of encouragement were making their way out of the prison and into the hands of Christians, they doubled the number of guards and never allowed a guard to stand outside Nee's cell more than once. They shortened shifts to six hours, hoping Nee would not have time to convert the guard.

Nee told the guard about the Father's love and willingness to send His own Son to die on the cross so the guard could live forever in heaven. "Communism cannot get you to heaven," he said. "Only the blood of Jesus Christ can do that."

Five hours into the sermon, with tears streaming from his eyes, the guard placed his trust in Christ. Yet another soul was won for the kingdom, and yet another of Watchman Nee's letters would be safely delivered.

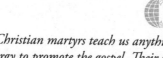

If Christian martyrs teach us anything, it is that we must use creative energy to promote the gospel. Their ingenuity, courage, and even craftiness ought to awaken our own spirit for spreading the Good News. While not everyone has the opportunity to smuggle Scriptures into restricted areas, we can still be willing servants for the kingdom. It might mean deliberately putting ourselves in new, often uncomfortable situations. We can't share Christ if we avoid interacting with unchurched people or hide our faith in their presence. A new method of witness always risks consequences. But we should always be willing to take the risk instead of settling for mediocrity. Which describes your evangelistic life today? Mundane and mediocre? Or creatively energetic for Christ?

eXtreme possessions

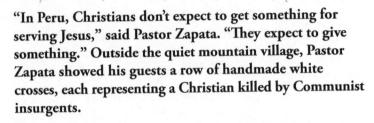

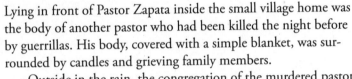

"In Peru, Christians don't expect to get something for serving Jesus," said Pastor Zapata. "They expect to give something." Outside the quiet mountain village, Pastor Zapata showed his guests a row of handmade white crosses, each representing a Christian killed by Communist insurgents.

Day 24

A man's life does not consist in the abundance of his possessions.

Luke 12:15

Lying in front of Pastor Zapata inside the small village home was the body of another pastor who had been killed the night before by guerrillas. His body, covered with a simple blanket, was surrounded by candles and grieving family members.

Outside in the rain, the congregation of the murdered pastor sang praise choruses. Their shoes were covered in mud. Guerrillas had destroyed their church and burned many of their homes. Yet they sang praise.

The Christians were not out of danger, because guerrillas could return at any time. Pastors were often singled out, since they strengthened the whole village to stand against Marxist incursion.

The pastor reminded the listeners that the Bible calls on us to seek God, not the material blessings that come from His hand. "Why do you buy a shirt?" he asked the people. "To use it. Why did Jesus redeem you and buy you with His own blood? To use you for His kingdom."

These impoverished believers were ready for God to use them.

When we are persecuted for our faith, it is easy to get overly focused on our losses. We may mourn former friends who have rejected us for our beliefs. We may miss the business opportunities we used to have. We feel sorry for ourselves when we are left out of social circles. However, there are many others who have lost far more than material possessions or superficial relationships. These stout believers focus on what remains to be given in Christ's service—not on what is already lost. Many of them have lost their churches, homes, jobs, and families to religious persecution. Yet they are willing to give more in sacrifice to the cause of Christ. They recognize their earthly loss is another person's opportunity to gain salvation.

eXtreme "fear"

LAOS: LU

The unwritten code of the police was clear: If you catch the Khmu or other tribesmen converting to Christianity, arrest them. If you catch anyone evangelizing the tribesmen, kill him.

Day 25

The LORD is my light and my salvation—whom shall I fear?

Psalm 27:1

After "Lu" had been shackled at the hands and feet and shamefully marched through the village, the Communist police threw him in a pit. "We will let you go," they said, "when one hundred Christians in your village renounce their conversion to Christianity." But they were unable to find believers willing to turn their backs on Christ.

Then tragedy struck the police. One officer's son broke both legs in an accident. His other son became critically ill. The officer who had beaten and harassed new Christians suddenly died of a heart attack.

Other officials fearfully pulled "Lu" from the pit and allowed him to return home. Government authorities were too frightened to take action against the Christians in the village after seeing what happened to their leader.

Seeing God's show of power, more Khmu became believers. Where there had been one hundred Christians, now there were seven hundred. They even sent Christians out to tell other villages about Jesus. While the Laotian authorities were controlled by their fear, the Christians in Southeast Asia overcame theirs.

Fear is one of the most basic human motivations. It drives stock markets and fuels wars. Its unruly energies can be used for great harm or channeled for great good. Professional boxers are often told fear is their friend. Fear can make them better fighters. It keeps them alert. It sensitizes their determination. In the same way, God can use our fears and make us better fighters for his cause. Whenever we are afraid, we have the potential to do the impossible. Why? That which is impossible in our own strength is made possible with God's help. Fear makes us more likely to forsake our own resources and rely on God instead. In this way, extreme fear can lead to extreme faith.

eXtreme jewelry

The brass shackle is called, in Arabic, a *bacle*. Peter held it out as if it were a sacred object. It was a reminder of his family's past and of Peter's great blessing.

His grandfather had made the bacle, but it was not a craft project. In fact, he was forced to wear it by his Islamic masters. Peter's grandfather had been captured in Southern Sudan and taken to Northern Sudan, where he was bought and sold as a slave.

Peter's grandfather, though harassed and tormented by his Muslim masters, would not join their faith. He held fast to his faith in Christ, and his body bore the scars of his refusal. Because he was not a Muslim, he was seen as nothing more than an animal.

Shortly before he died, Peter's grandfather had the bacle removed and gave it to Peter's father. "Our family will not always be slaves," he said, "but we must never forget."

Later Peter's father gave it to him, and he carried it with him when he escaped from his Muslim owner and fled to freedom. Today, it is no longer a sign of ownership, but a sign of God's overcoming power. It is a symbol of God's hand on a family, working through three generations to bring them to freedom.

"Never forget my people," he urged. "Never stop praying for persecuted Christians in Sudan."

Day 26

Pray continually.

1 Thessalonians 5:17

Forgetfulness is the number one enemy of prayerfulness. We are quick to offer our prayers of support. Unfortunately, our good intentions are rarely good enough to help us carry through on our commitments to pray for those in need. What can remind you to pray for those who are persecuted around the world? Perhaps a small sticker on the face of your watch will remind you. Each time you look at your watch throughout the day can be an opportunity for you to remember a people group who live under religious persecution. Whatever method you choose to be more mindful of the missed opportunities for prayer, follow through on it. Reading stories about extreme believers will not change anything. Praying for extreme believers can change everything —maybe even today.

eXtreme courage

ROMANIA: A YOUNG WOMAN

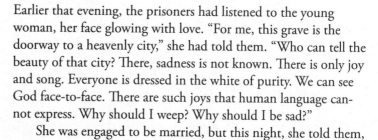

It was almost midnight as the women prisoners heard the Communist guards arrive. They quickly gathered around the condemned, a young woman of twenty who had been sentenced to die for her faith in Christ. They whispered hurried good-byes. There were no tears from the young Romanian woman, no screams for mercy.

Day 27

For to me, to live is Christ and to die is gain.

Philippians 1:21

Earlier that evening, the prisoners had listened to the young woman, her face glowing with love. "For me, this grave is the doorway to a heavenly city," she had told them. "Who can tell the beauty of that city? There, sadness is not known. There is only joy and song. Everyone is dressed in the white of purity. We can see God face-to-face. There are such joys that human language cannot express. Why should I weep? Why should I be sad?"

She was engaged to be married, but this night, she told them, instead of being with her earthly fiancé, she would meet her heavenly bridegroom.

The pitiless guards entered the cell, and the woman stepped toward them, ready to go. As she left the cell, surrounded by guards, she began to recite the Apostles' Creed. Minutes later, with tears streaming down their faces, the remaining prisoners heard shots. The executioners thought they had ended the young woman's life, but they had only sent her to live forever in a much better place.

Courage is the bridge that carries us from a nominal existence on earth to an inexplicable longing for a heavenly future. Those who fully understand the certainty of heaven's existence find it easier to exchange their comparably paltry lives on earth for eternal citizenship in heaven. Courage helps us to let go of all we cling to on earth—all the things that make us long to stay here. It takes courage to believe in a life after death. After all, this life on earth is all we can physically see and touch until the moment we die. We are courageous when we launch out in faith, believing Christ has made it possible for us to cross into eternity with Him. Once we have made that firm decision, we can face life with purpose and death with courage.

Day 28

We are not praying that our borders be opened.
We are praying that heaven be opened.

THE PRAYER OF A CONGREGATION
UNDER PERSECUTION IN VIETNAM

eXtreme missions

Pastor Norbu Promila was pleased with the service as he preached to the tribal people in the mountains of Bhutan. Those gathered seemed especially attentive and open to the Good News. Then in the middle of the sermon, police rushed in through every door, stormed the stage, and forcibly grabbed Norbu.

Day 29

Being confident of this, that he who began a good work in you will carry it on to completion until the day of Christ Jesus.

Philippians 1:6

Pastor Promila was thrown in prison and tortured, and the authorities ordered him to forsake his call to preach the gospel. He received massive head trauma, and when authorities finally let him go, there was permanent injury to his body. He returned home, where his wife and children were shocked at his bruised and bloodied face. Ten days later, he died as a result of his wounds.

Pastor Promila's congregation in this militant Hindu kingdom refused to give up his mission. Shortly after his death, they met together and called for volunteers to continue Norbu's work among the tribal people.

Five hands went up, one of which belonged to his wife. She answered God's call to missions while also caring for her five children. She ministered faithfully, and she and the other workers have seen many tribal people won to Christ. God provided for her needs and her children's. Mrs. Promila held fast to the knowledge that one day she would see her husband again and be rewarded for her faithfulness to Christ.

What we do for the Lord is not just a job—it's a mission. A mission is never about an individual's responsibilities. It is singly focused on Christ and His kingdom. Therefore, someone at the helm of God's work in a particular area may leave, but the mission itself never dies. God's work is never left undone; it goes on forever to its completion. Those who are willing to undergo persecution for their faith teach us about the meaning of mission. They recognize that there are only two things that last for eternity: God's work and human souls. When we are willing to invest our lives in these things, we are involved in a mission with eternal significance.

eXtreme assassin-part one

BANGLADESH: ANDREW

The evangelist, Andrew, stared into the gun, wondering why the man didn't fire. The assassin grew frustrated, then frightened, and finally he fled from the room.

The phone rang, and Andrew found himself talking to the man who had come to kill him minutes earlier.

"The Muslim leaders offered me a big reward to kill you," the would-be assassin explained. "I rode across Bangladesh to come to your office. The reward was mine. I was ready to shoot, but I couldn't move my arm. I couldn't pull the trigger." The evangelist praised the Lord for protection.

Andrew found it somewhat comical. "So what can I do for you now?" he asked.

"Sir, I still can't move my arm, and it's because of you! Can you help me?"

Right on the phone Andrew prayed, and instantly the man regained full use of his arm. Astounded by the miracle, he returned to the evangelist's office and began to ask questions about this Jesus of whom the Muslim leaders seemed to be afraid.

The evangelist patiently explained the Good News of Jesus' love and forgiveness, even offering tea to the man who'd come to kill him. After forty-five minutes, the man surrendered his life to Jesus. The former hit man's ministry now is to destroy the works of the devil. To this day, he is a fellow missionary in Bangladesh.

Day 30

I know that you can do all things; no plan of yours can be thwarted.

Job 42:2

The would-be assassin's murder attempt was a comedy of errors. If it were a movie, the audience would have cheered aloud when the protagonist, Andrew, came onto the scene. Like any good movie hero, Andrew did not just defeat his enemy's plans. He confounded them, even to the point of having tea with the hit-man-turned-convert. This was not going according to plan. The devil constantly has to go back to the drawing board to rethink his plans for our destruction. Andrew was not a victim of his circumstances, and neither are you. If he had been shot, his death also would have been a witness. The same is true of you. Unlike the devil's schemes, God's plans for your life cannot be thwarted.

eXtreme proclamation

Sabina Wurmbrand reached over and pinched her husband's arm. "Richard," she said fiercely, "stand up and wash away this shame from the face of Christ. They are spitting on his face!"

"If I do so," Richard Wurmbrand answered, looking intently at his wife, "you will lose your husband."

Her eyes bore into his. "I don't want a coward for a husband."

They sat in a Romanian national congress on religion shortly after Communist soldiers had stormed their country. The assembled Christian pastors, priests, and ministers of all denominations stood, one by one, and spouted praise to Joseph Stalin and to the new Communist leadership, who had put thousands of Christians in prison.

As Richard stood to speak, many were thrilled to see that this well-known pastor would join their cause. But instead of praising the Communists, he praised Jesus Christ as the only path to salvation. "Our first loyalty," he told the gathering, "should be to God, not to Communist leaders." The gathering was broadcast live across Romania, and thousands across the country heard Richard's challenge.

Realizing the damage Richard was doing, Communist officials rushed the stage. Richard escaped out the back door but was a hunted man from then on. He would later spend fourteen years in prison.

Day 31

I have fully proclaimed the gospel of Christ.

Romans 15:19

Most of us will probably never be challenged to make our stand for Christ in front of an entire nation. But we are all called to make a stand for Him wherever we are each day. It is not the size of the witnessing audience but the sincerity of our stand that matters. Our lives may not depend on what we say. But our jobs may depend on our decision to voice our convictions. It may mean losing a relationship. It may even mean estrangement from our families. In any case, it is far better to endure the consequences of our convictions than to regret their noticeable absence. When and where will you seize the opportunity to take a stand for Christ today?

eXtreme maturity

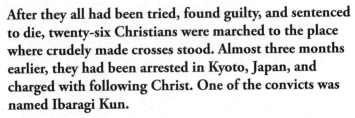

After they all had been tried, found guilty, and sentenced to die, twenty-six Christians were marched to the place where crudely made crosses stood. Almost three months earlier, they had been arrested in Kyoto, Japan, and charged with following Christ. One of the convicts was named Ibaragi Kun.

Day 32

Don't let anyone look down on you because you are young, but set an example for the believers in speech, in life, in love, in faith and in purity.

1 Timothy 4:12

Seeing how young Kun was, an official took him aside and urged him to recant his faith to save his life. Looking the official in the eye, Kun said confidently, "Sir, it would be far better if you yourself became a Christian. Then you could go to heaven with me."

The officer stared, startled by the young man's faith. Finally, Ibaragi asked, "Sir, which cross is mine?"

The bewildered official pointed to the smallest of the twenty-six crosses. Young Kun ran to the cross, knelt before it, and embraced it. When the soldiers began to nail his hands and feet to the cross, he did not cry out in pain. He courageously accepted the path God had laid out for him.

The crucifixion of the twenty-six Christians on November 23, 1596, was the beginning of a period of intense persecution of Christians in Japan. Over the next seventy years, as many as one million Japanese Christians would be killed for their faith. Many would embrace their own crosses to follow the example of Ibaragi Kun, a very mature twelve-year-old boy.

Spiritual maturity is not measured by a birth certificate. Chronological age has little to do with conviction. Rather, spiritual maturity is developed one day at a time. We measure our maturity by how well we daily apply our faith. Contrary to popular belief, spiritual maturity is not how much we know about the Bible. Many people are very familiar with the Bible, yet they remain strangers to spiritual maturity. Obedience to the Bible's commands is the mark of maturity. One question will help us know how well we are growing spiritually. We must ask ourselves each day, "How much more do we look like Jesus today than we did yesterday?" Our answer is a true reflection of our growth.

eXtreme willingness

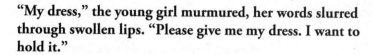

"My dress," the young girl murmured, her words slurred through swollen lips. "Please give me my dress. I want to hold it."

Day 33

For it is God who works in you to will and to act according to his good purpose.

Philippians 2:13

The Christians surrounding the girl's bed were sad. Because of her extensive internal injuries, doctors could do nothing for her. Weeks ago, the believers had bought her a white dress to celebrate her new life and pure heart in Christ Jesus.

Her father had not been pleased with his daughter's decision to follow Christ. One night, in a drunken rage, he attacked his daughter, beating and kicking her. He left her lying in the muddy street to die.

When she did not show up for church, her Christian friends went looking for her. They found the girl unconscious, lying in a heap, her formerly snow white dress now covered in blood and mud. She was brought to a doctor, but her injuries were severe.

Now she was asking for her dress.

"The dress is ruined," her friends told her. They tried to talk her out of it, thinking that seeing the ruined dress would break down the girl's spirit.

With the simple faith of a ten-year-old, she whispered, "Please, I want to show the dress to Jesus. He was willing to bleed for me. I just want Jesus to know that I was willing to bleed for Him."

Shortly afterwards, the young girl died.

God is not interested in our ability. We may be talented. Resourceful. Wealthy. Professional, popular, and punctual. Offering our various abilities in God's service, however, is nothing like offering our availability. Our abilities are about ourselves—we can see ourselves doing this or that for God. In contrast, our availability is about God alone—we can only imagine how God will use us in His service. Being available to God means being willing to obey no matter what the cost. God wants our willingness to serve Him regardless of our specific abilities. How do we become so willing? That, too, is God's gift. He gives us the "want to"—the will or desire to be available to Him.

eXtreme reminder

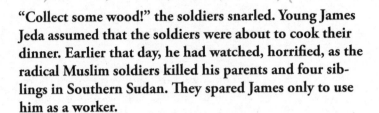

"Collect some wood!" the soldiers snarled. Young James Jeda assumed that the soldiers were about to cook their dinner. Earlier that day, he had watched, horrified, as the radical Muslim soldiers killed his parents and four siblings in Southern Sudan. They spared James only to use him as a worker.

Day 34

I thank my God every time I remember you.

Philippians 1:3

When the fire was well lit, James was surprised and terrified when they suddenly grabbed him. He tried to flee. But the soldiers were too strong, and soon they had tied his hands and feet.

"Good news for you, young one," said a soldier. "We are going to let you live. But you must join us by becoming a Muslim."

"I cannot become a Muslim," James said simply. "I am a Christian."

Infuriated by the young boy's faith, the soldiers picked him up and hurled him into the fire. They packed up their gear and left the area, assuming James would die.

Young James didn't die. He managed to roll out of the fire and find help.

Doctors were able to save James's life, but he will always carry reminders of that day. His body bears skin grafts and scar tissue, and one arm is partially deformed by the burns. In heaven, those scars will be honor bars, a reminder of the day when James Jeda refused to turn his back on Christ.

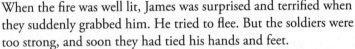

Most people cannot resist souvenirs. One can hardly make it through the gauntlet of gift shops at an airport or train station without succumbing to the temptation to buy a memento of the trip's experience. But what is there to remind us of our most significant life experience —our commitment to Christ? Some will look at their paycheck and remember the promotion they declined because they were not willing to compromise their morals. Others, upon seeing a public school classroom, will recall where they first learned what it was like to be persecuted. Still others will see a gravestone of a believer and be reminded of the meaning of commitment. These "souvenirs" are infinitely significant reminders of the price of faith in Jesus Christ.

Day 35

I had the physical sense of being prayed for. Even when I knew nothing and received no letters, I felt warmth as if sitting near a fire. Sometimes this happened in punishment cells, which are very cold. It was like hearing someone pray for me and think about me. This supported me so much. It is difficult to explain … I felt and knew I was not forgotten. This was sufficient to make me resist the most difficult moments.

IRINA RATUSHINSKAIA, CHRISTIAN POET
IMPRISONED IN THE FORMER SOVIET UNION UNTIL 1987

eXtreme injustice

ROMANIA: PASTOR FLORESCU

Pastor Florescu couldn't bear to watch his son being beaten by the Communist officers. He had already been beaten himself, and he had not slept for two weeks for fear of being attacked by the starving rats the Communists had forced into his prison cell. The Romanian police wanted Florescu to give up other members of his underground church so that they, too, could be captured.

Day 36

He will not falter or be discouraged till he establishes justice on earth.

Isaiah 42:4

Seeing that the beatings and torture weren't working, the Communists brought in Florescu's son Alexander, only fourteen years old, and began to beat the boy. While Florescu watched, they hammered his son's body unmercifully, telling the pastor that they would beat his son to death unless he told them the locations of other believers.

Finally, half mad, Florescu screamed for them to stop. "Alexander, I must say what they want!" he called out to his son. "I can't bear your beatings anymore."

His body bruised, blood running from his nose and mouth, Alexander looked his father in the eye. "Father, don't do me the injustice of having a traitor as a parent. Stand strong! If they kill me, I will die with the word 'Jesus' on my lips."

The boy's courage enraged the Communist guards, and they beat him to death as his father watched. Not only did he hold on to his faith, he helped his father do the same.

Is there no justice in this world? When we read of the horrible atrocities committed against the innocent, we can't help but wonder. We may falter in our faith when we hear about cruel suffering at the hands of evildoers. We may become discouraged when we long for the salve of mercy that seems to tarry. Is there no justice in this world? In answer to our cry, the Bible teaches the principle of "yes and not yet." Yes, some evildoers meet with swift justice here and now. However, God's mighty hand of infinite justice has yet to fall on this earth. That is saved for the end of time. We grow weary waiting, but He is undeterred.

eXtreme perspective

CHINA: SISTER TONG

Day 37

When VOM workers met Sister Tong in China, she had recently been released from prison after serving six months for hosting an unregistered house church meeting in her home. When they asked her to tell them about the prison, they expected to hear about hardship, discomfort, and suffering. "Oh, yes!" Sister Tong replied with a glowing smile. "That was a wonderful time."

We loved you so much that we were delighted to share with you not only the gospel of God but our lives as well.

1 Thessalonians 2:8

The VOM workers quickly looked at the translator, thinking there must have been some confusion in translating their question. After all, they had asked her about a Chinese prison cell, not some vacation spot or revival meeting.

But there was no translation error. Sister Tong had understood the question, and she'd answered it honestly. She thought prison *was* a wonderful time . . . because God had ministered to her heart while she was inside, offering her comfort and peace even in the midst of suffering. In addition, she'd had opportunities to share the gospel with other women in her cell, and several of them had accepted Christ.

Sure, it was hard to be away from her family. But for this Chinese Christian, the presence of Christ and the opportunity to minister in His name made even prison a wonderful time.

Instead of seeing hardship when she was sent to prison, Sister Tong saw opportunities to witness and a chance to experience the closeness of God's presence. We can't always control what happens to us or our circumstances in life. Bad things will happen to us. But even in difficult circumstances, we can be assured of God's presence and we can minister to those around us. Seek His face—especially in tough times—through prayer and reading His Word. And ask Him to open doors that will enable you to share His love with someone else.

eXtreme witnesses

For seven years, the radical Muslim clerics had tried to convince the "infidels" to follow Islam. But the Christians, locked in the brutal darkness of the prison, would not convert.

Day 38

And you will be my witnesses in Jerusalem, and in all Judea and Samaria, and to the ends of the earth.

Acts 1:8

"Mohammed is the greatest prophet," they tried to explain to the Christians. "He lived more recently than Christ and was the final prophet of Allah."

The Christians listened carefully and replied, "In your own legal system, a matter's legitimacy is determined by the number of witnesses. Jesus Christ had witnesses of His coming from Moses to John the Baptist. Mohammed only witnessed to himself."

Confounded, the Imams tried a different attack. "Surely Islam is the religion ordained by God, for our empire is far greater than the lands controlled by Christians," they said with smug smiles.

"If that were true," replied the Christians, "then the idol worship of Egypt, Greece, and Rome would have been true faiths, because at one time their governments had the largest empires. It is obvious that your victory, power, and wealth do not prove the truth of your faith. We know that God sometimes gives victory to Christians and sometimes leaves them in torture and suffering."

In 845, the Muslims near the Middle Eastern city of Ammoria finally gave up on seeing the Christians follow Mohammed. All seven were beheaded, and their bodies were cast into the Euphrates River.

Jesus commanded us to be His witnesses, and we do that by always being prepared to give an answer to everyone who asks us the reason for our hope. You might not have an answer to every nonbeliever's doubts and questions, but if you get to a point in a witnessing opportunity where you don't know the answer, say so. When the formerly blind man was asked questions about Jesus that he didn't have answres for he simply replied, "I don't know. One thing I do know. I was blind but now I see! (John 9:25). Like him, there are things we don't know, but we do know Christ and the change He has made in our lives.

eXtreme conviction

INDONESIA: PETRUS

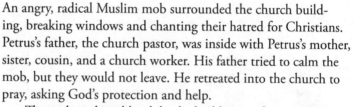

In a recent interview, an Indonesian Christian, Petrus, made this startling statement: "Because we have Jesus, it is not difficult to be a Christian, although there are many oppressions." While his statement seems obvious to many of us, following Christ has required great sacrifice for Petrus.

Day 39

Because our gospel came to you not simply with words, but also with power, with the Holy Spirit and with deep conviction.

1 Thessalonians 1:5

An angry, radical Muslim mob surrounded the church building, breaking windows and chanting their hatred for Christians. Petrus's father, the church pastor, was inside with Petrus's mother, sister, cousin, and a church worker. His father tried to calm the mob, but they would not leave. He retreated into the church to pray, asking God's protection and help.

The mob, seeking blood, lit the building on fire, screaming chants as they waited to attack anybody who came out. Indonesian police were too afraid to take action. The military were not available. It was another church burning in a nation where more than five hundred churches have been burned in the past ten years.

When Petrus arrived at the scene hours later, the church building and parsonage were ashes. The bodies of his loved ones were burned almost beyond recognition.

Later, a government official apologized to Petrus but urged him not to seek revenge. Petrus's desire is not for revenge but love. He wants to see Muslims in his country won to Christ's kingdom.

Persecution is often the final battleground in the fight between natural instinct and spiritual conviction. Instinct is interested in self-preservation. Conviction is above our own interests. Instinct says to take revenge upon our perpetrators. Conviction reminds us of the spiritual needs of those who persecute us. Most of us, after seeing our loved ones murdered for their beliefs, would find it instinctively difficult to share Petrus's convictions. However, the alternative to following Christ was more unbearable for Petrus. How could he not follow Christ? His story proves it is possible for our convictions to overrule our instincts. But this is only when our natural inclinations are reversed by the compelling love of Christ—a victory amid the battleground of persecution.

eXtreme assassin—part two

The Muslim leader was shocked to find Andrew, the Christian evangelist, sitting in his living room with his own family, sharing a meal together!

He was shocked because he had recently offered a large reward to have this Christian killed. Now Andrew was in his home telling his own family members about Jesus. "What's going on here?" he screamed. "What's this man, this infidel, this enemy of Allah doing in *my* home?"

His daughter-in-law began, "I asked him here because he, his Jesus, has healed your son—my husband." Her story continued in a rush of words. "He has been sick for eighteen years, but today this Christian, Andrew, came and prayed for him. He laid his hands on him, and now he is well! Jesus has healed him!"

The man saw his son's excitement as he told how he had felt the sickness leave his body. This was the first time in months that his son had gotten out of bed. For the first time in eighteen years, he felt no pain.

The man's anger was replaced with a sense of relief and happiness. He didn't choose to trust in Christ that day, but he has become an ally to the Christians in that area and has helped many avoid jail and persecution. The man who once put a contract on Andrew's head now welcomes him with open arms.

Day 40

But I, when I am lifted up from the earth, will draw all men to myself.

John 12:32

Christianity is a "see-for-yourself" type of experience. When the Muslim father walked into his home, Andrew was not preaching a three-point sermon on the triune God. He was not berating the man's wife and children for believing in Allah. He was having a meal after praying with the Muslim family. They had an empty sickbed to prove God was real. Likewise, we must remember that God's truths are self-evident. The pressure is not on us, as the messengers, to say and do the right things. We do the right thing whenever we proclaim the gospel to others. Jesus will draw their hearts to Him. We must let the evidence of Christ's reality speak for itself.

eXtreme truth

"Are you not afraid of what we will do to you?" the Communist colonel asked, his tone a combination of mockery and challenge.

Young Pastor Kochanga, having preached only one sermon in his career, stood before the colonel, knowing that the man held the power of life or death over him. He answered in a respectful, yet fervent tone.

Day 41

"Sir, truth is never afraid. Suppose your government would decide to hang all mathematicians. How much would two plus two be then? Two plus two would still be four.

"We have truth, as true as a mathematical equation. We have the truth that there is a God, and He is our loving Father. We have the truth that Jesus is the Savior of the world and wishes to save everyone, even you. We have truth that there is a Holy Spirit who empowers men and gives them light, and we have the truth that there exists a beautiful paradise.

Whoever acknowledges me before men, I will also acknowledge him before my Father in heaven.

Matthew 10:32

"Whatever whips and whatever instruments of torture you have, it will always remain so. Two plus two still equals four."

Kochanga was beaten almost beyond recognition and then was never seen again. Though his battered and bloody face was hard to recognize for the other prisoners, in heaven he was immediately known and welcomed.

"Tell the truth." Children learn this instruction at an early age, yet its wisdom is timeless. If we will return to simply acknowledging what we know to be true, we will always have the words to say when we are called upon to testify for Christ. Many people often feel unqualified to witness for Christ, saying they lack "training." We fear being asked a theological question we don't know how to answer. However, professing Christ doesn't require course credit in apologetics. Simply tell the truth about what you know—just as those who have experienced religious oppression. Testifying about Christ is easier than it seems. We must go back to the principle we learned in childhood. We are commanded to acknowledge Jesus Christ—to tell the truth.

Day 42

It is not until a man finds his faith opposed and attacked that he really begins to think about the implications of that faith. It is not until the church is confronted with some dangerous heresy that she begins to realize the riches and wonder of orthodoxy. It is characteristic of Christianity that it has inexhaustible riches, and that it can always produce new riches to meet any situation.

WILLIAM BARCLAY, *THE DAILY STUDY BIBLE*

eXtreme missionaries

ROMANIA: PASTOR RICHARD WURMBRAND

As the train began to pull out of the station, the Christians standing on the platform unbuttoned their coats and pulled out hundreds of gospel tracts. Quickly they tossed the tracts, handfuls at a time, through the open train windows to the Russian troops inside.

Day 43

Preach the Word; be prepared in season and out of season.

2 Timothy 4:2

The Russian soldiers, some of them no more than sixteen years old, laughed and whistled, especially at the attractive young women throwing things through the window. They grabbed at the tracts, wondering what was being thrown into an army train. When the political officer boarded the car, the soldiers quickly stuffed the tracts in their pockets. Soon enough they would read the strange booklet and find out more about this "King."

Back on the train platform, the Christians gathered, laughing nervously. When police officers took one aside, the believer opened his coat willingly because there was nothing inside. All the tracts he had brought to the Romanian train station were now on the train, headed to the heart of Communist Russia.

The train-car evangelism was just one of the methods that Richard Wurmbrand taught the youth of his church to reach Russians for Christ. These "allies" were stealing all of his country's wealth and murdering many of its people, yet Richard welcomed the soldiers. In each soldier he saw a mission field and sought a chance to harvest a soul.

A mission is not so much a place as it is an attitude—one's approach toward life. A missionary is simply someone who embodies this determination and single focus and expresses it in everyday living. Richard Wurmbrand was a man on mission, and his fervor spread through the ranks of young people who recognized his purposefulness. In that sense, we are all missionaries—ambassadors for Christ—wherever we are serving. Being on mission means you are always on the alert for new opportunities to further God's kingdom. At the watercoolers at work. At the grocery store. On the commuter train or bus. At school. The everyday world is your mission field when you are determined to further God's kingdom.

eXtreme legacy

INDONESIA: STENLEY

When Stenley got off the boat on the remote Indonesian island, he *felt* the spiritual darkness. The people practiced a combination of witchcraft and Islam. Stenley was fresh out of Bible school and ready for the work to which God had called him, reaching these island people for Christ.

Day 44

You are the light of the world. A city on a hill cannot be hidden.

Matthew 5:14

Stenley preached boldly, calling people to turn to Christ and then burn their idols and the relics of their old life. One Muslim burned his idol, but inside it was a scroll from the Koran. When radical Muslims heard of the burning of the Koran, they reported Stenley to area officials. Stenley was immediately arrested.

Although Stenley was horribly beaten and lay comatose, his mentor from Bible school, Pastor Siwi, came to see him and witnessed tears streaming from his eyes. Soon after, Stenley died from his injuries.

But even death could not end Stenley's ministry. When his story was told in his home village, eleven Muslims trusted in Christ as their Savior. Fifty-three villagers made the decision to attend Bible school, seven of whom asked to be sent as missionaries to the very village where Stenley had died.

Hoping to extinguish the gospel fire, village officials snuffed out Stenley's life. But even in the midst of their violence, God's hand was at work. Today the flames of the gospel burn brightly in that village.

"Leave the light on." That's what all who follow Christ should aim to do when they leave this world behind. A committed Christian leaves the light on for a world that is lost in darkness. It's called leaving a legacy. It seems we often hear of famous people who leave behind a legacy in film, sports, or some other public arena. However, while the lives of many Christian saints are extinguished in anonymity, their faithful lights still burn brightly throughout the world. Their legacy of faith, integrity, hope, and love cannot be doused by their death. In fact, death may even accelerate the flame. For a legacy like that is often willingly imitated by those who remain.

eXtreme family

The woman was one month away from graduating from Bible school along with her daughter. It was the same Bible school where her son, Stenley, had gone before he went to another Indonesian island as a missionary. Stenley was killed for carrying the gospel, but his testimony had prompted many others to go to Bible school and to accept God's call to share His love.

Day 45

Where, O death, is your victory? Where, O death, is your sting?

1 Corinthians 15:55

When they had completed their training, the woman and her daughter planned to go to the very village where Stenley had died. She hoped for a chance to show Christ's love, even to the men who had beaten her son to death. A visitor to the Bible school, hearing of her plans, was surprised.

"Are you not afraid to die?" he asked her.

The woman seemed confused by the question, as if it was something she had not thought of before. "Why should I be afraid to die?" she answered simply.

Her faith in God's goodness was complete. If He chose to use her in the village where her son died, so be it. And if He permitted her to die there, she would accept that call as well. Her death would bring her into the presence of the Christ she loved. Death was not an obstacle or a punishment, merely a doorway into the eternal presence of God.

Facing death can make us feel like children standing above the edge of a water hole. We hug our shoulders tightly to our bodies, shivering with the anticipation of the unknown. Will it hurt? Will I make it? We don't want to be the first to jump—not with all these uncertainties. Fortunately, we don't have to. History is full of family members who have leaped across the boundary between life and death. They are saints who died in full assurance of their destination. Jesus Christ, in fact, has gone where no other person has gone before—to death and back again. Christ, the head of our Christian family, has taken the terror out of death and replaced it with assurance. Heed the call to come on in. The water's fine.

eXtreme sides

RUSSIA: HYPOCRITES

Day 46

They were singing choruses when the two soldiers entered with rifles. The service came to a halt as the Russian soldiers stared at the believers with wild eyes.

"What are you doing here?" they shouted. "Worshiping your imaginary God?"

The church members cowered in the pews, wondering if there were more soldiers and more guns outside.

"All those who are faithful to God, move to the right side of the church," said one of the soldiers, his face a mask of hatred. "You will be shot for your faith. You who wish to go home and keep your life, stand on the left side. You must decide to live or die. Those who are faithful to this 'God' will die. Those who deny Him can live freely."

Ten minutes earlier, everyone had sung praises equally. Now it was a question of life or death. Some stood to the left, looking sadly or waving apologetically to those on the right. Some stood on the right, their eyes closed in last-minute prayers.

"You on the left are free to go," one of the soldiers said moments later. Those people filed out, taking one last look at those who would soon be dead.

When only those on the right remained, the soldiers put down their weapons. "We, too, are Christians," they said, "but we wish to worship without hypocrites."

He who is not with me is against me, and he who does not gather with me scatters.

Matthew 12:30

Defining moments come to us when they are least expected, and we cannot prepare for them. We must experience them "as is" and learn from the consequences. A defining moment is any situation involving a question of character. It may be as complex as a church service interrupted by perpetrators who demand our allegiance to their faith. Or it may be as simple as deciding whether or not to walk out of an offensive movie. Our response to a defining moment will side us with that which is Christlike or that which is questionable. Ready or not, we meet our real character face-to-face the moment we decide to take sides.

eXtreme prayer

BOHEMIA: JOHN HUSS

Day 47

The prayer of a righteous man is powerful and effective.

James 5:16

"O most merciful Christ," John Huss wrote while awaiting his execution, **"give us a courageous spirit, so that it may be ready. And if the flesh is weak, may your grace go before it, for without you we can do nothing, and above all, without you we cannot face a cruel death. Give us a bold courage and upright faith, a firm hope, and perfect charity, that we may give our life for you in all patience and all joy. Amen."**

Huss had called for reform in the fifteenth-century church, challenging priests who sold indulgences (the right to sin without consequence) and calling for biblical standards of justice. Huss was promised royal protection to present his defense. But he now sat in a dungeon, awaiting death, and cried out to God.

On July 6, 1415, Huss was stripped and chained to a stake. As the fire was lit around him, Huss prayed, "Lord Jesus Christ, it is for the sake of the gospel and the preaching of the word that I undergo with patience and humility this terrifying, ignominious, and cruel death."

As the flames rose around him, Huss, with his final breath, cried out, "Christ, Son of the living God, have mercy upon me."

Huss's witness was crucial in ending the practice of selling indulgences and in influencing Christians to return to biblical teachings.

Prayer—that which does the most, we often do the least. Prayer is our first defense against spiritual warfare, yet often our last resort. Those who are persecuted for their faith teach us the priority of prayer. Their last remarks are not fighting words. Their final actions on earth are not resistance. Instead, prayer is their dying breath, confounding their accusers and convincing others of their resolute faith. History shows persecuted saints' dying prayers can influence others for the gospel perhaps more than if they had lived. When you are in life's crucible and the "flames" are hot around you, will you turn to prayer? Will others see your first and last defense is your communication with your heavenly Father?

eXtreme encouragement

VIETNAM: PASTOR NGUYEN LAP MA

When Communists took over Vietnam, Pastor Nguyen Lap Ma refused to relinquish the Christian Missionary Alliance Church in Can Tho. For this "crime," he and his entire family were placed under house arrest in a tiny, rural village with no travel and with no mail for the first twelve years.

Day 48

I long to see you so that I may impart to you some spiritual gift to make you strong—that is, that you and I may be mutually encouraged by each other's faith.

Romans 1:11,12

Finally, when authorities loosened the mail restrictions, Pastor Lap Ma was thrilled to see letters arrive at his home. The Voice of the Martyrs published Pastor Lap Ma's story and his address. Students, housewives, pastors, and businessmen wrote letters of encouragement to the pastor and his family. Vietnamese police were shocked when Pastor Lap Ma received more than three thousand letters from all over the world.

"I read every letter with prayers and tears," Pastor Lap Ma said. "I devour every letter and meditate on the Scriptures shared in them. I then share these words of encouragement and the Scriptures in Vietnamese with my family. We are glad and encouraged by the messages in them.

"God has strengthened and helped us," the pastor continued. "So we keep hoping in Him and fixing our eyes on Jesus. We follow Him to endure the cross, scorning its shame to the point of death. While we are living, God uses us to comfort the other suffering Christians." The letters encourage them as they happily encourage other believers.

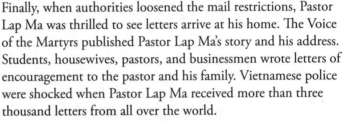

Encouragement is a necessary fuel for the Christian race. Without encouragement, as a runner without water, no one could endure the often grueling stretch for long. As we make our journey, we learn that encouragement is a two-way street. We give encouragement to others and so receive it ourselves from other believers and even from God Himself. A little encouragement goes a long way in strengthening the weary and motivating those whose faith is languishing. We often find that the spiritual encouragement we receive from the prayers of those around us rejuvenates us for the second mile. In some cases, that is another twelve years in prison for our faith. In other cases, it is merely the ability to endure another day.

Day 49

If you are not willing to die for what is in the Bible, you should not give money for Bibles. Because if you give, we will smuggle more Bibles. And if we smuggle more Bibles, there will be more martyrs.

PASTOR RICHARD WURMBRAND,
FOUNDER OF THE VOICE OF THE MARTYRS

eXtreme mother

ENGLAND: SUSANNA WESLEY

Susanna Wesley was born in 1668, in England, when the state church and government crushed any form of Christian worship or education not controlled by them. This determined Christian woman began programs of Christian education for adults in her kitchen and daily with her children.

Day 50

I have been reminded of your sincere faith, which first lived in your grandmother Lois and in your mother Eunice and, I am persuaded, now lives in you also.

2 Timothy 1:5

In 1662, six years before Susanna was born, the English government passed a law forcing the state church's Book of Common Prayer in all worship services. Two thousand clergy were forced to resign. Two years later, a law was passed forbidding more than five people who were not family members to worship together without a state official. In 1665, the Five Mile Act was passed aimed at Nonconformist ministers who were forbidden to come within five miles where they had founded a congregation. This law was upheld for almost one hundred fifty years. Soldiers destroyed meeting houses and took away furniture and Christian books. Five thousand Nonconformist Christians died in prison.

Although Susanna was associated at times with the official church, she refused to be a "Sunday-only" Christian. Her angry neighbors burned her fields and stabbed the three cows that gave milk to her family. They called her children "the little devils." One of her children, John Wesley, the founder of the Methodists, led a great spiritual awakening in England. He had learned perseverance from his mother.

Many believe the reason England did not experience a bloody revolution, in the same way that France was terrorized, is due to the Christian revival that began among the poor in Great Britain. This spiritual revival was led, in part, by John Wesley who also championed practical help, education, jobs, and food. Did the influence of his mother, Susanna, help to save England? Your influence for Christ does change history. Even if we don't have biological parents or grandparents like the Wesleys who pass down the Christian faith to us, God gives us a spiritual family to nurture and love us. Who is your spiritual mother or father—someone who taught you about Christ? To whom can you be a spiritual brother or sister?

eXtreme warmth

RUSSIA: NADEJDA SLOBODA

Day 51

But if I say, "I will not mention him or speak any more in his name," his word is in my heart like a fire, a fire shut up in my bones. I am weary of holding it in; indeed, I cannot.

Jeremiah 20:9

Nadejda Sloboda could hardly contain her enthusiasm. She had just learned about Christ from a shortwave radio program broadcast from Europe. As the first Christian in her Russian village, she desperately wanted to tell all of her friends about the God who had miraculously changed her heart. But she knew the local authorities strictly prohibited any talk of God or Christianity.

However, Nadejda was unable to contain her zeal, and soon a church was born. When the police were unable to squelch the church's growth even with road blockades, they arrested Nadejda and sentenced her to four years in prison. Her five children were taken by force to an atheistic boarding school, which tormented Nadejda. But she felt nearer to God than ever before and persisted in sharing Christ even with her fellow prisoners.

Because of her refusal to stop talking about Christ, officials put her in a solitary, unheated cell for two months. It was in the middle of winter and Nadejda was not allowed any bedding whatsoever. She was forced to sleep on the cold concrete floor. After she was returned to the common cell, her fellow prisoners asked her how she was able to stand the treatment.

She replied, "I fell asleep on the cold concrete floor trusting in God, and it became warm around me. I rested in the arms of God."

Most Christians can recall a time in their spiritual journey when it seemed like they could never get enough of God and His Word. Spiritual zeal was second nature. Fervor was a constant friend. Yet, somehow our faith grew cold along the way. Perhaps it was persecution that squelched our enthusiasm. Perhaps it was personal tragedy. Or perhaps it was nothing in particular—just ordinary activities that dampened our spirits and reclaimed our priorities. Are the flames of spiritual fervor now merely smoldering ashes? Has your zeal grown dormant? It is possible to ignite a new relationship with God and fuel the fire within. Ask Him to help you warm up to the idea today.

eXtreme "vision"

THE IVORY COAST: CHLOE

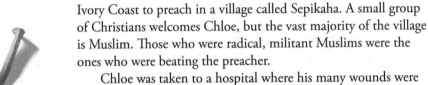

The blows seemed to come from everywhere, and Chloe tried to wrap his arms around his head to protect himself. Although he didn't know how many attackers there were, he felt the sharp thud of each blow as he lost consciousness. His attackers shouted at him, mocking his faith and his Jesus. Chloe prayed, silently crying out to God to give him strength.

Day 52

I pray also that the eyes of your heart may be enlightened.

Ephesians 1:18

Each week, Chloe walks more than twenty miles in his native Ivory Coast to preach in a village called Sepikaha. A small group of Christians welcomes Chloe, but the vast majority of the village is Muslim. Those who were radical, militant Muslims were the ones who were beating the preacher.

Chloe was taken to a hospital where his many wounds were treated. When police asked Chloe who had beaten him, he said he didn't know. Chloe has been blind for many years.

The week after he was released from the hospital, Chloe was back in Sepikaha, risking his life to preach to people he could not see. His eyes were blind, but Chloe's heart could see clearly. It saw a need for Jesus in the small village, and it saw young Christians hungry to grow in their faith. He returns, week after week, to Sepikaha. The faces that he cannot see now, he will see one day in heaven.

It doesn't take x-ray vision to see into the heart of those who are spiritually lost. Years of bad decisions are often in full view—etched across their tired faces. Spiritual vision means using the "eyes" of our hearts to notice others' needs. That's all. The power to notice is the first step toward making a difference. What do you see when you look into the faces of the people around you? Or do you even look? In today's culture, it is possible to be surrounded by a crowd in an elevator, airport, or shopping mall and never meet eyes with another human being. Do you see people who need to know Christ? Are your spiritual eyes trained to notice those in need around you? Ask God to help you develop the spiritual vision to take note and take action.

eXtreme parable

In a forest one day, three young trees all agreed to pray that they would be used for some noble purpose rather than decay from old age.

Day 53

Not only so, but we also rejoice in our sufferings, because we know that suffering produces perseverance; perseverance, character; and character, hope. And hope does not disappoint us, because God has poured out his love into our hearts by the Holy Spirit, whom he has given us.

Romans 5:3–5

The first tree wanted to become a manger where tired cattle could feed after a long day's work. God rewarded the tree for having such modesty. It became a very special manger—the one in which the Son of God was laid.

The second tree prayed that it might become a boat. The prayer was answered, and soon its fine wood sheltered a very special passenger—the Son of God. It heard Jesus calm a fierce storm by saying, "Peace, be still." The tree counted its life as worthwhile in order to witness such a scene.

The third tree, however, was made into a large cross to serve as an instrument of suffering. The tree was initially deeply disappointed in its fate. However, one day Jesus of Nazareth was nailed to its limbs. Strange, but the cross did not hear groaning and cursing as on other crosses. Instead it heard the Son of God offer words of love and divine forgiveness—words that opened paradise to a repentant thief.

The tree then understood that its part in the crucifixion of Jesus provided for the salvation of humankind.

In underground churches across eastern Europe, the parable of the three trees was often told as an encouragement to those suffering for their faith. These believers needed to see purpose in what they endured. They must have had such high hopes and aspirations when they originally said they wanted to be used by God for His glory. Yet, oppression seemed to have cut them off from God's plans. How could unjust suffering play into such a plan? Like the tree that formed the cross, they realized they were also being shaped into God's ultimate purpose for their lives. From this perspective, suffering is not seen as an interruption of God's plans for your life, but an integral part of the process.

eXtreme weakness

RUSSIA: REVEREND MIKHAIL

"If you will renounce your faith and trample the cross, you will go free," the Bolshevik gang said. "If you do not, we will kill you."

Reverend Mikhail had seen eighty thousand of his fellow Russian Orthodox leaders and lay people murdered by the Communists. Amid all that pain and suffering, he decided that God, if He did exist, would not have allowed such misery.

Day 54

I don't believe, he thought as he faced the gang. *What does a cross mean to me? Let me save my life.*

But when he opened his mouth to go along with the gang's orders, the words that came out shocked him. "I only believe in one God. I will not trample on the cross!"

The gang put a sack around his shoulders as a royal garment and used his fur hat for Jesus' crown of thorns. One of them, a former member of Mikhail's church, knelt before him, saying, "Hail, King of the Jews." They took turns beating him and mocking his God.

But he said to me, "My grace is sufficient for you, for my power is made perfect in weakness."

2 Corinthians 12:9

Silently, the reverend prayed. "If You exist, please save my life." As he was beaten, he cried out again, "I believe in one God."

His show of faith made such an impression on the drunken gang that they released him. When he arrived in his house, he fell face down on the floor, weeping and repeating, "I believe."

The Christian faith is full of paradoxes. Die to live. Lose to win. Be weak in order to be strong. In fact, unless we are willing to embrace our own failures, we cannot experience God's strength. When we undergo hardship and trial or even witness the unjust suffering of others from afar, we may begin to doubt God's goodness. That is a natural human response. However, God does not reject our human weakness. He restores our weakness with His strength. Therefore, we can rejoice in our failures because they remind us that human strength is no substitute for godly power. We may fail, but our God remains strong. What are you learning about your own weakness? What does that teach you about God's strength?

eXtreme wisdom

Witnesses falsely testified against him. "We heard him cursing Moses and God. This man talks nonstop against God's law. We even heard him say that Jesus of Nazareth would tear this place down and throw out all the customs Moses gave us."

Day 55

If any of you lacks wisdom, he should ask God, who gives generously to all without finding fault, and it will be given to him.

James 1:5

The chief priest of the high counsel turned to the defendant. "What do you have to say for yourself?"

Calmly Stephen rose, and his gentle tone changed. "Your ancestors killed anyone who dared talk about the coming of the Jesus. And you've kept up your religious traditions—you traitors and murderers, all of you. You had God's law handed to you by angels—giftwrapped!—and you squandered it!"

Screams and curses broke out in response, but Stephen was undeterred. He looked up into heaven and declared, "Oh! I see heaven wide open and the Son of Man standing at God's side!"

They blocked their ears with their hands, rushed him, and dragged him outside of the city. One of the Pharisees named Saul quietly collected the robes of the others so that Stephen's blood wouldn't stain them.

As the stones began to pound Stephen's body, he cried out, "Master Jesus, take my life." Then he knelt down, praying loud enough for everyone to hear, "Master, don't blame them for this sin"—his last words. Then he died.

(Paraphrased from Acts 6:11—7:60, *The Message*)

Keeping cool in the face of difficult situations is the wisest move. Things as trivial as being cut off in traffic, receiving a low grade in school, and being reprimanded on the job are all it takes these days to lose it. However, maneuvering through uncommonly stressful situations takes more than common sense. It takes divine wisdom. When faced with false accusations and even the threat of death, Stephen exercised true wisdom. He did not retaliate. He did not curse his accusers. He simply clung to what he knew to be true and what the Pharisees refused to believe—Jesus is the Son of God. This same Jesus who embraced Stephen as he died will also embrace you when you need the wisdom that comes only from God.

Day 56

I will preach until I die.

PASTOR LI DEXIAN, CHINESE HOUSE-CHURCH PASTOR
WHO HAS BEEN ARRESTED MORE THAN TWENTY TIMES
FOR PREACHING WITHOUT A LICENSE

eXtreme letters—part one

RUSSIA: MARIA

Dear Mom and Dad,

I greet you with the love of Christ. I am doing well and feel very blessed. One of my schoolmates, Varia, is a member of the Communist Youth Organization. I have been witnessing to her, and I think I am finally starting to get through to her. Recently she said, "I cannot understand you at all. So many of the students insult and hurt you, and you love them anyway."

Day 57

For, as I have often told you before and now say again even with tears, many live as enemies of the cross of Christ.

Philippians 3:18

I told her that God has taught us all to love, not only those who are kind to us, but especially those who are unkind—that they might see God within us. Varia has been one of the ones to join in the mocking and insults, but that has only made me pray for her even more.

Today, she asked me if I could really love her too! We embraced and both began to weep. I believe she is very close to receiving Christ. Please pray for her.

When you listen to those who loudly deny God, it seems like they mean it. But life shows that many of them really have a great longing in their hearts. And you can hear the groaning of the heart; they seek something and try to cover their inner emptiness with their godlessness.

I will write soon. Please send my love to everyone at home.

Maria

God created human beings with a spiritual space within them that can only be completely filled by Him. When we run across someone who is hostile to Christianity, we can remind ourselves of the tremendous needs in that person's life. Imagine a cavernous space in the chest cavity of your enemy—a body without a heart. This inner emptiness is what drives many people to a spiritual search. They either respond in faith, wanting to accept Christ's offer to fill the void, or they respond with bitterness, rejecting Christ altogether. Often, a Christian's presence simply reminds those who reject Christ what they are missing in their own lives. They are not resenting you personally. They resent what you represent.

eXtreme letters—part two

RUSSIA: MARIA

Dear Mom and Dad,

In my last letter I told you about the atheist girl, Varia. Now I am so happy to tell you the exciting news: Varia has received Christ! She is so different and is already witnessing openly to everyone.

Day 58

When Varia first believed, she still felt guilty inside. I think she was unhappy because for so long she believed and made a point of telling others that there is no God. She felt that she needed to suffer and pay for this.

We went together to the assembly of the godless (Communist Youth Organization meeting). Although I warned her to be reserved, it was useless. After refusing to join in the singing of the Communist hymn, Varia went forward to address the whole assembly. She courageously told everyone about accepting Christ as her Savior!

Therefore, if anyone is in Christ, he is a new creation; the old has gone, the new has come!

2 Corinthians 5:17

She begged everyone to give up the way of sin and come to Christ, and the whole place was silent. When she finished speaking, she sang with her incredible voice the old hymn, "I am not ashamed to proclaim the Christ who died, to defend his commandments and the power of his cross." I could only watch helplessly as they took her away. Today is May 9, and we haven't heard anything about her.

Please pray!

Maria

The greatest enemies of Christianity are prime targets for prayer. Like Saul of Tarsus, it is possible for a former enemy to become one of the greatest spokespersons for Christ. However, without prayer, it will remain only a possibility. Instead of being afraid of them or resenting them, we should pray for those in our community, country, and throughout the world who are vehemently opposed to Christ. Whenever we pray for nonbelievers—even atheists—we can envision the changes that would happen if their energies were redirected toward Christ instead of against Him. They could become the next evangelists to share a powerful testimony of God's grace. None of our enemies are beyond God's reach, and prayer keeps them within His grasp.

eXtreme letters—part three

RUSSIA: MARIA

Dear Mom and Dad,

Yesterday, August 2, I was able to speak with Varia in prison. She was thin and pale, but her eyes were shining with the peace of God and an unearthly joy.

My heart bleeds when I think about her. She is only nineteen. As a believer, she is still a spiritual babe. But she loves the Lord with all of her heart and chose to take the most difficult road right away.

Please pray for her. They have taken all of her things away except the clothes she was wearing. We have taken up collections and sent her packages, but I don't think she receives all the things we send.

When I asked Varia if she regretted what she did, she said, "No, and if they free me I would do it again. Don't think that I suffer. I am glad that God loves me so much and gives me the joy to endure for His name."

I thank God that we have the peace to understand this. If we are in Christ, no sufferings or frustrations should stop us. I can only pray that my faith would be as strong if I were in her place.

We now believe that Varia will be sent to a labor camp in Siberia. I believe God will give her the strength she needs to endure.

Your Maria

Day 59

But those who hope in the LORD will renew their strength. They will soar on wings like eagles; they will run and not grow weary, they will walk and not be faint.

Isaiah 40:31

Christianity is not a one-hundred-yard dash. It is an endurance marathon. Scripture teaches that there are times we soar like eagles and run without growing weary. However, there are also times in our lives where long, lonely stretches loom before us. At those times, we are doing well just to walk without fainting until we gather more strength. This is the image of those under persecution. During persecution, we are simply learning to take the next step without giving up. Simply enduring is a major victory that brings glory to God. If you are undergoing a trial you don't understand, hang on and hang in there. You are getting stronger each day—sometimes without realizing it. Soon, you will soar again.

eXtreme letters–part four

Dear Maria,

At last I am able to write to you. We arrived safely at the new camp, which is about ten miles from town. I can't describe life here, but I thank God that I am reasonably healthy and have the strength to work.

Day 60

I was put to work in a machine shop with another sister whose health is very bad. I have to do the work of both of us or we will both be punished. We work twelve to thirteen hours every day, and the food is scarce. But I don't want to complain.

I wanted to tell you that I thank God He used you to lead me to Christ. For the first time, I feel my life has a purpose, and I know for whom I suffer. I have a burning desire to tell everyone here about the great joy of salvation.

At work they curse and punish me because I cannot be silent. How could I be? As long as I am able to speak, I will witness to everyone about His great love.

Now I want you to know, brothers, that what has happened to me has really served to advance the gospel.

There are many believers here. Last night we were able to sneak out to the river, where seven brothers and I were baptized. I will never forget this wonderful day! Please don't weep for me. My purpose here is clear, and my faith remains strong.

Philippians 1:12

Love,

Your Varia

Some call it destiny. Some refer to it as fate. Regardless, most people long to give themselves to a certain cause. Christians know it as a "calling"—God's purpose for their lives. When we fulfill God's purpose for our individual life, we become part of a much bigger picture. We are satisfied that whatever we do and whatever happens to us advances the gospel of Jesus Christ. We are connected. Useful. For the first time in our lives, no matter what the circumstances are, we feel we are actually contributing to something beyond ourselves. Nothing can defeat someone once they have taken hold of this purpose. What do you sense is the greater purpose of your life?

eXtreme letters-part five

RUSSIA: VARIA

My Dearest Maria,

At last I have found an opportunity to write you again. I am happy to report that the sister who was so sick is feeling better. We have now been relocated to another camp.

In my last letter I told you of my baptism. But I never had the opportunity to ask you for forgiveness for all the times I wronged you before I received Christ. It is only through your gracious attitude of forgiveness that I am a Christian today. Please accept my apology.

Also, I want to thank you all for the packages you are sending. Thanks most of all for the Bible. Since the Lord revealed to me the deep mystery of His holy love, I consider myself to be the happiest person in the world. I consider the suffering I have had to put up with as a special grace. I am glad that God gave me this tremendous opportunity to suffer for Him.

Please pray for me that I may remain faithful until the end. May the Lord keep you all and strengthen you for the battle. Don't worry about us. We are glad and joyful because our reward in heaven is great!

Your Varia

I want to know Christ and the power of his resurrection and the fellowship of sharing in his sufferings.

Philippians 3:10

Varia was never heard from again, but her love and witness for Christ were never forgotten. Her young life was likely snuffed out by the cruel authorities who imprisoned her for her faith. However, her legacy burns brightly in the hearts of those who know her story. Her life brings irrefutable evidence concerning the strange level of friendship that suffering affords. Suffering for Christ can actually bring us closer to Him in ways no other experience could. The Bible calls it the fellowship of Christ's sufferings—an exclusive level of human experience. Growing closer to Christ through suffering is something best understood by firsthand experience. How have you seen your own personal suffering bring you into a closer walk with Jesus Christ? How did this happen?

eXtreme footsteps

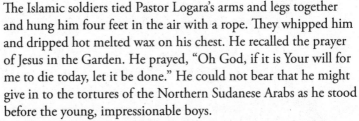

Jeremiah Logara never knew resignation, only determination. The Muslim soldiers had arrested six boys from his church and falsely accused them of being spies. When Jeremiah, their pastor, tried explaining that the boys were Christians, not spies, the soldiers decided to arrest him too.

Day 62

Whoever claims to live in him must walk as Jesus did.

1 John 2:6

The Islamic soldiers tied Pastor Logara's arms and legs together and hung him four feet in the air with a rope. They whipped him and dripped hot melted wax on his chest. He recalled the prayer of Jesus in the Garden. He prayed, "Oh God, if it is Your will for me to die today, let it be done." He could not bear that he might give in to the tortures of the Northern Sudanese Arabs as he stood before the young, impressionable boys.

But God's will was that he live on as a testimony for these boys. He was released. But the boys were detained. Pastor Logara imagines the boys were probably being forced to train as soldiers.

When the pastor reflected upon that incident, he recalled, "I thought of Jesus' death, that Jesus died to save the whole world. I thought my death could be part of the salvation of these boys as I followed in the footsteps of my Lord. I pray my example of suffering for them will encourage them to remain faithful to God."

Children love to walk in the footsteps of their parents. On sandy beaches, they strive and stretch to plant their tiny feet within the pattern of their mom or dad. Ever trusting, they follow the path wherever it may lead. Likewise, Jesus' footsteps may lead us through some trying terrain. We may follow Him through trials and tribulations that we never would have chosen for ourselves. However, if we are committed to following Jesus, we have released our right to choose our own destinies. Following Jesus provides a clear example for our children and other observers to imitate. The path we take matters. What impressions are you leaving in the minds of those around you?

Day 63

God, I do not ask You to make my life easy;
I do ask You to make me strong.

FROM A JEWISH CHILD, IN A NOTE FOUND IN THE RUBBLE OF A
JEWISH GHETTO IN POLAND AFTER IT WAS BOMBED BY THE NAZIS

eXtreme places

ROMANIA: PASTOR RICHARD WURMBRAND

Richard Wurmbrand, a Romanian pastor who suffered in prison for fourteen years, once told a story that he had heard from a fellow prisoner. It had helped him through his most difficult times of torture. The brother told him:

"I once went to a circus and witnessed a most impressive scene. An archery expert placed a burning candle on his wife's head. He then stepped out of the center of the arena and, from quite a distance, shot the candle off her head.

Day 64

Blessed are you when people Insult you, persecute you and falsely say all kinds of evil against you because of me.

Matthew 5:11

"After the show was over, I approached her and asked if she was ever afraid the arrow would strike her. She replied, 'Why should I be? He was aiming at the candle, not at me.'"

When Pastor Wurmbrand heard this story he thought, "Why should I be afraid of the torturers? They don't aim at me. They may beat my body but my real being is Christ within. I am seated with Him in heavenly places, and therefore they cannot touch my real person. From this incredible viewpoint I can look down and see the futility of their efforts."

Pastor Wurmbrand lived through years of suffering and was near death many times. But he was encouraged with this simple lesson and even flourished spiritually because he knew his place with Christ was secure, no matter what happened to his body.

Persecution, though indescribably painful, has its limits. Neither physical torment nor emotional trauma can destroy the deepest parts of who we are. What we carry on the inside is the most valuable part of ourselves—our souls. Christ's Spirit lives within us and protects our soul from emotional and physical harm. True, our enemies may strike us and even kill our bodies. However, when our enemies take a swipe at us, they are really maligning the name of Christ, the one who lives within. And He can never die again. However personal and pointed the opposition, it is really part of a bigger picture. The battle may involve us, but it concerns an overarching war between good and evil.

eXtreme wings

RUSSIA: A HUNCHBACK

"I spent many years in Soviet gulags," began the handwritten letter. **The text was neat, yet evidenced a small shake in the hand—a reminder of old age and years in prison.**

Day 65

So it will be with the resurrection of the dead. The body that is sown is perishable, it is raised imperishable.

1 Corinthians 15:42

"In the camp, I was forced to work under the ground in a mine. The labor was hard, and our guards were without sympathy or human decency. One day, in the mine, there was an accident. My back was injured, and since that day I have been a hunchback.

"One day," the letter continued, "there was a boy who would not stop staring at me. 'Mister,' he asked, 'what do you have on your back?'

"I was sure that some harsh joke at my expense was coming, but nevertheless I said, 'a hunchback.'

"The child smiled warmly. 'No,' he said, 'God is love. He gives no one deformities. That is not a hunchback you have; it is a box below your shoulders. Hiding inside the box are angels' wings. One day, the box will open, and you will fly to heaven with your angel wings.'

"I began to cry for joy. Even now," the letter concluded, "as I write to you, I am crying."

Many persecuted Christians bear the marks of their experience on their bodies. Sometimes God must remind them, even through the voice of an innocent child, of the hidden blessings beneath these scars.

There is only one reminder of earth in heaven. Jesus, even in His resurrected body of glory, still bears the scars of His own persecution. Jesus showed His scars to the disciples soon after His resurrection. Thomas touched the wound in His side and the scars on His hands. One day, His nail-scarred hands will embrace us, too, when we enter heaven. They will serve as a loving reminder of the blessings brought forth from His sufferings. However, the scars from our own difficult lives will be erased in our new, heavenly bodies. Those who have endured sufferings, insults, and injustices for His sake will exchange their scars, one by one, for God's richest blessings.

eXtreme return

CHINA: PASTOR WANG MIN-DAO

"I will not allow it," Chinese pastor Wang Min-dao said to the Japanese soldiers. "I will not hang that picture of the emperor in my church."

Several years later the Communists demanded that Pastor Wang hang a picture of their leader, Chairman Mao, in his sanctuary. "I do not even have a picture of Jesus in my church," the pastor said. "I refused to hang a picture of the Japanese emperor, and I refuse to hang one of Mao."

Wang was arrested in 1955, and for two years he was subjected to severe torture and brainwashing. Driven nearly insane by the torture, he finally signed a "confession" outlining all his "crimes" against the People's Republic. With the confession, Pastor Wang secured his release from prison.

But outside the prison he had no peace. He told himself, "I am Judas. I am like Peter when he denied Christ." Finally, he went back to the Chinese police.

"I renounce my confession," he told them. "Do with me as you will."

The guards were not satisfied to merely imprison Wang again. So they put his wife in prison as well. In a letter from the prison, he wrote, "Do not be anxious about me; I am of more value than many sparrows."

Wang Min-dao was only guilty of loving his Savior.

Day 66

Return to the LORD your God, for he is gracious and compassionate, slow to anger and abounding in love.

Joel 2:13

Who wouldn't want to be brave like Peter, impulsively striking those who came to arrest Jesus Christ? Yet, who isn't also weak like Peter, denying Christ in almost the same instance under the threat of opposition? God does not chide us for our humanity. He accepts our weakness and works with us until we are strong again. Just as God restored Peter and other believers like Wang Min-dao to a position of faith, He can restore our stout courage again as well. Have you suffered from the memory of a missed opportunity to stand up for Christ? Ask God to restore you today. He will begin to prepare you even now for your next opportunity to stand strong.

eXtreme outlook

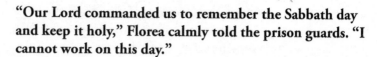

"Our Lord commanded us to remember the Sabbath day and keep it holy," Florea calmly told the prison guards. "I cannot work on this day."

The Romanian prisoners were forced to labor every day, but each Sabbath Florea refused. For his refusal, the guards routinely beat him so bad he lost the use of his arms and legs. He could only move his head.

Day 67

Because he could no longer labor, Florea was forced to sit in his cell all day long. He had to rely on other prisoners to feed him. In spite of his situation, Florea was not downcast.

When other prisoners would complain about their situation, Florea would encourage them. "If the outlook is bad," he would say, "try the 'uplook.' When Stephen was stoned, he looked up and saw Jesus standing at the right hand of God. This comforted Stephen's heart, and it will comfort yours too." He encouraged his fellow prisoners not to "look out" to their circumstances but to "look up" at Jesus.

Your attitude should be the same as that of Christ Jesus.

Philippians 2:5

One of Florea's fellow prisoners was Richard Wurmbrand, who was released from the prison and found Florea's nine-year-old son. He told him what a blessing his father had been in prison.

The boy smiled and replied, "I would like to become a sufferer and encourager for Christ as my father has been."

A Christian is not privileged with a certain set of circumstances. Nice home. Perfect family. Good health. No, a Christian is a person with a certain attitude toward any and all circumstances. A person's attitude makes the difference, regardless of circumstances. A heavenly attitude focuses on God's presence amid trials. Fixating on our hardships distracts us from a heavenly outlook. We feel burdened. Depressed. Hopeless. In contrast, a godly outlook on our troubles brings confidence that God is at work. We relax in God's presence, waiting to see how He will work out our concerns. Are you undergoing a trial right now? Where are you focused? Ask God to redirect your energies so you can look beyond your troubles and feel His presence near you.

eXtreme chains

"Sign the statement!" screamed the Cuban officer, forcing a pen into the Christian prisoner's hand. "Sign the statement!"

The written statement in front of the prisoner contained accusations about other Christians. His signature was all the government needed to arrest the others.

Day 68

Therefore, since we are surrounded by such a great cloud of witnesses ... let us run with perseverance the race marked out for us.

Hebrews 12:1

"I cannot sign this paper," the Christian said, calmly looking the officer in the eye.

"Why not?" asked the captain, with exaggerated calm, before swearing at the man. "Do you not know how to write your own name?"

"It is because of the chain, my friend. The chain keeps me from signing this."

Grabbing the prisoner's hands roughly, the officer held them in front of his face. "But you are not in chains, you idiot!" he screamed.

"Oh, but I am," said the believer. "I am bound by the chain of witnesses who throughout the centuries have given their lives for Christ. I am yet one more link in this chain, and I will not break it."

Though he was threatened and roughed up, the prisoner refused to sign.

Christian martyrs leave behind a rich testimony of incredible poise in the midst of horrific circumstances. Their strength is heroic. Their words are wise. Their calm is unshakable. Thomas Aquinas wrote, "Words pronounced by the martyrs before authorities are not human words, the simple expression of a human conviction, but words pronounced by the Holy Spirit through the confessors of Jesus." Life by life, link by link, the words spoken through the power of the Holy Spirit in the midst of oppression are forming a powerful testimony. You, too, have the potential to add your own chapter to the pages. You, too, are a link in the chain of believers. Will you hold it together?

eXtreme school

LITHUANIA: NIJOLE SADUNAITE

The mood was somber, almost harsh. The Lithuanian court was meeting to determine the sentence for Nijole Sadunaite. Her "crime," like so many others', was simply being a Christian in a Communist nation.

Day 69

Take my yoke upon you and learn from me.

Matthew 11:29

Then the judge offered her a final chance to speak. He eagerly waited for the young woman to tearfully beg for mercy. Perhaps she would even renounce her ridiculous faith in God. Yet he was in for a surprise.

There were no tears from Nijole. Her face shone, and a beautiful smile began to form. Her eyes held warmth, even for her accusers.

"This is the happiest day of my life," said the condemned woman. "I am on trial for the cause of truth and love toward men."

Now, every eye in the courtroom was on her. "I have an enviable fate, a glorious destiny. My condemnation here in this courtroom will be my ultimate triumph."

The passion in her voice was unmistakable. "I regret only that I have done so little for men. Let us love each other, and we will all be happy. Only the one who has no love will be sad."

She turned her attention away from the judge and peered into the eyes of other believers who watched the trial. "We must condemn evil, but we must love the man, even the one in error. This you can learn only at the school of Jesus Christ."

When it comes to learning about those who have been persecuted for the sake of Christ, take notes. Class is in session. From the relative safety of our homes and communities, we may read the stories of Christian martyrs. We may even shudder as we turn the pages. However, are we ready to enroll in the school of Jesus Christ? Are we ready to study side by side with those who have walked the lonely path of oppression? We must apply what we learn from them about faith, love, holiness, and endurance. Only when we identify with the sufferings of Christ through the experiences of others can we truly call ourselves "Christians," meaning "little Christs." Only then will we be ready to pass the test.

Day 70

Suffering may prevent sin,
but sin will never prevent suffering.

A HANDWRITTEN COMMENT FOUND IN AN
1800S EDITION OF *FOXE'S BOOK OF MARTYRS*

eXtreme declaration

"You are lying!" Lieutenant Grecu screamed at the imprisoned pastor, Richard Wurmbrand. "Tell us the truth about your Christian activities and about others in your church! Here, you must write out for me all the rules that you have broken in the prison."

Day 71

Now, Lord, consider their threats and enable your servants to speak your word with great boldness.

Acts 4:29

Wurmbrand sat and quietly wrote down all of the prison rules he had broken. When he was finished, he added one final paragraph: "I have never spoken against the Communists. I am a disciple of Christ, who has given us love for our enemies. I understand them and pray for their conversion so that they will become my brothers in the faith." He signed his name boldly at the bottom.

Grecu read the "declaration." His face softened as he got to the end, overwhelmed that Wurmbrand could write about loving a government that had arrested and tortured him. "This love," he said. "That is one of your Christian commandments that no one can keep."

"It's not a matter of keeping a commandment," Richard replied gently. "When I became a Christian it was as if I had been reborn, with a new character full of love. Just as only water can flow from a spring, only love can come from a loving heart."

In the following months, Wurmbrand spoke of Christ's love many more times to Lieutenant Grecu, who eventually gave his life to Christ!

Declaring your faith in Christ is simply saying it loud enough for others to hear and receive it. It doesn't mean you're obnoxious. It doesn't mean you must be extraordinarily extroverted. It simply means you are an open book for others to read about Jesus Christ. And you're willing to read it aloud. We are often hesitant in our witness for Christ. We don't wish to offend. We don't want to be ill received. And yet our taciturn testimony may cause us to miss the opportunity to lead someone to faith in Christ. What would it mean for you to declare your faith in Christ today? To whom should you define and deliver God's message of grace?

eXtreme reunion

Though he was being burned at the stake on the order of Spanish authorities, Antonio Herrezuelo's pain was in his spirit. He realized his wife had renounced her faith in Christ to escape a similar death.

Day 72

Antonio could have saved his own life and received life in prison like his wife. Perhaps he would have someday been pardoned and been reunited with his wife.

But he would not recant. The last words he uttered, before soldiers gagged him, were pleas for his wife. "Please return to Christ and be forgiven. We will be united together in heaven. Please return!" he yelled to his wife. Although he had no earthly hope of reunion, he wanted to be with her in eternity.

After her husband's death, Mrs. Herrezuelo was brought back to the prison to serve out her life sentence. For eight years she wrestled with God and her own spirit. She could not find peace about her fateful decision.

Finally, she publicly returned to faith in Christ, taking back her previous denial even as the sixteenth-century inquisitors threatened her. A judge sentenced her to death at the stake—now for the second and final time.

She was eager to die and be reunited with her husband. Mrs. Herrezuelo, though dying, was once again at peace. Her first words would be to tell him of her return to the faith.

After this I looked and there before me was a great multitude that no one could count, from every nation, tribe, people and language, standing before the throne and in front of the Lamb.

Revelation 7:9

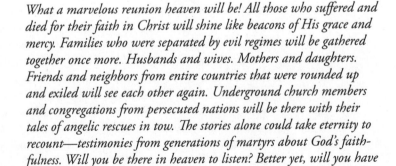

What a marvelous reunion heaven will be! All those who suffered and died for their faith in Christ will shine like beacons of His grace and mercy. Families who were separated by evil regimes will be gathered together once more. Husbands and wives. Mothers and daughters. Friends and neighbors from entire countries that were rounded up and exiled will see each other again. Underground church members and congregations from persecuted nations will be there with their tales of angelic rescues in tow. The stories alone could take eternity to recount—testimonies from generations of martyrs about God's faithfulness. Will you be there in heaven to listen? Better yet, will you have your own story to tell?

eXtreme grace

KENYA: A WIDOW

"Before we finish this funeral service," her words rang out clearly to the thousand people in attendance, **"I want to tell you what my husband told me before dying. He asked me to tell all his murderers that he goes to heaven loving wholeheartedly everybody, including his assassins. He has forgiven all for what they have done because Jesus loves and will also forgive them."**

Day 73

Bear with each other and forgive whatever grievances you may have against one another. Forgive as the Lord forgave you.

Colossians 3:13

She stood over her husband's coffin. There were tears in her eyes, but her voice was strong. The bruises on her body told the mourners that she, too, had been beaten.

As Christians, she and her husband had refused to take a Kikuyu tribal oath that wasn't consistent with their Christian faith. For this, her husband was beaten to death, and she was beaten and hospitalized.

The crowd was still, silenced by the power of the widow's words, and her will. Many living in Kenya in 1969 had also faced harassment and attack for valuing their faith over tribal loyalties.

"I, as his widow, also tell all of you, in the presence of my dead husband, that I hate none of those who killed him. I love the killers. I forgive them, knowing that Christ has died for them too."

No one in attendance that day would ever forget the widow's words or her example of extreme forgiveness and grace.

Forgiveness is an extreme example of what it means to be like Christ, to extend His grace to others. No one has ever had to forgive more than Jesus Christ. Nothing can compare to the weight of an entire world's sins on His shoulders at Calvary. Therefore, when we forgive those who hate us, we are never more like Jesus than at that moment. Forgiveness does not make the wrongs that were done to you right. Forgiveness makes you all right. Forgiveness does not mean letting your perpetrators off the hook. Forgiveness means letting yourself off the hook and getting released from the tyranny of vengeful thoughts. Forgiving others for their wrongs gives you a chance to shine for Christ like never before. Where will you shine the light of God's forgiveness today?

eXtreme kindness

ROMANIA: BARTO

Barto was on the brink of starvation. Once a Communist Party official and prosecuting attorney, he was now considered expendable by the same Party. He was sentenced to labor in a Romanian prison camp. His stomach, once full, was now wasting away. He wondered how much longer he could go on.

Day 74

Or do you show contempt for the riches of his kindness, tolerance and patience, not realizing that God's kindness leads you toward repentance?

Romans 2:4

Seeing Barto's frail stature, a fellow prisoner came up to him and offered to share his rations of food. "Thank you, my friend," he said to the other prisoner. "How long must you be here?" Barto asked as he wolfed down the food.

"Twenty years," replied the prisoner. His eyes seemed to question Barto.

"What crime did you commit?"

"I was tried and sentenced for giving food to a fugitive pastor who was being chased by the police," the man stated calmly. Barto noticed his voice didn't carry bitterness like Barto had heard from so many others.

"Who gave you such a harsh punishment for doing a good deed?" demanded Barto.

The prisoner replied humbly, "Sir, you were the state prosecutor at my trial. You don't recognize me now, but I remember you."

The man went on. "I am a Christian. Christ taught us to reward evil with good. I wished then for you to realize that it is right and good to give food to a hungry man—even your enemy. Now, I can show you." Barto began that day to understand that his own spiritual needs far outweighed his physical ones.

Kindness is the way to our enemies' hearts. And it may do something for their souls. God uses kindness as His strategy of choice when dealing with us. Instead of giving us exactly what we deserve for our offenses against Him, He deals with us kindly. His kindness is an example of how we should fashion our own approach to those who offend us. Kindness arrests their attention. It is as unexpected as it is undeserved. Like Barto, our kindness toward an enemy may awaken a spiritual hunger for the source of our compassion. However, regardless of their response, we must follow the example of our Lord when dealing with our enemies. Who needs your kindness today?

eXtreme children

Day 75

In restricted countries, Christian children frequently suffer alongside their parents. When fathers and mothers are arrested because of their church activities, the children are often left as orphans. If they are lucky, their family members or friends can care for them. However, at worst, they are sent to orphanages or state-run institutions. No more bedtime Bible stories and no more family prayers before meals.

I tell you the truth, anyone who will not receive the kingdom of God like a little child will never enter it.

Mark 10:15

However, the letters from the children to their imprisoned parents display tremendous courage and tenacity during the difficult times of separation. Their words convey hope of a reunion.

"God bless you, dear Mommy. Don't be troubled by our temporary separation—it won't last forever. Our joy will return soon—let that thought encourage you. Mommy, I can't imagine the feast we will have when you return. I have been keeping up with my schoolwork. Now it is night—tomorrow will be another day. Day after day it drags on, but I know we will be together soon. I embrace you. Your loving daughter."

"Dear Mom, when you come home, I will not think about the loneliness and pain anymore. I beg you not to cry, Mommy. I love you. I wrote a little poem for you:
> You have a heart of gold,
> You are young at heart, not old.
> The Lord observes you from on high,
> We'll be together soon, you and I."

Children are often the last ones considered when it comes to the effects of persecution. For every imprisoned parent, there is a child left behind. However, as Jesus pointed out on numerous occasions, a child's faith is significant. If a child can demonstrate incredible courage amid intense circumstances, then what is our excuse? Instead of growing resentful toward the circumstances that are beyond their control, the children of persecuted Christians are growing in grace. Can we say the same about our lives? As adults, we risk focusing too much on the blows and beatings life brings. We could benefit from modeling the resilient faith of children. In what ways do you need to grow in childlike faith? Begin today by remembering the children.

eXtreme protest

RUSSIA: BAPTIST CHRISTIANS

Day 76

In everything set them an example by doing what is good ... so that those who oppose you may be ashamed because they have nothing bad to say about us.

Titus 2:7,8

It was like no protest the world had ever seen. Most riots around the world are violent, with slogans being yelled, signs and banners being waved, and even rocks being thrown. But on May 16, 1966, five hundred Soviet Baptists gathered in the courtyard of the Communist Central Committee. However, unlike most protestors, they did not shout slogans or demands.

They stood together praying and singing hymns. Georgi Vins and Gennadi Kryuchkov presented a petition to the Soviet government on their behalf, requesting the official recognition of their churches, a plea to stop governmental interferences, the release of imprisoned believers, and freedom for Soviet citizens to teach and be taught religious faith.

On the morning of the seventeenth, soldiers and KGB agents surrounded the peaceful gathering. Around 1:00 p.m., a number of buses closed in and the soldiers attacked, beating them and forcing them into the buses. No one fought back. Instead, the demonstrators linked arms and started singing again over the screams of the attacking soldiers. All of this was done in public with many bystanders gathering around to watch the steadfast faith of the Christians. They were then taken to prison.

Even in prison they continued to pray and sing. The Communists had refused the pleas of these peaceful protestors, but they had not broken their spirits.

People who turn Christianity into a cause run the risk of confusing violence for obedience. However, nothing could be further from the true description. Radical obedience means we protest whatever is contrary to Christ's teachings. However, like the Soviet Baptists, we desire to bring peace and not to provoke harm. Those who are persecuted for their faith leave an example of peaceful demonstration and determination. They do not return evil for evil, yet they calmly accept the consequences of their obedience to Christ's commands. If you want to be a radical Christian, you must fully obey Christ's commands. In what area of your life is God calling you to radical obedience for Him? What does it mean to you to be a radical Christian?

Day 77

The cause, not the suffering,
makes a genuine martyr.

Sᴛ. Aᴜɢᴜsᴛɪɴᴇ

eXtreme instruments

A COMMUNIST PRISON: A CHRISTIAN PASTOR

"Why is it that so many Christians sing only once a week? Why only once? If it is right to sing, sing every day. If it is wrong to sing, don't sing on Sunday."

Day 78

Come, let us sing for joy to the LORD; let us shout aloud to the Rock of our salvation.

Psalm 95:1

The pastor had spent several horrifying years in prison at the hands of the Communist authorities. He was jailed for his belief in Christ, and though he remembered the tortures there, he did not focus on them much. Instead he spoke of the times of joy in the presence of his Lord. He and his fellow Christian prisoners formed a community of praise—in the middle of prison.

"When we were in prison we sang almost every day because Christ was alive in us. The Communists were very nice to us. They knew we liked to praise God with musical instruments, so they gave every Christian in prison a musical instrument. However, they did not give us violins or mandolins—these were too expensive. Instead, they put chains on our hands and feet. They chained us to add to our grief. Yet we discovered that chains are splendid musical instruments! When we clanged them together in rhythm, we could sing, 'This is the day (*clink, clank*), this is the day (*clink, clank*) which the Lord has made (*clink, clank*), which the Lord has made (*clink, clank*).'" What a joyful noise unto the Lord!

To those who have yet to experience it, persecution seems to focus entirely on loss. The loss of freedom. The loss of hope. Even the loss of life. However, those who have suffered for their faith in Christ overlook what's missing and focus on new discoveries. They relish what little freedoms they have instead of regretting what they lack. In this story, Communist captors robbed believers of most of life's freedoms and dignity. However, these stout believers focused on what remained—their joy in the Lord. If it is good to sing to the Lord when you have everything, it is good to sing to Him when you have lost it all, too. What will you do today to make sure you do not lose your Christian joy?

eXtreme example

COLOMBIA: CHET BITTERMAN

Day 79

Follow my example, as I follow the example of Christ.

1 Corinthians 11:1

The hooded and armed guerrillas, members of the Marxist revolutionary group known as M-19, tied up the twelve adults and five children who were present in the Wycliffe Bible Translators headquarters in Bogota, Columbia. "Where is your director? Where is Al Wheeler?" the leader shouted into the face of one of the secretaries. "We want Wheeler!"

"Don't hurt her," came a quick reply. "Wheeler is not here."

The Marxist bristled as if to hit him, then reconsidered. "All right, we'll just take you instead. Let's go!"

Their demands arrived several days later. "If your organization does not leave Columbia by February 19, we will execute our prisoner." The guerrillas even called President Reagan and demanded that their manifesto be published in the *New York Times* and the *Washington Post* or Mr. Chet Bitterman would die.

As the date approached, prayer chains were formed. A tape was received at a local radio station confirming that Chet had been witnessing to the guerrillas. His wife, Brenda, received a letter requesting a Spanish Bible.

Chet reached his goal in life—to broadcast the gospel wherever it was needed. Chet's body was eventually left on an abandoned bus by the terrorists. Columbians, along with Christians all across America, commemorated his death by stepping forward to fill the gap left by Chet. The following year, applications to serve with Wycliffe Bible Translators doubled.

Leading by example is a popular executive training principle. A company's priorities ought to be modeled by the highest level of staff. When it comes to Christianity, leading by example is equally important. In fact, Jesus commanded it. He demonstrated how Christian leaders must model the faith for other believers to follow. He didn't just give us His teachings—He lived them. How many of us are willing to live out a standard of radical obedience to Christ? If we are, we won't control our own destinies. We will be an example to others as we follow the example of Christ. Who is observing your life today? What are they learning from your example about how closely you follow Christ?

eXtreme preparations

SUDAN: SUDANESE CHILDREN

Foxholes in a schoolyard—they are all too common in Southern Sudan. In the midst of a play area surrounded by children running and laughing sits a large metal cylinder, with fins on its tail, buried halfway in the ground. A flag sticks out from the unexploded bomb as a reminder for the children to stay away from it.

Day 80

He who has the Son has life; he who does not have the Son of God does not have life.

1 John 5:12

A missionary team recently delivered assistance to this elementary school in Yei County. Like most areas in Sudan, this school is barely able to function for lack of supplies and qualified teachers. This particular school is in an area regularly bombed by the Islamic government of Sudan.

These children have dug more than twenty foxholes by hand around the schoolyard. They have prepared themselves with some means of protection for when the bombers come. When they hear the engines of the bombers, they run for the holes, watching out for flying shrapnel.

Some succeed in getting to the foxholes safely, but some do not. When the missionary team asked what could be done for the children, the answer was simply, "Pray for their protection."

The Bible teaches that many believers lived a precarious existence in order to maintain their faith in Christ. To these children, suffering or even dying for their faith is an everyday reality. To us, they are brave soldiers for Christ.

The children in Sudan are prepared to enter earthly battle. More importantly, they are prepared to one day enter heaven's gates. They have secured protection within the earth from fly-by raids from enemy camps. Yet their faith in Christ has secured eternal protection within the arms of God. Perhaps, like the Sudanese children playing near an undiffused bomb, you have learned by now that life often takes place a step away from disaster. You may have taken steps to pad and protect your life on earth, hoping for the best amid uncertain times. However, have you also followed their example of being prepared for life in the hereafter? Are you prepared for eternal life through a personal relationship with Jesus Christ?

eXtreme revolution—part one

ROMANIA: THE CHRISTIANS OF TIMISOARA

When Romanian poet Constantin Ioanid wrote the poem entitled "God Exists," he could not have known the significance his words would have in Romanian history.

Day 81

One night in 1989, Christians were protesting in the town of Timisoara. A bishop who had become a puppet for the Communists had fired the reformed Pastor Tokes for faithfully preaching the Word of God.

On the day Pastor Tokes was to leave his home and church, the Christians surrounded his house to prevent the police from evicting him. Quickly the crowd grew, and the army was called out to stop them.

The soldiers began shooting, and many were killed or wounded. Then an amazing thing happened. The entire crowd, instead of fighting the army, knelt down and prayed. The shocked soldiers were overwhelmed and refused to shoot anymore.

Then you will know the truth, and the truth will set you free.

John 8:32

Meanwhile, the whole town had gathered, and a local pastor addressed the crowd from the balcony of the opera house. He recited Brother Ioanid's poem, and the whole crowd began shouting, "God exists! God exists!" Leaflets with the poem's text were passed around, and those who knew the music composed for the words began to sing. Soon thousands were singing it again and again.

The song became the beginning of the Romanian revolution that led to the fall of Communist dictator Nicolai Ceaucescu.

A revolution is a new resurgence of belief in a very old idea—whether freedom, personal dignity, or even the existence of God. These self-evident principles remain unchanged during the cycle of oppression. Though they may go "underground" for a time, their existence is unchallenged. A spiritual revolution resurrects the belief in the existence of God—although God Himself was never dead. The revolution begins with God's revelation of truth. We all need courage to resurrect our faith in the basic, powerful, and life-altering proposition that God exists. We are part of a revolution when we join other Christians who begin to live like they believed it. What would spiritual revolution look like in your own life?

eXtreme revolution—part two

ROMANIA: THIRTEEN CHILDREN

After hundreds had died needlessly in Timisoara in 1989, other demonstrations spontaneously broke out in different cities all across Romania. During one protest, a group of thirteen children made a human barrier with their bodies to keep the soldiers from advancing on the crowd. When the soldiers began to advance anyway, the children knelt and shouted, "Please don't kill us."

Day 82

The soldiers ignored the innocent children and began shooting them. Yet the children did not retreat. They just kept begging, "Please don't shoot us." A memorial was erected where the children were killed.

A legend has circulated around Romania that angels actually started the revolution by surrounding the children and giving them the holy courage they needed to stand in the face of evil.

In every town, tanks and troops were called out to stop the uprisings. But eventually, the soldiers succumbed to the peaceful crowds. In the town of Sibiu, soldiers and officers joined in with the crowd of thousands as two ministers atop tanks asked everyone to kneel for prayer. They were just as fed up with the government as the people were, and it soon became impossible to repress the uprising.

And he said: "I tell you the truth, unless you change and become like little children, you will never enter the kingdom of heaven."

Matthew 18:3

It is believed that the martyrdom of a small group of children gave the country victory over a generation of Communist oppressors.

When we become childlike in our faith, we deeply desire to accomplish that which Christ has set before us. Like children, we must seize the moment and make the most of it. The Romanian children unsuccessfully begged for their lives, but they were undeterred in their mission. Is there a circumstance or consequence that threatens your allegiance to your mission? What are you willing to sacrifice in order to abandon yourself to Christ's cause?

eXtreme step

"...seven, eight, nine—you! Step out!" The Nazi guard yelled at the woman. The commandant had ordered every tenth prisoner executed as punishment for two women's escape the previous night.

"Please have mercy on me! I have a child," the tenth woman pleaded.

Day 83

Mary Skotsobaugh stood next in line. In her heart Mary heard, "Step forward and say you wish to die in her place." She replied to the inner voice, *Why? She is not a Christian. She is a Jewish Communist. When the Nazis are overthrown and the Communists come to power, they will be as bad as the Nazis.*

Then Mary remembered that it was Good Friday. The voice said, "On this day I died not for the good ones but for the bad ones, for sinners."

Mary then stepped forward. "I wish to die."

The officer laughed. "If you are stupid enough to die in her place, all right, you come forward. Her turn will come soon enough."

As Mary went to be executed and burned in the ovens, she told them, "When God took His people out of slavery in Egypt, it is written in our Bible that He walked before them in a column of fire. I pray when my body burns it would be a column of fire that will show you the way to God."

A man's steps are directed by the LORD. How then can anyone understand his own way?

Proverbs 20:24

One step forward can make all the difference. Christians often live their lives precariously balanced on the ledge between safety and the unknown. Those who have taken the small step forward into the unknown have always found the faithfulness of God. Noah. Moses. Abraham. Deborah. Ruth. Mary. Paul. The list of biblical examples goes on and on, not to mention a host of history's hall of fame. One step of faith changed their lives from ordinary to extraordinary. Is God calling you to step forward in faith today? Do you hear His voice in your heart? Listen up. Prepare to move. Your small step of obedience could show others the way to God.

Day 84

The true martyr is he who has become the instrument of God, who has lost his will in the will of God, not lost it but found it, for he has found freedom in submission to God. The martyr no longer desires anything for himself, not even the glory of martyrdom.

T. S. ELLIOT, *MURDER IN THE CATHEDRAL*

eXtreme secrecy

ROMAN CATACOMBS: EARLY CHRISTIANS

Day 85

For whatever is hidden is meant to be disclosed, and whatever is concealed is meant to be brought out into the open.

Mark 4:22

Early Christians were known for two things: prayer below ground and persecution above ground. The whole known world was against the Christians in the Roman Empire. Marcus Aurelius Antonius signed a decree in AD 162 stating, "Anyone who professes to be a Christian is worthy of the most painful death!" A period of almost four centuries of extreme secrecy began for the church. The church literally went underground, creating the Roman catacombs.

A vast network of rooms and corridors was constructed beneath Rome for the burial of the dead. Yet these became the covert cathedrals of the early church. Believers could find a place of unhindered and unguarded worship and prayer.

The catacombs show the dedication of early believers to find a place to worship Christ. The broken and burnt bones of their tombs show the intensity of the persecutions they suffered. Perhaps most significant are the secret notes of victory and peace inscribed on the walls. Despite the cruelty shown them above ground, below they decorated the walls with symbols of their faith and peace through the cross.

It is not unusual to see cryptic inscriptions such as the following on tombs: "Victorious in *peace* and Christ" or "Being called away, he went in *peace*" or "Here lies Maria, put to rest in a dream of *peace*." The key to their triumph is no secret: perfect peace in Christ Jesus.

Many people keep their faith a secret their whole lives. They claim religion is a private matter, something between God and them alone. However, this was not so in the early church. Believers were so open in their faith that they were easily identified and persecuted. The Roman catacombs served as a private place for worship; however, above ground their allegiance was no secret. This is why so many of them were martyred for their faith. The consistent and open prayer below ground gave them the peace they experienced in persecution above ground. Has your faith been "underground" for the duration of your Christian life? It's time for the secret to come out. No matter the consequences, don't keep Christianity concealed.

eXtreme confidence

NEW YORK CITY: AMERICAN CHRISTIANS

"Now I want you to know, brothers, that what has happened to me has really served to advance the gospel ... Because of my chains, most of the brothers in the Lord have become encouraged to speak the word of God more courageously and fearlessly ... For it has been granted to you on behalf of Christ not only to believe on him, but also to suffer for him" (Philippians 1:12,14,29).

Day 86

Such confidence as this is ours through Christ before God.

2 Corinthians 3:4

If American Christians were more active in evangelism, would the United States see an increase in persecution within its borders? Metro Ministries, an evangelistic ministry that reaches out to the most difficult areas of New York City, has seen this effect in their own ministry. As their evangelism penetrates deeper into the city, they have faced more resistance. Certain staff members have been beaten, stabbed, and raped while carrying out their mission. One staff member was even killed.

Their director, Pastor Bill Wilson, has been stabbed and beaten on a number of occasions. Yet, the threat of evil has not kept him at arm's length from the people he loves. He also contracted tuberculosis from ministering to homeless people.

Debbie, a fifteen-year-old in one of the poorer neighborhoods of Brooklyn, New York, speaks for many young people who have experienced persecution within the states. She says, "It is very hard to openly be a Christian in my school. I am constantly harassed and pressured to join one of the gangs."

In many restricted nations, Christians are not persecuted because they believe in Jesus but because they tell others about Him. In these nations, evangelism produces persecution, which often produces stronger witnesses for Christ. What was meant to destroy them actually makes them more determined. Similarly, evangelism in America and other open nations is not always safe. Yet, should this reality dampen our enthusiasm for the task? A nation such as America, founded on religious freedom, is wholly unaccustomed to suffering and persecution. Instead of using this principle as a buffer to keep us safe, we should rely on it to make us bolder. As a person living in a free democracy, you have even more reason to share your faith with boldness and confidence. Will you speak up today?

eXtreme dedication

INDIA: GLADYS STAINES

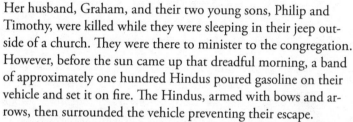

Gladys Staines had every reason to be bitter and angry. No one would have blamed her for leaving India. But when fanatical Hindus in the Indian town of Manoharpur murdered her husband and two sons, Gladys and her thirteen-year-old daughter, Esther, decided to stay. She would continue her work with the lepers in the area.

Day 87

But those who live in accordance with the Spirit have their minds set on what the Spirit desires.

Romans 8:5

Her husband, Graham, and their two young sons, Philip and Timothy, were killed while they were sleeping in their jeep outside of a church. They were there to minister to the congregation. However, before the sun came up that dreadful morning, a band of approximately one hundred Hindus poured gasoline on their vehicle and set it on fire. The Hindus, armed with bows and arrows, then surrounded the vehicle preventing their escape.

Gladys said that Graham had never set out to evangelize among the Hindus. He was simply there demonstrating the love of Christ. As a result, the Australian couple had seen many convert to Christianity and burn their idols. The dangers of their witness never deterred their dedication to demonstrate the love of Jesus Christ.

At the memorial service for Graham, Philip, and Timothy, Gladys and Esther sang:

> Because he lives, I can face tomorrow,
> Because he lives, all fear is gone,
> Because I know he holds the future,
> And life is worth the living just because he lives.

("Because He Lives" by William J. and Gloria Gaither.)

Extreme dedication is never daunted by danger. It isn't weakened by worries. It isn't even concerned about consequences. Dedication only knows one thing: the task at hand. For many people, losing their family to hostile foreigners would be a rational excuse for abandoning their mission. Not so for those driven by extreme dedication. Although they may be devastated by the trial, their determination to move forward is undeterred. God alone can give us the spiritual strength necessary to resume our mission in spite of misery. Do you find yourself trying to determine whether or not to continue in God's work? Has something happened to take you off course? Ask God for daily dedication to stick to the task.

eXtreme teen

CUBA: ROSE

Day 88

"I was born in a Communist home where no one could even mention the word *God*. My parents are atheists. My father is in the Cuban Communist Party leadership. My mother is secretary of the Committee for the Defense of the Revolution. You might say my home is a nest for communism. However, my grandmother loves God and taught me about the Lord. She sowed the seeds of God's Word into me. On several occasions I tried to go to church with her, but my parents did not allow it.

"One day, I received the Lord Jesus Christ as my Savior. My life started to change. Even the way I dressed changed. My mother did not accept it. She never beat me before, but now she often does. When my father learned that I was a Christian, he told me to choose God or him. I chose God because I have understood that He is the only one worth living for.

"Now, even though I am only fourteen, I have to study far away from my home. When I first came to this place I was the only Christian, but I have sown God's Word and now there are four of us. We meet under a tree—hidden—to share God's Word. We keep sowing and waiting, believing that soon we will be many."

But the one who received the seed that fell on good soil is the man who hears the word and understands it. He produces a crop, yielding a hundred, sixty or thirty times what was sown.

Matthew 13:23

Rose's childhood would have been one destined for Communist indoctrination and atheism, had it not been for her grandmother's influence. She is an extreme teen because she followed in the footsteps of her grandmother, who took a risk to share Christ with her. Now, Rose takes the same risk with those at her boarding school, sharing and sowing the Word of God. She is working on one believer at a time to make a difference. However, Rose has discovered, like many Cuban teenagers living under communism, faith comes with consequences. But she believes, despite the odds, that some of her seed will fall on responsive soil. In whose life will you sow seeds of God's Word and wait for a harvest?

eXtreme conquerors

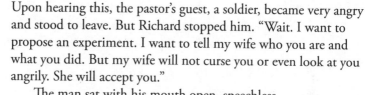

"My wife is sleeping in the other room because she has been ill," Pastor Richard Wurmbrand began. **"She and I are both Jewish. Her family perished in the same Nazi concentration camp where you just boasted of killing Jews with children still in their arms. Perhaps you murdered my wife's family."**

Day 89

And now these three remain: faith, hope and love. But the greatest of these is love.

1 Corinthians 13:13

Upon hearing this, the pastor's guest, a soldier, became very angry and stood to leave. But Richard stopped him. "Wait. I want to propose an experiment. I want to tell my wife who you are and what you did. But my wife will not curse you or even look at you angrily. She will accept you."

The man sat with his mouth open, speechless.

The pastor continued, "Now if my wife, who is only human, can forgive you—then how much more will Jesus love and forgive you?"

The man buried his face in his hands. "What have I done? How can I go on living with the guilt of so much blood? Jesus, please forgive me." The soldier surrendered his life to Christ.

Then Richard went and woke his wife, Sabina. "This is the murderer of your sisters, your brothers, and your parents," he introduced the man. "But now he has repented." She wrapped her hands around his neck and kissed him on the cheek.

"Love conquers all" is a popular saying. Christians, however, know the truth of this saying firsthand. When we are at the mercy of our anger, we are consumed with hatred. But when we have allowed God (who is love) to control our lives, we find that our natural emotions like anger submit to Him. We don't even feel like getting upset over situations that used to enrage us. Love must conquer anything within us that is contrary to the character of Christ. The end result is that we are so consumed with love that even our worst enemy benefits from our transformation. Are you experiencing victory over bitterness and vengeance? Ask the God of love to conquer your anger today.

eXtreme tenderness

CAMBODIA: A TEENAGE GIRL

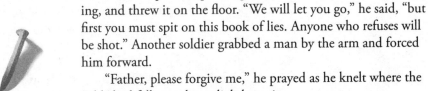

The Khmer Rouge soldiers burst into the room, brandishing their weapons and shouting insults and threats. When the Khmer Rouge took over Cambodia in 1975, thousands of Christians were killed. Children were even thrown before alligators so the soldiers could "save their bullets."

Day 90

If you have any encouragement from being united with Christ . . . if any tenderness and compassion, then make my joy complete by being like-minded.

Philippians 2:1,2

None of the members of the small congregation moved. An officer walked up to the pastor, grabbed the Bible he had been reading, and threw it on the floor. "We will let you go," he said, "but first you must spit on this book of lies. Anyone who refuses will be shot." Another soldier grabbed a man by the arm and forced him forward.

"Father, please forgive me," he prayed as he knelt where the Bible had fallen and spat lightly on it.

"Okay, you can go." Then the officer pointed to a woman. She too knelt by the Bible. She moistened the Bible just enough to please the officers.

A teenage girl suddenly stood up and walked toward the Bible. Tearfully, she knelt and picked up the Bible, taking the hem of her dress and wiping it clean. "What have they done to your Word?" she said. "Please forgive them." The soldier lowered his revolver to the back of her head and squeezed the trigger.

The Christians who were initially allowed to leave were also shot. Their actions did little to save them.

One act of tender resolve can inspire a congregation more than any number of betrayals. The teenager in this story prompts a vision of what it means to be united in Christ. Instead of rebuking her weaker brothers and sisters, she merely led by example in her tender treatment of the Bible. Imagine if everyone in that church had acted in the same like-minded manner. What a strong witness for Christ! Whenever we act together, we are stronger. Tenderness and compassion, combined with a strong example, will lead those who are weak to join together in greater commitment. If you are frustrated with others who struggle in their commitment, remember God calls you to unite with those who are weaker and help them along.

Day 91

For Christians, persecution is not about human rights, it is a rite of passage.

<small>STEVE CLEARY</small>

eXtreme patience

"This gift is for you."

"What is it?" the missionary asked his friend while preparing to go into North Korea.

"Just take it. You'll know when to open it."

Disguised as a businessman, the missionary journeyed into North Korea. He was assigned a Communist guide with a penchant for long naps.

Day 92

Seeing his opportunity, the missionary quietly left the hotel while his "guide" slept. He entered a nearby village and met up with a small group of believers. As soon as they realized the young missionary was an ordained minister, they said, "You must baptize us! We have waited for someone to baptize us!"

Trust in him at all times, O people.

Psalm 62:8

In a land where possessing a Bible can mean a fifteen-year sentence, a formal baptism could mean certain death. Without any lake or river nearby, the missionary simply prayed over the believers one by one as a symbol of their faith. But to his amazement they were not satisfied. "We have waited forty years for Communion."

One of the believers immediately brought out some rice cakes. The missionary thought, *They had had a baptism without water, maybe they could have Communion without drink.* Then he remembered the gift his friend handed him before going into North Korea. He quickly grabbed his travel bag and took out the package. It was a bottle of wine! Speechless, each villager wept openly, praising God for His timely gift.

While most people in modern culture could not imagine life without a calendar and a clock, God keeps His own time. He is not driven by the tyranny of the urgent. However, we must learn patience in order to happily live within His timing. Patience means trusting God is at work, even when we don't see the evidence. Patience is the principle of delayed gratification. When we wait for God's blessings in our lives, we appreciate them so much more. What we wait for, we value more. Whether it is a rice-cake Communion or a specific need in our lives, God's timing is certain. What concerns you regarding God's timing in your life? Is it time for you to trust Him?

eXtreme evangelism

UGANDA: BISHOP HANNINGTON

"The only chance a torturer has to be saved may be through a Christian prisoner. They never go to church or read the Holy Bible. But a Christian prisoner can speak love to them, even while being beaten." Such is the belief of an underground church member.

Day 93

I am not ashamed of the gospel, because it is the power of God for the salvation of everyone who believes.

Romans 1:16

Another woman who had spent her years serving Christ under danger of torment said, "Throughout church history, many Christian prisoners have brought their tormentors to heaven. There is a plaque in a Roman jail containing the names of those converted while Paul was in prison there. They would be in hell if Paul had not given them the chance to beat him." She paused. "I don't mind suffering if the salvation of torturers is the result."

Bishop Hannington knew the risk was high when he decided to bring the message of Christ to the cannibals in Uganda. A few weeks after the bishop arrived, the cannibals rejected his message and executed him. Before Hannington died, the cannibals heard the following words in a loud voice, "Love your enemies . . . pray for those who spitefully use you and persecute you."

This was the same message the bishop's two sons carried with them when they set out for the same village after their father's death. They were determined to continue evangelizing the same people who had killed their father.

Some suppose Christ's death and resurrection to be merely a hoax made up by wishful thinkers who wanted the memory of their beloved teacher to live on. However, how does that explain the martyrdom of most of His disciples and generations more after them? It seems reasonable that they would admit their folly at the moment of their arrest and certainly before their sure death. Why would they willingly carry a supposed hoax that far? In fact, history documents their attempts to convert their torturers right down to the last minute. Their extreme evangelism was evidence of their conviction: This was the very gospel of God. How convinced are you of the gospel message? Are you willing to carry it as far as the brink of the extreme?

eXtreme mission field

JAPAN: FRANCIS XAVIER

Day 94

I tell you the truth, if you have faith as small as a mustard seed, you can say to this mountain, "Move from here to there" and it will move.

Matthew 17:20

Japan, a country surrounded by beautiful mountains, was blessed by the faith of brave Christian brothers and sisters who decided to risk it all to be the first to bring Christ's message of love and forgiveness to Japan.

In 1549, Francis Xavier was the first missionary to Japan. Under his ministry, many were converted and the church grew rapidly. But Japanese officials saw Christians as a threat, and severe persecution began. The opposition to Christianity grew like a jagged mountain against the skies of Japan, overshadowing the believers below. In cities like Unzen, Christians were boiled in volcanic lava. Others were crucified on wooden crosses in the town of Nagasaki. Japanese soldiers rounded up all known Christians in 1637, around thirty thousand of them, and killed each one.

Following this, the church went underground in hopes of protecting those who managed to survive. The church struggled for several years. However, by God's grace the church survived. Faithful missionaries did not stop coming. They heard about the mountainous persecution and answered the call to minister to the few faithful believers who were left.

Japan now has 1.7 million active Christians, and the church is adding believers every day. Xavier and the modern missionaries represent the faith of a mustard seed that moved a mountain of opposition so a nation could be changed.

Life is full of obstructed views. Believers often face a mountain of opposition from worldly family members who don't accept their beliefs. Many Christians come across the Alps of atheism in the workplace. Towering peaks of persecution from their own governments overshadow believers in restricted nations. However, a beautiful view is just beyond each mountain of opposition that faces the church today. The scene is of thousands of men, women, and children who hunger for the gospel. Faith can clear the way for others to be saved. Many Christians before you have been persecuted to demonstrate that truth. Will you continue their work with a faith that can move mountains? What mountain of opposition will you focus on today?

eXtreme places

RUSSIA: ZOYA KRAKHMALNIKOVA

A fellow prisoner who was a priest in a Russian prison had betrayed Zoya. He made false accusations about her so that he could be released from prison and escape his own torture. During the trial, Zoya refused to say one word against him. She said, "When Judas betrayed Jesus, he was a treacherous man. But Jesus called him 'friend' in Gethsemane. Should we not learn from Christ's example and behave like this toward those who betray us?"

Day 95

Do your best to present yourself to God as one approved, a workman who does not need to be ashamed and who correctly handles the word of truth.

2 Timothy 2:15

Zoya Krakhmalnikova spent six years in a Russian prison for sharing Christ with others. Her time there gave her a unique insight into God's Word and how it applies to the harsh realities of life.

"In prison, every cell door has a hole called the Judas hole. Through it the guards can control you every five minutes. They watch you closely, inspecting you and instructing you. This helped me to understand, if the Communists are so diligent about keeping an eye on me, would not God and His angels do so with even more diligence?"

Zoya could have easily allowed bitterness to rule her heart. But she took the lessons in Scripture and directly applied them to her own life. They were hard lessons. But they served to make her life and the lives of those around her a little brighter.

Going on an extended trip without packing one's things is a seemingly ridiculous proposition. Who would travel unprepared? Yet Christians make a spiritual journey every day without being adequately spiritually prepared for their trek. We need to be prepared with God's Word in our hearts in order to apply them when needed. Many of us struggle to succeed in spiritual tests because we have not studied God's principles ahead of time. We end up feeling like failures when we could have been victorious like Zoya by applying God's Word to our situation. Your faith in Christ may take you to extreme places. Are you prepared for the journey? Make sure you have plenty of God's Word—you'll need it.

eXtreme guerrilla

Juan was sentenced to serve fifteen years in the Miguel Castro prison for his terrorist activities. Juan understood how terrorists think. He was a militiaman for the Communist group known as the "Shining Path." His greatest commission was teaching others how to kill and destroy. He was a high-ranking official and an expert in dynamite, weapons, and annihilation. His job gave him a sense of inspiration and destiny.

Day 96

But whatever was to my profit I now consider loss for the sake of Christ.

Philippians 3:7

Juan continued his work even in prison. As he worked to enlist a young man named Fernando into the militia, he found that many of the Marxist ideas were not working on him. In turn, Fernando asked Juan a penetrating question: "If you died tonight, my friend, where would you spend eternity?"

Juan had witnessed or orchestrated the countless deaths of others, but he had never considered his own death. Fernando's question began to bother him. Fernando continued to speak with him each day about the love of Christ and His sacrifice. Finally, Juan became a believer.

Fernando encouraged the new disciple: "As you gave your life to the revolution, today give it to Christ your Lord."

Eventually, Juan pastored a flock in prison. In his past, he enlisted people in the militia school; in prison he organized Sunday school. His mission of death changed to helping others find eternal life.

People's passions give them a sense of inspiration and destiny. Some people have a passion for their job. Others are passionate about their families. Still others are passionate about causes that directly oppose the cause of Christ. Those who persecute Christians cannot be accused of apathy. Their relentless determination would almost be admirable were it not misdirected. God is in the business of exchanging old lives for new ones, however. With the same passion he once felt for Marxism, Juan began to enlist others for Christ. God took his perverse passion and turned it into a passion for Christ. Pray for God to transform anything that competes for your spiritual devotion. Ask Him for a burning desire to further His kingdom.

eXtreme choice

THE PHILIPPINES: PETER

Peter felt it was worth the risk. He loved traveling with his Uncle Michael, an evangelist in the Philippines, to the remote villages where people were so hungry to hear about Christ.

Day 97

If anyone chooses to do God's will, he will find out whether my teaching comes from God or whether I speak on my own.

John 7:17

The trips to villages were adventurous and sometimes dangerous, traveling through the thick forests for hours on end. People in the Philippines had been terrorized for many years by the New People's Army, the arm of the Communist Party. Peter and his uncle often had to hide to keep away from danger. Peter loved the children and enjoyed seeing their eyes light up when they finally understood how much God loved them.

On Good Friday, the New People's Army sought to put an end to his Uncle Michael's ministry. So they captured Peter and threatened to put him to death if his uncle would not stop talking about Christ. Peter's parents replied, "We cannot tell Michael to cease his work. However, we beg you to please return our son. He has done nothing wrong."

Finally, with his hands tied behind his back, Peter heard his parents tell the soldiers, "To live is Christ and to die is gain." And with those words, Peter went home to meet his Savior that somber Good Friday. His Uncle Michael still tells the mountain villagers about the power of Christ's love and about his young, faithful nephew named Peter.

Risks are all about choice. Some people choose to risk their fortunes, betting on the most mundane activities. The outcome of a football game. The winner in a lap around the racetrack. The number of baskets a certain player makes in a night. Others risk their very lives by choosing self-serving activities with no eternal significance, like drugs and alcohol. Jesus calls people to another choice altogether. He says we must choose to risk our earthly security in order to gain a heavenly reward for doing His will. Doing His will brings a greater reward than a cash payout at the racetrack or an artificial high from the latest drug. Have you experienced Jesus' reward for risking your faith? Why or why not?

Day 98

We don't pray to be better Christians,
but that we may be the only kind of Christians
God means us to be: Christlike Christians,
that is, Christians who bear willingly
the cross for God's glory.

FROM A LETTER SMUGGLED OUT FROM THE
UNDERGROUND CHURCH IN ROMANIA

eXtreme hymn

The young, brown-eyed girl looked up at her mother. What would her mom decide?

Earlier that morning, the young girl's mother, their pastor, and twenty-six others in her North Korean village of GokSan were bound and taken before a screaming crowd of Communists.

Day 99

One of the guards ordered Pastor Kim and the other Christians, "Deny Christ, or you will die." The words chilled her. How could they ask her to deny Jesus? She knew in her heart he was real. They all quietly refused.

Then the Communist guard shouted directly at the adult Christians, "Deny Christ, or we will hang your children." The young girl looked up at her mother. She gripped her hand knowing how much her mom loved her. Her mother then leaned down. With confidence and peace she whispered, "Today, my love, I will see you in heaven."

For God so loved the world that he gave his one and only Son, that whoever believes in him shall not perish but have eternal life.

John 3:16

All of the children were hanged.

The remaining believers were then brought out onto the pavement and forced to lie down in front of a large steamroller. The Communists gave them one last chance. "Deny this Jesus or you will be crushed." The Christians had already given up their children; there was no turning back.

As the driver started the heavy piece of equipment, the singing from the villagers started softly. "More love, O Christ, to thee, more love to thee."

More. It's what God gave when He sent His Son. More. It's what Jesus gave when He was crucified. More. It's what believers give simply out of love for Christ. They want to give more to the One who gave so much to them. In a worldly age that values giving only what one must to get by, believers set a new standard. "More love to thee" is more than just words in a traditional hymnal. It's a lifestyle without limit. Each day is a path of discovering how to give more love to Jesus Christ. For some believers, this path has led to their death. For others, "more love to thee" has meant financial sacrifice. What does "more love to thee" mean to your everyday life?

eXtreme movie

PAKISTAN: CHRISTIAN WORKERS

Now everyone wanted to see the movie. They whispered about it in the market and even in the mosque. "What is it about?" "Is it really that bad, that people should get arrested for having it?"

Day 100

"For my thoughts are not your thoughts, neither are your ways my ways," declares the LORD.

Isaiah 55:8

The movie in question was the *JESUS* film—a high-quality film that portrays the life, ministry, death, and resurrection of Jesus Christ. It shows the plan of salvation on the big screen, bringing the story of Jesus to life. In Jacobabad, Pakistan, two men were arrested for distributing the film and other Christian materials. Both men were beaten, and local mullahs, Muslim religious leaders, urged that charges be filed against them and others who had been involved in distributing the materials. Then they went one step beyond, encouraging Muslims in the city to take action against all Christians. Soon, a local pastor's possessions were stolen, and shots were fired near a Christian school. The town seemed on the verge of outright violence.

However, things soon began to change. Instead of boycotting the movie, everyone in town wanted to see the "sinful" film. They wanted to know about all the fuss firsthand. Black-market copies began making the rounds, and eventually the *JESUS* film was even shown on local television. The city judge watched the movie, and he declared that it was not anti-Islam.

Through the unintentional efforts of the mullahs, the gospel message reached an entire community. They planned to erase the JESUS film from their country. However, their campaign actually promoted the ministry. God does not turn evil into good by conventional methods. He blesses the efforts of His servants, but not in ways we might anticipate. Christians in restricted nations are learning this the hard way, but they rejoice to see the mystery of God at work in their nations. God makes a way for us even when it doesn't make sense. There are times when everything seems to be going wrong. Are those the times when you trust God the most? He knows what He is doing even when you do not.

eXtreme pardon

The paper was dirty, torn at the edges. The black ink marched across the page in an almost-illegible scrawl. At the bottom, the letter was signed "Ricardo."

Day 101

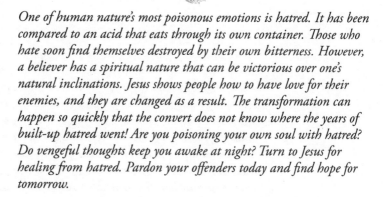

If anyone says, "I love God," yet hates his brother, he is a liar. For anyone who does not love his brother, whom he has seen, cannot love God, whom he has not seen.

1 John 4:20

"I write from a Communist guerrilla camp in Peru. Recently, I searched for some radio programs to cheer me up. The hate-filled programs of my comrades were empty to me. Then I came across your program, 'The Gospel in Marxist Language.' You said that Jesus, the great teacher, talked about pardoning one's enemies.

"That passage drove itself into the deepest part of my being. Suddenly, I experienced peace, and I wept like a child. I don't understand what has happened.

"My parents had been victims of an exploiting landowner, and I had hated the rich all my life. But for some reason, I don't hate anymore. I can't explain it. Is it *possible* for me not to hate?

"That was the first time I heard your program. How happy I have become. Now I shall not miss a single one. I want to read the book you spoke about."

Later, Ricardo left the guerrillas to join a church. Two years later, he returned to the camp, hoping to tell his former comrades about his Savior. He has not been heard from since. If he died, he did so with love for those who killed him.

One of human nature's most poisonous emotions is hatred. It has been compared to an acid that eats through its own container. Those who hate soon find themselves destroyed by their own bitterness. However, a believer has a spiritual nature that can be victorious over one's natural inclinations. Jesus shows people how to have love for their enemies, and they are changed as a result. The transformation can happen so quickly that the convert does not know where the years of built-up hatred went! Are you poisoning your own soul with hatred? Do vengeful thoughts keep you awake at night? Turn to Jesus for healing from hatred. Pardon your offenders today and find hope for tomorrow.

eXtreme treasure

ROMANIA: THE VILLAGERS OF DOBROGEA

Nicolai Ceaucescu had a brainstorm called "collectivization." As the vicious dictator of Romania, he probably thought it was a good idea to get the people to voluntarily surrender all of their possessions to the state for the common good of all.

Day 102

For you are a people holy to the LORD your God. The LORD your God has chosen you out of all the peoples on the face of the earth to be his people, his treasured possession.

Deuteronomy 7:6

Farmers, landowners, and peasants everywhere lost everything: fields, sheep, cattle, houses, and furniture. The once-thriving agricultural sector of Romania was destroyed. Every farmer now became a slave of the state, working for pathetic wages on the state's fields. Families stood in line just to obtain bread.

To keep the people from becoming resistant to his strategy, the dictator himself helped in the initial launch. In the Romanian province of Dobrogea, all the villagers were gathered together in the town center and asked to willingly give up their possessions. When no one volunteered, Ceaucescu shot ten people with his own gun. The vote was taken again: "Who is willing to give up all of their possessions?"

They played military music and chanted the praises of communism. As the people were forced to dance, a video was made propagating their enthusiastic adherence to socialism. One farmer who had lost everything reported later, "They thought they took everything. But they left something very important: our hymnals. So we sat down and sang praises to the Lord."

People often play games to get new people talking and learning about each other. One of the more revealing questions is to ask people what one thing they would bring if they were stranded on a deserted island. Most people have a hard time deciding and have to be reminded that this is only a game. However, the people of Romania did not have the luxury of playing a game; they were experiencing real life. Their government didn't even allow them one possession. However, the villagers realized the presence of those overlooked hymnals brought joy to their village, which now resembled their own deserted island. The people treasured the hymnals, and God treasured the people.

eXtreme offering

LEBANON: MARY

Mary was only seventeen when Muslim fanatics raided her village in Lebanon. Mary and her parents were confronted with a grueling choice: "Become a Muslim, or you will be shot."

Mary boldly told the man, "I choose God. Go ahead and shoot." Mary and her family were shot and left for dead. Two days later, the Red Cross arrived in the village and found a miracle. Mary was alive—but paralyzed by the bullet.

Devastated and grieving, Mary clung to her faith and prayed. Finally a strange peace came over her. She made this commitment to God: "Everyone has a job to do. I can never marry or do any physical work. So I will offer my life for the Muslims, like the ones who killed my father and mother and tried to kill me. My life will be a prayer for them."

Her prayers and her undeniable witness of Christ brought many Muslims to faith in the Son of God. In Lebanon, 1990 was the fiercest year of the fifteen-year civil war. Thousands were killed or wounded, and hundreds of thousands fled. However, Mary's offering of her wounded life encouraged many Christians to stay and take a stand for Christ.

Day 103

But even if I am being poured out like a drink offering on the sacrifice and service coming from your faith, I am glad and rejoice with all of you.

Philippians 2:17

The greatest gift to God's service will not fit in an offering plate. When we view our entire lives as offerings to God, our resources to benefit His kingdom are unlimited. Many of those who have been persecuted like Mary share a similar story. They continue to offer their lives, as an act of worship, to serve those who oppress them. Therese of Lisieux once noted, "Sufferings gladly borne for others convert more people than sermons." The majority of Christians will find it easy to make the usual excuses for offering their lives: "too busy" and "too much going on." However, God can reveal unique ways that we can be witnesses for Him.

eXtreme sadness

The Communist prison of Jilava was especially harsh. The broken windows let in the bitter winter cold. Some of the prisoners had even frozen to death. There was no sympathy for Christians at Jilava. In fact, they often endured "special" beatings from the cruel guards.

Day 104

Yet now I am happy, not because you were made sorry, but because your sorrow led you to repentance. For you became sorrowful as God intended.

2 Corinthians 7:9

One of the new prisoners, Archmandrite Ghiush, was a pastor in the city of Liberty, Romania. As Archmandrite anxiously looked around his new "home," he noticed a familiar face—a man who had served with him in Liberty. It was Pastor Richard Wurmbrand. "How could he still be alive?" Archmandrite wondered. "No one has heard from him in nearly eight years." The two faithful pastors embraced. Archmandrite smiled, grateful for an old friend to help him through the horrific sufferings he was about to endure.

But Pastor Wurmbrand did not smile. He felt saddened to see such a fine pastor in prison. He began to worry about him. Would he survive the cold and the cruel treatment? Would he go mad, as others had done? After eight years in prison, Wurmbrand knew what was to come.

The two friends sat silently for a while. Finally Richard broke the tension and softly asked, "Are you sad?"

To his amazement Archmandrite simply replied, "Brother, I know only one sadness: That is not being fully given to Jesus."

It is difficult to read the true stories of Christian martyrs without feeling emotionally drained. The natural reaction is one of sadness and a sense of pity for the innocent who died such horrific deaths. However, the heroes and heroines of the stories would wish for an altogether different response. They hoped their sacrifices would inspire others toward like-hearted commitment, not pity. Certainly, their deaths touch our hearts. But the realization of our own paltry faith ought to break our hearts in two. That is truly sad. Are you challenged beyond earthly sympathy toward repentance for your own complacency? Do you have a divine sense of determination as a result of your reading? Ask God to stir your resolve to live for Him today.

Day 105

Faith is not even worthy of the name
until it erupts into action.

<small>Catherine Marshall</small>

eXtreme forgiveness

ROMANIA: DEMETER

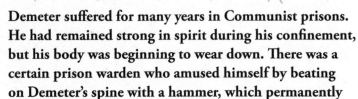

Day 106

Demeter suffered for many years in Communist prisons. He had remained strong in spirit during his confinement, but his body was beginning to wear down. There was a certain prison warden who amused himself by beating on Demeter's spine with a hammer, which permanently paralyzed him. But Demeter's Christlike attitude never wavered, and he was eventually released from prison.

Twenty years later, he heard a knock at the front door of his home. He was shocked to see the same prison warden who had so cruelly beat on his spine and paralyzed him years earlier standing before him. Still, Demeter did not waver in his expression of faith.

Even before Demeter could offer a greeting, the former warden said, "I realize I can never be forgiven for what I have done to you. It was too heinous. But please just listen to my words of apology and then I will leave."

Demeter paused only for a moment as he gazed with compassion and wonder at the man. He replied softly, "For twenty years I have prayed for you daily. I have waited for you. Twenty years ago, I forgave you already."

If we are willing to show love and forgiveness to everyone —even those who have hurt us—then the love of Christ can conquer all.

Bear with each other and forgive whatever grievances you may have against one another. Forgive as the Lord forgave you.

Colossians 3:13

Most people will never suffer deliberate physical torment. However, the wounds that others inflict upon us emotionally can be just as devastating. Memories of unkind words, a betrayal by a friend, a bitter divorce, can stay with us for a lifetime. We are tempted to hold a grudge, or even perhaps to exact revenge against the offender. Forgiveness does not come naturally to us, but it is inseparable from God's nature. If we have tasted God's grace, then we can allow others to share in God's forgiveness. Forgiveness does not depend on the offender asking for it first. It is an act of obedience, as well as an act of faith. Ask God to open your heart to the miracle of true forgiveness.

eXtreme visitation

EASTERN EUROPE: JON LUGAJANU

A young Christian man in Eastern Europe, Jon Lugajanu, returned to the prison after his court hearing. His cell-mates anxiously asked him, "What happened?"

He answered, "It was just like the day the angel visited Mary, the mother of Jesus. Here she was, a godly young woman sitting alone in meditation, when a radiant angel of God told her the incredible news. She would carry the Son of God in her womb."

Day 107

Curious about how this story tied in to Jon's courtroom experience, the other prisoners listened closely. Jon went on to share the gospel of peace through the story of Mary.

"For all the joy Jesus brought her, Mary would have to one day stand at the foot of a cross and watch Him suffer and die for the sins of the world. God resurrected Jesus, where He now reigns in heaven. Mary knew once she was in heaven, she would be with Jesus again and experience eternal joy."

Because he suffered death, so that by the grace of God he might taste death for everyone.

Hebrews 2:9

The other prisoners were puzzled at this. "But we asked you what happened in court?" they reminded Jon.

Jon looked at them, his face shining with peace, and said, "I was given the death penalty. Isn't that beautiful news?" Jon realized the news the angel delivered to Mary was just as bitter-sweet—after Jesus had suffered there would be rejoicing in heaven. He anxiously anticipated his eternal joy in Jesus' presence.

In many cultures, death is a taboo subject. People often go to great lengths to insulate themselves from the inevitability of their own death. They like to use phrases like "passed away" instead of "died." We resist making a will or buying life insurance, thinking, "It will never happen to me." Corporations make huge profits selling us products that promise eternal youth. God does not give us the option of ignoring death, but He gives us the key to facing it. Mary's angelic visitor did not shirk from telling her she would suffer great grief at the cross. However, she was also given the hope of resurrection to make her grief bearable. As Christians, God's promise of eternal life helps us accept our own death both realistically and courageously.

eXtreme defense

RUSSIA: GEORGE JELTONOSHKO

George Jeltonoshko knew his government did not want people propagating the gospel of Christ, but he had a stronger conviction to obey the commandments of Christ—even if it conflicted with the laws of his country.

Day 108

It was not a huge surprise to him when the police came to his door. He figured it was inevitable that they would find out about his ministry activities because of the literature he had been spreading. When his trial date came, he was given a state-appointed Communist attorney. George boldly told the judge, "I don't want a lawyer. I feel I am right, and righteousness needs no defense."

The judge asked him, "Do you plead guilty?"

He replied, "No. To spread the Good News of God's love is the duty of all Christians."

Commit your way to the LORD; trust in him and he will do this: He will make your righteousness shine like the dawn, the justice of your cause like the noonday sun.

Psalm 37:5,6

The judge then asked him to join the ranks of the "official churches," which were nothing more than state-run puppet churches. But George refused. The state church followed the commandments of the state, not the commands of God.

The judge was getting frustrated. "Where do you meet for worship?" he demanded.

"True believers worship everywhere."

George Jeltonoshko was sentenced to three years in prison where he continued to carry out his work and worship. He was right. Righteousness needed no defense.

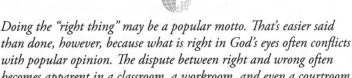

Doing the "right thing" may be a popular motto. That's easier said than done, however, because what is right in God's eyes often conflicts with popular opinion. The dispute between right and wrong often becomes apparent in a classroom, a workroom, and even a courtroom or church. We can't rely on our environment to tell us what is right. People can persuade us to confuse compromise with righteousness. God's Word is the only defense for determining what is right in every situation. Others may not understand or agree with the choices we make. However, God promises to honor our commitment to doing what is right. Those who observe us will see the light and feel the warmth of our righteous actions.

eXtreme fire

SIBERIA: VICTOR BELIKH

"With the flames of love's fire that Jesus kindled in my heart, I caused the ice of Siberia to melt. Hallelujah!"

Bishop Victor Belikh's face lit up as he spoke these words. He had learned the powerful secret of letting God take over one's heart even in the worst of circumstances. For twenty years he had suffered in the lonely prison cell in Communist Russia without a visit or news from his family or friends.

Every evening, a simple straw mattress was placed in his small cell. He was allowed to sleep for seven hours before the mat was removed. He spent the remaining seventeen hours of each day walking circles in his pathetic little space, and if he stopped or broke down, guards would beat him or throw water on him until he continued. After twenty years of such incredible hardship, he was sent to a forced-labor camp for another four years in Northern Siberia, where the ice never melts. He survived only because he allowed the fire of God to melt away all bitterness and anger.

Victor's situation is rare, but his resolve through Jesus Christ is available to everyone who suffers. Jesus stoked the fire of love in Victor's heart—a godly furnace that was able to keep him warm for twenty years.

Day 109

For our God is a consuming fire.

Hebrews 12:29

Fire. The mere word ignites powerful images. It implies danger when shouted in a crowded building. It embodies comfort when camping on a frosty night. It is connected with strong emotions during the "heat" of the moment or a "fiery" temper. Fire is also used to refine and to harden metals through the smelting process. Fire illuminates and consumes darkness. In all these images, one thing remains constant. Fire is associated with change. Like an encounter with fire, an encounter with God is life changing. Has the fiery love of Christ ignited, sustained, refined, comforted, and ultimately liberated you as it did Victor? Human cruelty can never extinguish the flame of God's love. Is the flame of God's love alive in you?

eXtreme reputation

JERUSALEM: JAMES

James "the Just" faithfully served as head of the newborn church following Jesus' resurrection. It is said that no unbeliever could endure his teachings without either converting or fleeing his presence.

Day 110

So then, those who suffer according to God's will should commit themselves to their faithful Creator and continue to do good.

1 Peter 4:19

For this reason, the high priest and other Jewish leaders placed James on the pinnacle of the temple and told him to deny Jesus and His resurrection before all the people gathered or be thrown to the ground. This only gave James another opportunity to preach to a captive audience.

"Listen, all you people! Jesus is the promised Messiah, the Son of God, and our Savior! He is sitting at the right hand of God and shall come again to judge the living and the dead!"

Below, some began to praise God and magnify the name of Jesus; others were stunned at his boldness and conviction. He certainly was a just man! Immediately, he was pushed over the edge—falling to his certain death.

The crowd hushed; then someone shouted, "Look! He lives!" James was not dead but rather kneeling in prayer. Many had collected rocks to stone him, when one of the priests rushed forward and begged, "What are you doing? 'The Just' is praying for us, and you would harm him?" As he said this, another came from behind him with a large rod and struck James in the head, killing him instantly. He was buried in the spot where he had fallen.

Behind every event one reads about in history, there is a story. The nuances and the feel of the situation may have been lost, but it's easy enough to imagine them from the facts recorded in history. This story about James captures the essence of his personality and his forthright witness for Jesus. Those who knew him best knew his commitment to Christ. And those who did not know him at all had heard of his reputation as a courageous preacher. His death is one more testimony of an unswerving faith in Christ. Christian history attests to the faithfulness of Christ's followers with inarguable evidence. What will history have to say about you? What's the story you would like generations from now to tell about your faith?

eXtreme baptism

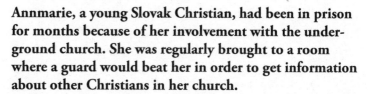

Annmarie, a young Slovak Christian, had been in prison for months because of her involvement with the underground church. She was regularly brought to a room where a guard would beat her in order to get information about other Christians in her church.

Day 111

By God's grace she was able to resist. She even used these times to tell the guard about the love of Jesus. The guard mocked, "If you don't tell me secrets of the underground church, I will beat out of you all your loves."

Annmarie responded, "I have a boyfriend, the sweetest of all. He is love. His love does not seek pleasure but seeks to fill others with joy. Since knowing this boyfriend, I, too, can only love. You love hatred now. I beg you to love Love."

This water symbolizes baptism that now saves you also —not the removal of dirt from the body but the pledge of a good conscience toward God.

1 Peter 3:21

The guard was so angry that he slapped her until she passed out. When she came to, she saw him sitting quietly as if in deep thought. Finally he asked, "Who is this boyfriend of yours?" Annmarie told him all about Jesus and why He came.

When he asked how to make Jesus his friend too, she told him that he must repent and be baptized. "Then baptize me immediately or I will shoot you," he demanded.

Annmarie did baptize him, and he later became a prisoner with the very ones he used to beat.

When people are in love, they let everyone know it. They tell their families, their friends, their neighbors, and anyone else who will listen. Love so consumes them that they cannot help but talk about their beloved. In the same way, one's baptism is a public announcement of being identified with Christ and His community, of being in love with Jesus. Baptism of an adult is a sign to all who witness it— even if only by another prisoner in a cell—that one is ready to follow Christ at all costs. Our love for Christ motivates us to proclaim our commitment to the world. Even if not threatened, do we have courage to tell of our love for Jesus?

Day 112

*Faith is never passive. It demands a response.
It asks for a mission. It demonstrates the
indwelling presence and power
of the Holy Spirit.*

PASTOR RICHARD WURMBRAND

eXtreme courage

ROMANIA: A MOTHER AND DAUGHTER

All the prisoners were upset to see the little girl in prison with her mother. Even the prison director said, "Why don't you take pity on your daughter? If you will give up being a Christian, you both can go home."

Day 113

Have I not commanded you? Be strong and courageous. Do not be terrified; do not be discouraged, for the LORD your God will be with you wherever you go.

Joshua 1:9

The woman was understandably torn inside. She had been imprisoned with her child after protesting the arrest of her pastor, but she agreed to deny her faith to keep her daughter from suffering. Two weeks later, the Communists forced her to shout from a stage in front of ten thousand people: "I am no longer a Christian."

On their return home, the little girl turned to her mother and said, "Mommy, today Jesus is not satisfied with you." The mother tried to explain that she did this out of love. The little girl looked at her mother with conviction beyond her years and said, "I promise if we go to prison again for Jesus, I will not cry."

Her mother wept, overcome with pride and love for her daughter and conviction for her own weakness. As she cried out to God for strength in a difficult decision, she went back to the prison director and said, "You convinced me to deny my faith for my daughter's sake, but she has more courage than me." They both returned to prison, and the little girl kept her promise.

Joshua of the Israelites faced a difficult challenge: picking up where Moses left off and leading God's chosen people onward. Was it dangerous? Undoubtedly. Was Joshua apprehensive? Probably. Joshua received God's promise to be with him, giving Joshua the same confidence as the child in the story. Both Joshua and the child realized early in life that they would need God's presence to succeed. God commands us to fortify ourselves with courage and the knowledge that He will never forsake us. In the face of trials, courage often flees. In times of trouble, choose to trust God's promise that He will be with you. Be obedient and courageous today.

eXtreme advice

ALBANIA: VALERII NASARUK

In Albania, the first self-declared atheist state in the world, a young Christian by the name of Valerii Nasaruk was arrested for boldly tattooing a cross on his hand. He wanted everyone to know from the first handshake that he stuck to his faith in God. Valerii was frustrated, however, by not being allowed to verbally tell others about God's love.

Day 114

May I never boast except in the cross of our Lord Jesus Christ, through which the world has been crucified to me, and I to the world.

Galatians 6:14

At the trial, the judge told Valerii's mother, "Tell your son to change his ways so he can go free."

She thought for a while before responding through tearful eyes, "Valerii, my advice to you is to stand firm and not deny Christ, even if it means your death."

In a subsequent letter to the underground church, she wrote, "I attended the trial, which was so hard on me. I wished I could have taken his place. The hardest thing was when they asked me in court to advise Valerii to change his ways, but I could not do it. The world accuses us, his parents, for his being sentenced, saying it is the result of our influence. Even some Christians can't understand why I did what I did, but then I remember that Jesus was misunderstood. When I struggle with depression, I am reminded that Peter advised Jesus about saving his own life. God gives me the power to bear everything. Please pray for me."

God loves us, and He has great plans for our lives. The problem is, everyone else has plans for us, too. Do this. Do that. Try this. Try that. Words of advice are cheap and plentiful. The time comes, however, when words are costly. Any time another believer encourages us to carry on with God's call on our lives despite the consequences, we know we have heard from a godly person. Anything to the contrary, even well intentioned, is bad advice. To whom do you listen for spiritual guidance? Recall and record the last bit of spiritual advice you received from a trusted friend. How well have you followed through?

eXtreme focus

CHINA: ME LING

"I purified my heart of the fear of men, and I learned to see God."

Me Ling was young when she was arrested for her Christian activities in Communist China. During times of interrogation, the police would torture her to try to force her to betray friends in the underground church.

Day 115

Set your minds on things above, not on earthly things.

Colossians 3:2

At first Me Ling was extremely fearful, and she could not see the purpose that God had for her in that terrible place. But then she remembered the teachings of her pastor who had said, "Real suffering lasts only a minute, and then we spend eternity with our awesome Savior."

When asked how she was able to keep from going crazy during those terrible times, she replied, "When I closed my eyes, I could not see the angry faces of the men or the instruments of pain they were using. I kept repeating the promise of Christ to myself: 'Blessed are the pure in heart, for they will see God' (Matthew 5:8). I also found that when I purified my heart of the fear of men, I learned to really see God. I took courage from all the others who had gone before me and focused on Him until everything else faded away. When the officials learned of my defense, they taped my eyelids open. But it was too late because my vision was secure."

We admire people whose professions require a great deal of concentration and focus. The skilled neurosurgeon, the Olympic athlete, and the corporate visionary share a common trait: they are focused. The discipline of focus transcends intelligence, athletic agility, or charisma. Without focus, these people would be merely smart, athletic, or interesting at best. Their ability to stay focused contributes greatly to their success. Developing an earthly focus can bring earthly success, but what about matters of eternity? If you are more focused on the temporary things of this world you will miss the goal. What can you do today to ensure you are focused on Christ and on spreading His Good News?

eXtreme letters

THE UKRAINE: THREE CHRISTIANS

The Soviet newspaper *Molodoij Gruzii* reported the imprisonment of three Christians. Their crime was starting an organized chain letter to help people all across the Soviet Union understand the teachings of Jesus Christ.

Day 116

Your word, O LORD, is eternal; it stands firm in the heavens.

Psalm 119:89

Unable to publish Bibles or Christian books, they had begun sending out multiple copies of these letters and asking recipients to make copies and pass them on. Through this creative method of spreading the gospel, thousands of letters had reached into many areas of the Soviet Union. The children especially liked them because they were not allowed to attend church, and the letters became an integral part of their Christian teaching.

In addition, these letters helped to bolster the faith of Christians throughout the country during that time. After years of government repression and interference in their churches, they were ready to try something bold and new. They sincerely wanted everyone to know about the love of God, and despite the restrictions placed upon them, their brilliant simplicity allowed the message to spread throughout the town of Tbilisi and even into some areas of the Ukraine!

Another newspaper article stated, "The Christians have flooded our town with their writings." It described this coordinated effort as "an offensive on the part of the believers."

Who could predict the far-reaching effects of a mere chain letter!

After fifty years of tyranny against Christianity, Soviet officials felt threatened by a chain letter. Their cowardly response demonstrates the power contained in God's Word. Oppression does not yield to human effort. It does not soften with feelings of sympathy. It only resists the powerful Word of God—alive and active in the lives of believers. Satan trembles at the power contained in God's Word. Are we as aware of its power as our adversaries are? If it has been a long time since you experienced awe when reading Scripture, ask God for a second chance. Ask Him to show you His power and experience the Word's effect on your life today.

eXtreme volunteer

CHINA: SISTER KWANG

After requiring many hours of hard labor and providing a near-starvation diet, the Chinese prison guards demanded that someone volunteer to clean the bathrooms daily. None of the women prisoners spoke up.

Day 117

And whatever you do, whether in word or deed, do it all in the name of the Lord Jesus, giving thanks to God the Father through him.

Colossians 3:17

Finally, Sister Kwang stepped forward and volunteered to do the despicable task. She saw it as the ultimate opportunity to share her faith with fellow prisoners whom she would otherwise never see. During her time in that prison, she led hundreds of women to Christ.

Kwang's devotion was evident to all who knew her, but it came through much suffering. Before her imprisonment, she and her husband had volunteered to organize groups of evangelists who traveled around China forming small house churches.

When Communist officials discovered Kwang's activities, they beat her twelve-year-old son to death. Still, she refused to deny Christ and even continued to build the house-church movement after her release.

Finally in 1974, the Communists decided to make an example of "Mother Kwang," as her church members now knew her. She was sentenced to life in prison, put in an underground cell with a bucket for sanitary needs, and fed only dirty rice.

She was miraculously released after ten years and always looked back on her prison time as a gift—a special opportunity to share the love of Christ with people who might never have heard otherwise.

Volunteerism is almost a professional occupation for some people. They volunteer at their children's school, assist with parent/teacher nights, and help coach their children's soccer teams. Volunteering for the not-so-popular opportunities can be more of a challenge. Often the volunteer spirit is nowhere to be found. Nursing homes, orphanages, and shelters are the last places many people want to spend their time. The smell, depressing environment, or other discomforts drive them away. But where do you suppose Jesus would spend most of His time? Nearly any volunteer position involves necessary and admirable work, but listen carefully for the opportunities less traveled and with those less fortunate. Try being the first to volunteer the next time one comes your way.

eXtreme audience

Even when Romanian pastor Richard Wurmbrand was placed in a solitary prison cell devoid of light and sound, he continued to preach to an unseen audience.

After his miraculous release from prison and his eventual migration to the United States, Pastor Wurmbrand wrote several books describing his prison experience and the sermons that he composed and memorized while in solitary confinement. After a few years, he received this letter:

Day 118

You do not have, because you do not ask God.

James 4:2

> Dear Pastor Wurmbrand,
>
> I was raised in a godly home, but I strayed and eventually ended up in prison here in Canada. I wanted to return to God but didn't know how, so I prayed, "God, if somewhere in the world there is another lonely prisoner who knows you, please bring me his thoughts." I heard an inner voice telling me to sit quietly and confidently and that God would reach me.
>
> Miraculously, night after night I began hearing a kind of sermon that seemed to come from far away. I repented, and after my release from prison, I ran across your book *Sermons in Solitary Confinement* in a Christian bookstore. I immediately recognized these sermons as the same ones I had heard in prison. Thank you for delivering them!

Pastor Wurmbrand received two other letters from different countries that contained nearly identical stories. Truly, angels had carried the sermons to others crying out to God.

It is said that Christians often leave angels unemployed because of their lack of faith. Too often believers are content to live good lives with occasional blessings. But God longs to give us more than what is good for us. He longs to bring us to better things and even what is best; however, He has reserved His best blessings for those who ask in faith. Why should we ask God if He already knows our needs? We must ask in faith to demonstrate our dependence on Him. Have you been content with the good things God has given to you? Then ask in faith for better. Settle for nothing less than His best in your life.

Day 119

If all mankind had been righteous and only one man a sinner, Christ would have come to endure the same cross for this one man. He so loves every individual.

St. Augustine

eXtreme "coward"

TARSUS: JOHN MARK

Day 120

Get Mark and bring him with you, because he is helpful to me in my ministry.

2 Timothy 4:11

"He cannot come with us!" Paul insisted. "He is a coward and of no use to the ministry."

Barnabas responded, "You may have given up on him, but God has not."

Paul was still resolute. "You cannot force my hand, Barnabas. I will only bring people on whom I can depend. He is not welcome on this journey to share the faith."

"Then neither am I. It is your decision, Paul. God has given you the direction of the journey. Let us part in peace. When the church feared you, by God's grace I came to you and showed them that you would do great work for the kingdom of God. God has the same call on John Mark."

Paul hesitated. "So be it then. I hope you are right, my old friend, though I cannot believe it myself." Thus Paul and Barnabas parted ways.

Eventually Paul and John Mark ended up in prison together in Rome, and Paul found his young friend's true worth in Christ as a faithful servant. John Mark had written the Gospel of Mark and proved himself anything but a coward as he and Paul faced the daily rigors of prison. Through the toughest of times, Mark stayed the course, which Paul acknowledged in a letter to Timothy shortly before his death.

God often brings trying situations our way to demonstrate one of two truths: He will use trials to show us how far we have come in our spiritual development, or He will allow problems into our lives to show us exactly where we could use some more growth. John Mark's transformation from an apparent coward to a committed follower reminds us that spiritual growth is a process. We may point to past failures where we wish we could have been stronger. But actions in the past do not have to affect our future. Like Mark, do you need a second chance to show your commitment to Christ? Pray for opportunities that will help you to grow spiritually.

eXtreme sermon

"Shoot them, and we will let you live!"

Day 121

The pastor had struck a deal with the Communists in the Chinese prison where they were being held. But the two Christian girls standing before him were resolved not to renounce their faith. A fellow prisoner who watched the terrible scene described their faces as pale but beautiful beyond belief—infinitely sad, but sweet. They were determined to face death rather than turn their backs on Christ.

The pastor reasoned, "Why should we all three die? If I kill you and they let me live, then I can continue to work among the churches."

Be kind and compassionate to one another, forgiving each other, just as in Christ God forgave you.

Ephesians 4:32

The girls spoke to him softly, "Before you shoot us, we want to thank you for all you have meant to us. You led us to Christ, baptized us, and gave us Holy Communion. May God reward you for all the good you have done. You also taught us that Christians are sometimes weak and commit terrible sins, but they can be forgiven again. When you regret what you are about to do to us, don't despair like Judas but repent like Peter. And remember that our last thoughts of you are not of hatred and anger, but of love and forgiveness. We all pass through times of darkness. We die gladly."

But the pastor's heart was already hardened, and he shot them. Immediately afterward, the Communists shot him.

People who are faced with the prospect of a sudden death may find their thoughts turning to friends and family or to unfulfilled dreams. Some recall seeing their lives "flash before their eyes." This total recall, however, is likely interrupted for those who fall victim to the ultimate betrayal—being murdered by someone they considered a friend. Anger, bitterness, and hatred for the supposed friend would all seem justifiable. Would forgiveness factor in at all? As Christians, we must choose to extend forgiveness in every circumstance, even those involving life and death. Like the girls in this story, your reaction to betrayal preaches an effective sermon. How might your choosing to forgive point the way to Jesus for someone you know?

eXtreme shield

PAKISTAN: TAHIR IQBAL AND RAYMOND LULLY

"I will kiss the rope but never deny my faith!" exclaimed Tahir Iqbal. The soldiers lifted the paralytic pastor out of his wheelchair and slipped the noose around his neck. Today he walks freely in heaven with Christ.

Day 122

In addition to all this, take up the shield of faith, with which you can extinguish all the flaming arrows of the evil one.

Ephesians 6:16

In Pakistan, another seasoned pastor heard a gunshot right outside his house. The bullet narrowly missed him and lodged into the wall behind his chair. He thanked God for another day that he could share Christ in the Muslim-dominated nation.

Raymond Lully left a comfortable position as an Oxford professor and spent most of his life suffering for the gospel. He wrote, "Once I was fairly rich and tasted freely the pleasures of this life. But all these things I gladly resigned that I might spread the knowledge of truth. I have been in prisons; I have been scourged . . . now, though old and poor, I do not despair; I am ready, if it be God's will, to persevere unto death."

Believers like these have a unique understanding of the term "shield of faith." They realized it would not necessarily prevent their suffering, but it gave them courage to face it if necessary. The shield of faith gave them the resolve to continue doing spiritual battle for the cause of Christ no matter what it cost them here on earth.

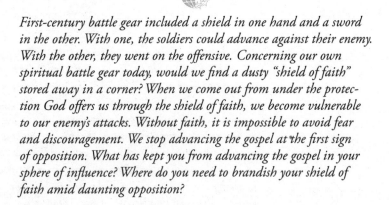

First-century battle gear included a shield in one hand and a sword in the other. With one, the soldiers could advance against their enemy. With the other, they went on the offensive. Concerning our own spiritual battle gear today, would we find a dusty "shield of faith" stored away in a corner? When we come out from under the protection God offers us through the shield of faith, we become vulnerable to our enemy's attacks. Without faith, it is impossible to avoid fear and discouragement. We stop advancing the gospel at the first sign of opposition. What has kept you from advancing the gospel in your sphere of influence? Where do you need to brandish your shield of faith amid daunting opposition?

eXtreme opportunity

ROMANIA: PASTOR RICHARD WURMBRAND

Pastor Wurmbrand worked his way through the other prisoners to where another pastor sat motionless on the floor. He had just been thrown into the cell. He was badly beaten, and Wurmbrand did not know if he would survive the night.

Day 123

Be wise in the way you act toward outsiders; make the most of every opportunity.

Colossians 4:5

With loving compassion Pastor Wurmbrand knelt down beside the beaten pastor and asked, "My brother... can you say the prayer, 'Father, forgive them'?"

The man winced with pain, touching his swollen, bruised face. It was difficult to speak. The words came out slowly, "I cannot."

Just as Pastor Wurmbrand began feeling sympathy for the man, the beaten pastor began to speak again. With tears in his eyes he said, "My prayer is not 'forgive them.' My prayer is... 'Father, forgive them and me.' If I had been a better pastor, perhaps there would have been more converted torturers."

This weary pastor expressed his concern for the missed opportunities to convert his enemies to Christ. Both pastors realized a young member of Romania's Communist Youth Organization was once arrested and unmercifully beaten by a supposedly Christian police officer. This incident hardened his heart toward Christ for the rest of his life. This missed opportunity for the gospel finally became the dictator of the former Communist nation of Romania. Nicolai Ceausescu was responsible for the torture of countless Christians, including Pastor Wurmbrand and his fellow beaten pastor.

No regret is greater than that involving a missed opportunity. Unfortunately, life often brings missed opportunities, like the birth of a child, a Christmas morning, or even that last flight out going home. However, nothing compares to the missed opportunity to change another person's eternal destiny. We never know how the seemingly nominal person sitting next to us on the train one day might affect the world for Christ—if only we said something. Equally true is the possibility that breaking our silence might detour a determined Christian opponent. You may count many missed opportunities for the gospel in your past. However, you can change your future by seizing the opportunities given to you each day to share your faith.

eXtreme purpose

CHINA: CAI ZOUHUA

Day 124

Pastor Cai Zouhua, age thirty-four, was arrested on September 11, 2004, for printing Bibles and Christian books. In November 2005, he and his wife, Xiao Yun Fei, and two more relatives were sentenced to prison terms. Pastor Cai's mother, Cai Laiyi, sitting with her son's picture by her side says gently, "I pray for him, and for all of us. We are simple people, but we do know this: in the Bible, it says follow your leaders, but first follow your God."

Then the word of God spread, and the number of the disciples multiplied greatly in Jerusalem, and a great many of the priests were obedient to the faith.

Acts 6:7

Today in many nations, Christians can write their own books, take them to a printer, and give copies to their friends with no fear of any government reprisal. Many older translations of the Bible have no restrictions or copyrights and can be printed and distributed by anyone. Pastor Cai and his family were not selling these books for earthly gain but giving them away to others for their eternal gain.

Pastor Cai follows the footsteps of William Tyndale, an Englishman who was captured in October 1536 and imprisoned by authorities of the English Church and the government. Tyndale was later executed for printing the New Testament and smuggling copies into England. It was against the law to print without government permission.

Pastor Cai and his flock courageously continue to follow Christ. Chen Rufu, a church member said, "My whole family has become believers in Christ, and we have all become one big community, loving each other. When my wife had an accident last year, no one did anything for us except our church."

Believers can be lulled into a false security, believing once they are committed to Christ, life will be easy. After all, they are "doing God's will," and shouldn't that mean hard times are behind? However, Jesus promised that we would be hated for His name's sake. We may even suffer physical harm, imprisonment, or death because of our faith. We don't have a choice of the trials we will encounter, but we do have the choice of how we will react and in whom we will trust and seek comfort and counsel. As we spread the gospel, we walk in the joy of the Lord. No one or no thing can block us from God's love.

eXtreme contrast

RUSSIA: CLAUDIA VASILEVNA

Secret Soviet police documents show that in Butovo, a suburb of Moscow, forty-four thousand people were shot in groups of two hundred and buried secretly. One night during the slaughter, Claudia Vasilevna opened her door to a haggard woman who was supposed to be shot for her Christian faith but managed to escape. She begged Claudia to hide her.

Day 125

So that you may become blameless and pure, children of God without fault in a crooked and depraved generation, in which you shine like stars in the universe.

Philippians 2:15

Fearful, Claudia refused. She closed the door and left the woman outside, sealing the woman's death sentence. For over fifty years, Claudia has struggled to forget the image of the woman.

In contrast to Claudia's struggle, Romanian church members enjoyed peace in their hearts by helping two Germans soldiers who had escaped en route to a Soviet jail. They sought refuge in the church of Pastor Richard Wurmbrand. At the end of World War II, Romania was ruled by harsh Nazi Germany. As Germany was losing the war, the Russian army entered Romania and began taking Germans as prisoners of war. Hiding or helping a German was punishable by death.

The soldiers still wore the German uniforms and were candidates for death. The church families agreed to help protect them because it was not their place to judge but to help every person in mortal danger. They also reached out to German children during this time, knowing that they were only doing what Christ would do in their place.

Christians often have to choose between trouble for their bodies and trouble for their souls. It's the difference between earthly trouble and eternal regret. Extreme Christians live in such contrast with the rest of the world that sometimes it is hard to relate. Their circumstances are often so extreme. Even within our relatively ordinary circumstances we may face decisions that require extraordinary courage. Will we choose earthly security over eternal significance? Will we take an earthly risk that may result in a spiritual gain? When you are faced with situations that require courage beyond your means, ask God for help. He will provide the wisdom you need at the right time to make the right decision.

Day 126

For it has been granted to you on behalf of Christ not only to believe on him, but also to suffer for him.

PHILIPPIANS 1:29

eXtreme travels

CHINA: BOB FU

Chinese professor Bob Fu and his wife held secret Bible studies in remote villages. The inhabitants' hunger for God's Word never ceased to amaze him.

Day 127

My soul thirsts for God, for the living God. When can I go and meet with God?

Psalm 42:2

One memorable trip began with a twelve-hour bus ride on which a church leader stood in front of the broken window for hours to keep the rain out so that Fu could rest. The next night, they drove a small van on rough, muddy roads until the van got stuck; then they drove a tractor for hours in the pouring rain until the tractor also got stuck. After that, they walked all night by the light of the moon, slipping and falling in the muddy fields.

They arrived early the next morning to a warm welcome. Villagers began arriving at the house church to pray for two hours before the service. Some had walked fifty miles just to hear God's Word. The house had no chairs, so the church members sat on rocks or pieces of wood. In this area, they had another blessing: it was too difficult for the police to follow.

For a few days, they could worship freely! Each had overcome extreme travel conditions to worship, and none considered it a sacrifice. They just had a desire like David, who was drawn to worship with every fiber of his being.

For those in restricted nations, church is not optional; it is essential. In contrast, in free nations many people make up their minds each week whether or not they will attend church. Do they have time? Is it raining? Would they rather sleep late? What's the sermon topic anyway? Shamefully, we often run through a gamut of questions trying to decide whether church is worth our time. For David and others, going to meet with God was not optional. In fact, they would not let anything keep them from it. When was the last time you asked God to give you a desire for worship like this? Ask Him today, and make plans to attend church this week and meet with God.

eXtreme composer

RUSSIA: NICOLAIE MOLDOVAE

Drunken Russian guards entered the cold cell one harsh winter afternoon. One prisoner, Nicolaie Moldovae, was a poet and composer as well as a devout believer and leader of an evangelical movement in the Orthodox church. He received a five-year sentence in the brutal Russian prison for his ministry work.

Day 128

Hear this, you kings! Listen, you rulers! I will sing to the LORD, I will sing; I will make music to the LORD, the God of Israel.

Judges 5:3

"Lie on your belly!" a guard yelled to Nicolaie. In his thin shirt and shorts, he lay on the freezing floor. The guards then stepped on his back, legs, and feet with their heavy boots for an hour.

When the guards left, fellow prisoners knelt beside Nicolaie to see how badly he was hurt. To their amazement, Nicolaie said, "I have written a new hymn while I was being walked upon." He began to sing, "May I not only speak about future heavens, but let me have heaven and a holy feast here."

After Nicolaie was released from prison, the Communist police searched his home and confiscated a unique book of manuscripts that Nicolaie had worked on for several years. Hundreds of hours of precious work, writing, and devotion were immediately taken. After this, Nicolaie composed another hymn. "I worship You with gratitude for all You ever gave me, but also for everything beloved You took from me. You do all things well, and I will trust in You."

Today, Nicolaie Moldovae's songs are celebrated throughout his nation.

It has been said that life is ten percent what happens and ninety percent how one responds to what happens. In that light, the actual circumstances of life do not matter as much as a person's attitude toward them. Circumstances are beyond anyone's control. But an attitude or response is a choice. Life may bring us a disharmonious jumble of notes and melodies in a minor key. With God's help, however, we can choose to arrange the notes to produce a song of worship and victory. We can choose to hear melody in the madness of our lives. How would you describe the current circumstances in your life? What is your attitude toward your situation? What do you need to do to change your tune?

eXtreme violence

ALEXANDRIA: JOHN MARK

After writing the Gospel of Mark, John Mark traveled, sowing the seeds of the faith throughout Northern Africa and Egypt, and finally settled in Alexandria and established a church there.

Day 129

For our struggle is not against flesh and blood, but against the rulers, against the authorities, against the powers of this dark world and against the spiritual forces of evil in the heavenly realms.

Ephesians 6:12

On April 21, AD 64, Mark preached a sermon remembering the suffering and death of Christ as part of Passover, or what we would consider Easter Sunday. He had been at odds with the local heathen priests, and they took this day to incite the general population to rise up against him.

The rebels stormed the church and seized John Mark. Using hooks and ropes, they dragged him out through the congregation, into the streets, and out of the city. He left a trail of blood and flesh that stained the rocks over which they dragged him. Blood flowed from virtually every spot on his body as the mob jeered and mocked him. With his last words, he commended his spirit into the hands of his Savior and died.

Even with Mark's death, the crowd's thirst for violence was not satisfied, and the priests called for his body to be burned instead of buried. Suddenly, a rainstorm erupted, scattering the mob in every direction, and Mark's body was left where he had died. A group of Christians then came and took the body and gave Mark a proper burial.

Jesus never led a military campaign, never incited a rebellion, and never spoke words of war, yet His followers have been and continue to be violently opposed. Jesus' message speaks of love, peace, and reconciliation, yet public and government officials have banned the gospel as if it were a declaration of war. In reality, we are engaged in a war—with our Savior and Satan locked in a spiritual battle. The evil one will make every effort to thwart the kingdom by bringing a violent end to Christianity. Will you be on the winning side when the battle is over?

eXtreme favor

ROMANIA: A FORGIVING JEWESS

The Romanian pastor and his wife had hidden Soviet soldiers during the Nazi occupation of their country. Now it was Nazi soldiers who needed refuge.

Day 130

Three German officers hid in the little building behind their house. The pastor's wife sneaked them food and emptied their waste buckets at night. As a Jew, she felt hatred for their actions —they had murdered her entire family. But as a Christian, she felt compelled to aid the refugees and offer them physical and spiritual support.

The show of favor intrigued the captain: "I wonder why a Jewess should risk her life for a German soldier? I do not like Jews, and I do not fear God. I must tell you that when the German army recaptures Bucharest, and it surely will, I will never return the favor to you."

Serve whole-heartedly, as if you were serving the Lord, not men.

Ephesians 6:7

The pastor's wife was undaunted by his cold heart. She continued preaching to him, "Even the worst crimes are forgiven by faith in Jesus Christ. I have no authority to forgive, but Jesus does, if you repent."

The officer replied, "I won't say I understand you. But perhaps if more people had this gift of returning good for evil, then there would be less killing."

The officers soon escaped to Germany, still unrepentant. But the pastor and his wife had done their part in showing them the true meaning of Christianity.

Jesus shared a parable about a farmer who sowed seeds in different types of soil, producing different results. In His story, the seed is the Word of God. Like birds who gobble up the trampled seeds outside a garden, the devil wants to take God's Word away from those who hear it. In contrast, those who represent good soil receive God's Word and respond. Whenever we share the gospel with others, we don't know what type of "soil" is in their hearts. We can't be responsible for their response, positive or negative. Are you discouraged because someone did not respond to the gospel? You have done your part. Now let God do His.

eXtreme preaching

ROMANIA: PASTOR RICHARD WURMBRAND

Day 131

You intended to harm me, but God intended it for good to accomplish what is now being done, the saving of many lives.

Genesis 50:20

In 1991, the Communist Romanian government put on a new face. They feared being overrun by their citizens who hated their activities. They begged Romanian pastors to preach, even in public places. However, they ordered the pastors to preach a specific message—love for one's enemies—so the people would forgive them. The government felt they could manipulate the Christian message for their own gain.

The Christians gladly took up the call and began preaching openly, although they knew that the government's motive was for its own self-preservation. But some thought, *Why should we teach the oppressed to love their oppressors?* They thought this message of forgiveness would strengthen the hand of the government.

It was to this atmosphere that Pastor Richard Wurmbrand returned to Romania after twenty-five years of exile. He was invited to preach on Romanian television where he stressed the message of "love your enemies."

The church was convicted by his words: "Love, just because it is love, exposes itself to all risks—even the risk of being misused by the wicked—in order to win all. We must not give up teaching love for one's enemies, even though, for a time, God-haters profit at our expense. We believe that the Word is God and in the end this Word will change the hearts of even those who hate God."

The Bible is full of stories with surprise endings... right up to the last chapter. Just when it looks like evil is getting the upper hand and all the circumstances are stacked against those who are righteous, God brings the righteous to victory. Fortunately, God is the author of our lives as well. It's not up to us to question how the script is evolving. We may feel we are not being effectively used for God's work. We may even feel our best efforts to evangelize are thwarted by others. However, our role is to faithfully preach His message and let Him deal with the challenging circumstances. God is still writing the story, and the best is yet to come!

eXtreme remembrance

TIBET: WILLIAM SIMPSON

Day 132

I thank my God every time I remember you.

Philippians 1:3

"Your son has been killed."

Mr. Simpson received the terrible message that day. His missionary son, William, had built a small school on the Tibetan border where he had been teaching God's Word to children. William's father lived nearby and immediately rushed to the school after receiving the news. As he looked around, the memories of his son's ministry flooded his mind.

William had traveled four thousand miles a year on horseback to share the gospel with the people of Tibet. Muslim fanatics had slaughtered fifty thousand people in one Tibetan city, but even this did not scare his son away.

William had written, "All the trials, the loneliness, the heartache, the pain, the cold and fatigue of the long road, the discouragement and all the bereavements, temptations, and testing seemed not worthy to be compared with the glory and joy of witnessing these 'glad tidings of great joy.'"

William's father walked slowly through the destroyed school and found his son's mangled body lying on the floor. He later learned that a horde of Muslim army deserters had attacked the Christian school, showing its founder no mercy.

As a missionary himself, Mr. Simpson was very proud of the example of Christ William had been to others. Under his son's body was a piece of paper smeared with blood. He gently picked it up and read the fitting words, "In Remembrance of Me."

Memorials are scattered throughout every country of the world. Each one commemorates an act of heroism, bravery, and personal sacrifice amid trials. People from every era in history have erected memories and remembrances. It's part of human nature. We don't wish to forget those who paid the ultimate price while preserving our ideals of freedom, justice, love, and honor. Our hearts contain the memorials of Christian martyrs who died for the sake of Christ and His gospel. No military honors are awarded at their funerals. No statues erected in their place. Yet we read their stories and we vow never to forget. Take time to remember them today and praise the God who inspired them.

Day 133

If you could show us that you are the true church of Christ, we would pass immediately to your side because we wish to be with Christ. But you did not come with arguments for the truth. You put us in jail. You can take our lives but not our faith.

BISHOP JOHN BALAN, IN RESPONSE TO ORTHODOX/COMMUNIST
LEADERS WHO TRIED TO CONVINCE HIM TO PLEDGE HIS ALLEGIANCE
TO THE ORTHODOX CHURCH OF ROMANIA

eXtreme confirmation

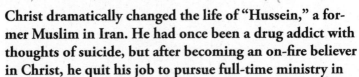

Christ dramatically changed the life of "Hussein," a former Muslim in Iran. He had once been a drug addict with thoughts of suicide, but after becoming an on-fire believer in Christ, he quit his job to pursue full-time ministry in the underground church. He was assigned to "shadow" a Christian couple in their ministry work as he learned and grew in his calling.

Day 134

Let us hold unswervingly to the hope we profess, for he who promised is faithful.

Hebrews 10:23

At one of the first houses he and the Christian couple visited, a young woman in the home began to weep as soon as she saw the three Christians standing outside her door. Confused by her response, the Christians wondered if she'd just suffered some great tragedy or if they had offended her in some way.

Then, through tears, she explained. She had wanted to see Jesus in her dreams, and just that week she finally had a dream in which Christ appeared to her. In the dream, Christ led her to a table and invited her to sit down with three people already sitting at the table. And now, only hours later, those same three people—whom she had never met before—were knocking on her door!

She invited them in, and before they left she had committed her heart and life to following Jesus. Hussein had been confident that God had called him into ministry work. And by the time he left that young woman's house, God's amazing work had obliterated any remaining shred of doubt in his mind. Hussein never again questioned God's plan for his life, even when he was arrested and imprisoned for his faith.

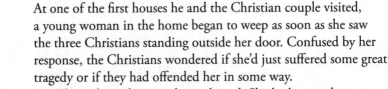

Sometimes God makes His will so plain it's as if He's written it in neon across the sky. Other times, we "see in a mirror, dimly," as Paul wrote to the Corinthian church. V. Raymond Edman, former president of Wheaton College, advised students to "never doubt in the dark what God told you in the light." Hussein saw clearly God's call on his life, confirmed in neon by the girl's dream. He hung onto that clarity and remained faithful to Christ, even in police stations, prison cells, and Iranian courtrooms. What truths has God revealed to you that you need to hold onto more tightly today?

eXtreme sacrifice

ROMANIA: A FAITHFUL PRISONER

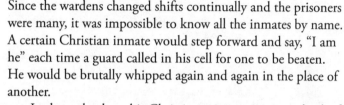

In the jail at Gheria, Romania, the names of prisoners believed to have broken the rules were noted, and each was given twenty-five lashes. There was a special day set aside when the painful punishment was administered. On that day, an officer would pass from cell to cell, gathering those who were to be flogged.

Day 135

Greater love has no one than this, that he lay down his life for his friends.

John 15:13

Since the wardens changed shifts continually and the prisoners were many, it was impossible to know all the inmates by name. A certain Christian inmate would step forward and say, "I am he" each time a guard called in his cell for one to be beaten. He would be brutally whipped again and again in the place of another.

In the end, when this Christian prisoner was near death after one of the sacrificial floggings, the other prisoners tried to comfort him. They told him, "Brother, be happy now. Soon everything will be over. You will be in heaven. There will be no more pain, only joy!"

He turned, looked at them with love and replied, "May God do to me as He wills . . . but if He were to ask me, I would tell Him not to take me to paradise. I would prefer to remain in jail. For I know that above are unspeakable delights, but in heaven one thing is missing: to sacrifice oneself for another."

In a world that values hoarding over sharing, the biblical principle of sacrifice seems like a strange idea. "Get as much as you can as quick as you can" is the name of the game when it comes to worldly ideals. The Bible teaches another means of success. It's called sacrifice—laying down one's life for another. It's not natural. It does not sound appealing to our lower nature. Once we try, however, it becomes a compelling way of life. God's Holy Spirit inside of us helps us to put ourselves second behind others. In fact, His Spirit even helps us want to do it. Are you willing to put others' needs above your own?

eXtreme legend

In an old legend, Jesus said to His follower named Gorun, "Go pitch a tent on Mount Carmel, and stay there for a time of meditation and prayer." Gorun did as Jesus asked.

Day 136

One day Gorun went into the nearest village and asked, "Please give me a blanket. Rats have gnawed on my old one, and I can't sleep." The villagers gladly gave him a blanket, but Gorun returned repeatedly because the same thing had happened. Someone finally suggested, "We'll give you a cat to solve your problem for good."

After a few days, Gorun was back. "Could you please give me some milk for the cat?" Realizing the need would be ongoing, the villagers decided to give him a cow.

Gorun returned again, "I need something to feed the cow." They gave him a plot of land. Gorun then asked for workers for the land, then for materials to build houses for the workers, and so on.

Be careful, or your hearts will be weighed down with . . . the anxieties of life, and that day will close on you unexpectedly like a trap.

Luke 21:34

Years later, Jesus went to see His beloved disciple. A fat man greeted him and asked, "What business brings you here? What would you like to buy?" Gorun, now a rich businessman, didn't even recognize his master.

Christians tell stories like this in persecuted nations where government officials often try to entice Christians to give up their faith and ministry activities in exchange for important jobs and more money.

Sometimes we need a story to see something in a different light, to remind us of what is important and keep us focused on the task ahead. We may not be offered a cat or a cow, but our adversary often tempts us in other ways to get us off track. He offers security in our homeland so we'll resist going to other countries with the gospel. He will use God's blessings as distractions—a mate, a family, or a job— to make us so preoccupied with life that we neglect our mission. What does this story reveal in your life that could be drawing you away from the Master? Have you been so busy with earthly tasks that you've neglected your spiritual mission?

eXtreme time

Day 137

Teach us to number our days aright, that we may gain a heart of wisdom.

Psalm 90:12

A man was walking late one night to a distant town when he stumbled upon something in the road. Reaching down, he picked up a small bag full of stones. He looked around and stared through the darkness, attempting to see if anyone had dropped them. Seeing no one, he decided to take the bag along with him on his long journey on a moonless night.

To pass the time, he started dropping the small stones in the river bordering the road. *Plop...plop...* the sound was harmless amusement for the bored traveler. When he reached his destination, he had only two stones left in the bag. Entering the town, he drew closer to a street lamp off the square. Cupping the two remaining stones in his palm, he looked at them under the yellow lamplight and saw an odd twinkle and luster to the stones. He peered closer. To his shock and dismay, the small stones were actually diamonds!

A wise prison pastor who was able to lead many of his fellow prisoners to Christ related this brief story on numerous occasions. He learned through suffering that every minute could be used to further God's kingdom, no matter what the circumstance. He often admonished others, "You can regain lost money, but not lost time. Use your time wisely in God's service."

Thirty-two million seconds in every year, and each second we live is a precious gift from God to use for his purposes. If we waste them, the seconds return to God, but they will not return to us. They are gone forever, like the diamonds in the silt of the river bottom. Jesus, even while being crucified, spent his final breaths offering salvation to the robber and speaking words of comfort to his mother. He even ministered to his murderers by offering them forgiveness. Imagine how precious that time was to the thief who joined Jesus in heaven that day. Are you filling your precious moments with purpose? Ask God to show you how to redeem your time, not waste it.

eXtreme risks

CHINA: TWO CHURCH BUILDERS

The two women traveled week after week to attend secret house-church meetings. They were tired and frustrated that no church existed in their own village.

After praying for months for a church nearby, one of the women finally said, "Maybe God is waiting for us to build a church. Why should He listen to our constant complaints if we are not willing to do something ourselves?"

Day 138

So they decided to take a risk. The two women and their husbands built a church in their little village in the Anhui province of China. The government immediately threatened to tear the building down unless they registered with the religious affairs bureau. They complied, and fortunately their rural area was not as closely supervised as some of the larger city churches. They even dared to invite other house-church pastors as guest speakers without first acquiring written permission.

In fact, everyone who wants to live a godly life in Christ Jesus will be persecuted.

2 Timothy 3:12

The women evangelized by visiting the local hospital and finding the patients that had no hope of recovery. Then they would pray and ask God to heal them. In one year, the budding church grew to over two hundred!

One of the sisters said, "We prayed twenty days straight for one man, and he wasn't healed until the very end. The family started threatening violence against us, saying that we were angering the gods. You have to be willing to take risks for God."

The gospel of Jesus Christ is controversial, plain and simple. Why else would the devil isolate Christianity as the number one religion on restricted nations' hit lists? For example, Buddhists do not have the extensive Christian underground church system that is forced to exist in restricted nations. New Age meditation experts do not fear for their lives in persecuted countries. Christianity is controversial because it is powerful over the enemy. Satan does not waste his time on false religions. Are you a spiritual risk as far as Satan is concerned? Or do you play it safe? Are you a threat to his plans because of your faith? If so, expect controversy. But rejoice that you are part of the truth!

eXtreme love

ROMANIA: JEWISH CHRISTIANS

Day 139

But love your enemies, do good to them, and lend to them without expecting to get anything back.

Luke 6:35

At the end of World War II, the German soldiers knew the Soviets would take them to a labor camp in Siberia and that many of them would die there. The Soviet army had just taken the city from the Nazis, so when the two soldiers found an opportunity, they ran away from the group. They wandered fearfully through the dark streets of Bucharest, Romania.

When they spotted the Lutheran chapel, they were ecstatic, because the Romanian Lutherans were of German descent. But when they discovered the people inside were Jewish, their fears returned.

The pastor immediately calmed their fears. "We are Jews but also Christians, and we don't give anyone seeking refuge into the hand of their enemies."

At that time, if any Romanians were caught hiding Germans, they would be put to death immediately. But to the kind pastor, the Germans—still in their Nazi uniforms—were lost souls in need of a Savior. He would help them just as he had helped persecuted Jews.

He told them, "We have suffered greatly under the German occupation. Whether or not you are personally guilty, we are not your judges. We offer you our home and civilian clothing so you can make your way to Germany. We do this to prove God's great love and mercy for you. He alone can offer you freedom from your guilt."

Love makes people do strange things. A couple in love will go to great lengths to demonstrate their exclusive devotion. Likewise, a mother loves a child like no other person on earth. Yet the love between Christ and the believer is not just between the two of them. It is the strangest love of all, for it does not thrive on being exclusive. In fact, it is the only love relationship that grows by being inclusive of others. We must love others with Christian love in order to show our devotion to Christ. We show Christ extreme love if we are willing to love those who have not loved us back. Who is God asking you to love today for His sake?

Day 140

God will not judge us according to how much we endured, but how much we could love. The Christians who suffer for their faith in prisons could love. I am a witness that they could love both God and men.

FORMER UNDERGROUND CHURCH PASTOR
WHO WAS IMPRISONED FOR HIS FAITH

eXtreme hero

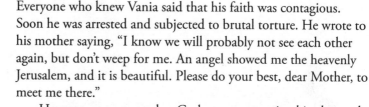

As a soldier in the Soviet Red Army, Vania Moiseev was constantly reprimanded for sharing his faith. Many men in his regiment came to Christ through his testimony. When his commander ordered him to keep silent about his faith, he replied, "What would a nightingale do if ordered to stop singing? It could not, and neither can I."

Day 141

Everyone who knew Vania said that his faith was contagious. Soon he was arrested and subjected to brutal torture. He wrote to his mother saying, "I know we will probably not see each other again, but don't weep for me. An angel showed me the heavenly Jerusalem, and it is beautiful. Please do your best, dear Mother, to meet me there."

He went on to assure her God was encouraging him by sending angels to his side. He described the various encounters he had with angels. "Angels are transparent. When you have one in front of you and a man stands behind, the presence of the angel does not block the view of the man. On the contrary, you see him better. When you see through an angel, you can understand and appreciate even a torturer."

In the end, Vania was killed for his faith at age twenty-one. He was a young martyr whose courageous life enabled him to become a hero all over Eastern Europe.

Do not forget to entertain strangers, for by so doing some people have entertained angels without knowing it.

Hebrews 13:2

Angels are everywhere. Their likeness is in books, shaped into candleholders, hung as Christmas ornaments, and formed into cookie cutters. Many people regret they have never seen real angels, God's heavenly messengers. Yet everyday angels are often overlooked. An unlovely person in need of our acceptance just may be an angel. The enemy who hurts us may be the angelic being we are looking to see. Even if a person turns out to be an ordinary human after all, our love for that person will still bring us one step closer to heaven. Like Vania, are you looking at your life through a heavenly perspective? Are you looking for angels where you previously saw only an enemy? Look for potential angels to love today.

eXtreme meals

EASTERN EUROPE: THE HUNGRY PRISONER

The imprisoned Christian was hungry and irritated. A lieutenant had come to interrogate him again, and he was in no mood to be questioned. He thought, *Why should I be the one who is always interrogated?*

Day 142

So he pelted the officer with questions, "Do you believe in God? What will happen to you when you die? How did this beautiful world come into existence?" Eventually, he was able share the complete salvation message with the interested officer. To the prisoner's surprise, the lieutenant immediately gave his life to Christ!

The officer also gave his lunch to the hungry prisoner. The Christian was thankful that God would feed him and use him, even in his irritable mood.

Another time, this same man was in solitary confinement and, again, particularly hungry. Then he remembered the words of Jesus about rejoicing under persecution because it is a blessing. He immediately got up and started praising God and dancing around his small cell. His rejoicing soon got the guard's attention.

Blessed are you when men hate you, when they exclude you and insult you and reject your name as evil, because of the Son of Man.

When the guard checked on him, he was sure the Christian had gone crazy. Guards were instructed to treat the crazy ones kindly, so he brought the Christian some cheese and a loaf of bread.

Luke 6:22

Once again, God had provided. The thought struck the Christian prisoner, *It is better to be a fool in Christ than to be a "wise" man who is foolishly angry about things that cannot change.*

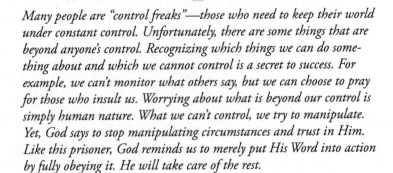

Many people are "control freaks"—those who need to keep their world under constant control. Unfortunately, there are some things that are beyond anyone's control. Recognizing which things we can do something about and which we cannot control is a secret to success. For example, we can't monitor what others say, but we can choose to pray for those who insult us. Worrying about what is beyond our control is simply human nature. What we can't control, we try to manipulate. Yet, God says to stop manipulating circumstances and trust in Him. Like this prisoner, God reminds us to merely put His Word into action by fully obeying it. He will take care of the rest.

eXtreme "superstition"

ROME: PLINY

The following is a letter from a governor named Pliny to the Roman emperor on the growth of Christianity less than one hundred years after the crucifixion of Christ:

Day 143

If we had forgotten the name of our God ... would not God have discovered it, since he knows the secrets of the heart?

Psalm 44:20,21

I have never been present at any of the Christians' trials, and I am unaware of the methods and limits used in our investigation and torture. Do we show any regard to age or gender? If a Christian repents of his religion, do we still punish him or pardon him?

Currently, I am proceeding thus: I question them as to their religion; if they state they are Christian, I repeat the questioning, adding the threat of capital punishment. If they still persist, I order them to be executed. I do not believe that their stubbornness should go unpunished.

I recently questioned a group of Christians who, after interrogation, denied their faith. From this event, I could see more than ever the importance of extracting the real truth, with the assistance of torture, from two female prisoners. But I was able to discover nothing except depraved and excessive superstition.

I therefore thought it wise to consult you before continuing with this matter. The matter is well worth referring to you, especially considering the numbers endangered. This contagious superstition is not confined to the cities only, but has also spread throughout the villages.

Nevertheless it still seems possible to cure it.

Are Christians easily "cured" of their Christianity? When push comes to shove, are most believers incurably faithful to Christ or merely running a mild fever? Persecution is one sure way to discover the truth. Only God knows a person's heart. However, persecution introduces us to our real selves and helps determine whether we will forsake Christ or remain faithful. If we are truly committed to Christ, then He will give us the stamina we need to endure for His sake. If we are more committed to an ideology than the person of Jesus, we will find ourselves faltering under pressure. Are you an incurable case for Christ or will your beliefs turn out to be "excessive superstition" instead?

eXtreme seed

ROME: EARLY CHRISTIANS

"The Christian blood you shed is the seed you sow; it springs from the earth and increases all the more."

Day 144

I tell you, open your eyes and look at the fields! They are ripe for harvest.

John 4:35

The Christians in the early church thrived in the face of intense persecution by cruel government authorities. Their brothers and sisters were being tortured, maimed, burned, and murdered for the sake of Christ. Each martyred believer gave the other remaining believers even more resolve. They looked past their own fears for their lives and saw only the fields white for harvest, as Jesus described those who are ready to trust Him. They gave the following daring response to the judges and authorities in charge of the persecution:

And now O judges, go on with your show of justice, and you will be righteous in the opinion of the people as often as you make a sacrifice of Christians.

Crucify, torture, condemn, and grind us to powder. Your injustice is illustrious proof of our innocence, for the proof of this is that God permits us to suffer.

But do your worst, and create your inventions for tortures upon the Christians; it serves no purpose. You do, however, attract the world and make it more in love with our faith. The more you mow us down, the quicker we rise.

The Christian blood you shed is the seed you sow; it springs from the earth and increases all the more.

Though these words were written centuries ago, this message is still being fulfilled today. Over forty nations of the world are currently experiencing religious persecution. In many of these nations, however, the church is flourishing with new believers every season and increased boldness among its members. Persecution has not accomplished its goal of reducing the followers. In fact, it has often served to increase the number of those willing to sacrifice. As followers of Christ, we can view the opposition that patrols the fields of souls waiting to accept Christ as giants waiting to devour us. Or we can view the opposition as mere scarecrows—counterfeit images of fear. Will you enter the harvest fields to labor for Christ?

eXtreme growth

CHINA: HOUSE CHURCHES

Songs of praise filled the crisp air. "It is four in the morning. Where are they coming from?" one man almost laughed in amazement.

"The harvest is plentiful, my friend. It is going to be a long day but a good one for the kingdom," said the pastor as he smiled. "Let's get to work."

Day 145

The sea of believers at the river seemed to have no end. The pastor spoke compassionately as he baptized them, each with hands lifted up to a new life in Christ. He and his associates baptized eleven hundred new believers that day.

God is moving in China in a powerful way. Believers are being added to the fold daily. In 1995, in a city of Northern Shanxi, several hundred Christians attended house churches. Now that number has grown to seventy thousand. In another city of fifty thousand, there is heavy persecution, yet three thousand devoted believers meet every week in underground churches.

All over the world this gospel is bearing fruit and growing.

Colossians 1:6

One pastor commented insightfully, "We believers are stronger than before. The more they want to pull down the banner of Christ, the higher it flies."

For decades, the church in China has suffered consistent persecution. The government instituted a "strike-hard" policy in a vain effort to curb the growth. Today's membership in the underground church is considerably higher than the membership in the Chinese Communist Party!

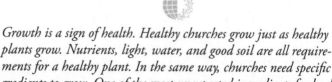

Growth is a sign of health. Healthy churches grow just as healthy plants grow. Nutrients, light, water, and good soil are all requirements for a healthy plant. In the same way, churches need specific ingredients to grow. One of the most unexpected ingredients for healthy church growth can be a fair amount of persecution. Persecution purifies the believers and makes them appreciate the value of their faith. As the pastor in this story illustrates, the more a church is persecuted, the more its members rise up as a testimony to the steadfastness of Christ. Are you bitter or better because of persecution? Are you using it to your advantage to grow the kingdom?

eXtreme "angel"

ROMANIA: ANGELA CAZACU

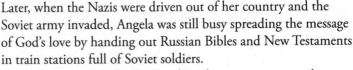

Angela Cazacu was just an ordinary woman living in Romania during World War II when the Nazis invaded. All too quickly, life for Jews and Christians became a daily terror. Angela kept busy stealing Jewish children from the ghettos and smuggling food and clothing to female Christian prisoners in the prisons around her city.

Day 146

Later, when the Nazis were driven out of her country and the Soviet army invaded, Angela was still busy spreading the message of God's love by handing out Russian Bibles and New Testaments in train stations full of Soviet soldiers.

When Pastor Richard Wurmbrand was a prisoner in the Tirgul-Ocna jail in the winter of 1951, he was severely ill. His skeletal body shivered from the constant cold of the worst winter on record. Each prisoner was allowed only one blanket, and food was scarce because no one was able to get to the prison through the heavy snow.

Therefore, as God's chosen people, holy and dearly loved, clothe yourselves with compassion, kindness, humility, gentleness and patience.

Colossians 3:12

It was during this bleak time when Pastor Wurmbrand received a package containing desperately needed food and warm clothing, which he gladly shared with others. The package that he thought must have been delivered by an angel probably saved his life.

Once again, Sister Angela (meaning "angel" in Romanian) was busily going about her Father's business. Ordinary? Maybe. But God delights in using ordinary people as His angels of mercy.

Years ago, in response to the increasing news coverage of random acts of violence, a bumper sticker began to appear that suggested practicing "random acts of kindness." An act of kindness or mercy to a stranger may be as seemingly insignificant as giving up a prime parking place at a shopping center or taking the time to make eye contact with the clerk at the store. However, God can use you to transform even the most ordinary act of kindness into a powerful gift of grace in someone else's life. Ask God to help you commit a random act of kindness in His name today. You may never know it, but you might be someone's "angel."

Day 147

Just like shaving a tiger's hair doesn't do away with its stripes, so I am still a Christian. I still have meetings. At first there were only five meetings in my house; now there are more than a dozen.

MRS. VO THI MANH, A VIETNAMESE GRANDMOTHER
IMPRISONED FOR HER FAITH

eXtreme sufficiency

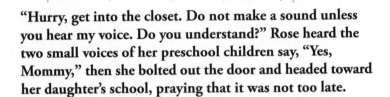

"Hurry, get into the closet. Do not make a sound unless you hear my voice. Do you understand?" Rose heard the two small voices of her preschool children say, "Yes, Mommy," then she bolted out the door and headed toward her daughter's school, praying that it was not too late.

Day 148

But he said to me, "My grace is sufficient for you."

2 Corinthians 12:9

At the proclamation of Sharia, or Islamic law, by the Nigerian government, pockets of violence broke out against Christian groups because they had opposed the laws. Rose's oldest daughter was still at school during the rioting, and Rose was sure she would not be safe there. When she arrived at the school, she learned her daughter had been taken to a military base for safety. Eventually, Rose found her, and they returned home where the two younger children were waiting safely.

The following day, when her husband left for a Christian gathering, it was the last time she saw him alive. Roughly 260 churches were destroyed during these riots, and more than 460 Christians were killed.

In the months since her husband's murder, Rose has drawn comfort from the book of Acts. She said, "The same God who allowed Stephen to be stoned also allowed Peter to escape from prison. God has been faithful, and His grace has been sufficient." Today Rose continues to work in the church where her martyred husband pastored, and she busily raises her three children.

It has been said God will never lead us where His grace cannot keep us. We must realize that sometimes His plan does not include a miraculous deliverance from illness, death, or oppression. Yet His grace is sufficient, and He has not abandoned us. We must trust that God would not lead us to a place of ministry or work without an adequate measure of His grace to make it. Sometimes His plan involves simply seeing us through an ordeal instead of delivering us from it. Have you come to a point where you are willing to entirely rely on Him? You'll likely never say that God's grace is all you need until His grace is all you have.

eXtreme vision

INDONESIA: DOMINGGUS

Day 149

The LORD is my light and my salvation—whom shall I fear?

Psalm 27:1

The twenty-year-old Bible student was asleep when he was awakened by shouts of *"Allah-u-Akbar!"* (Allah is Almighty!) Radical Muslims entered his room and beat him nearly unconscious. As Dominggus fought to escape, a sickle came down on the back of his neck, almost severing his head. The attackers left him in a growing pool of his own blood, assuming he would soon die.

Dominggus said that his spirit left his body and was carried by angels to heaven, and he witnessed his own corpse lying motionless on the ground. He no longer felt fear or pain, but rather peace. Then he heard, "It is not time for you to serve Me here."

The next voices Dominggus heard were those of Indonesian emergency medical workers. Since they did not know whether he was Christian or Muslim, they were discussing where to take his body.

Dominggus prayed to God for strength to speak. Finally, the words "I am a Christian" came out. One can only imagine the look on the workers' faces as the "dead" student answered their question.

Today, Dominggus has fully recovered. His physical scars remain, but his spirit has a renewed faith and a message of forgiveness. Dominggus stated he is closer to God, and now, he is actively praying for his Muslim neighbors—even those who attacked him.

In an uncertain world of violence and threats, Christians are commanded to face the future without fear. Fear only aggravates a bad situation without alleviating any pressure. We can confidently face the future's uncertainties on earth because we know our eternal destination is secure. We know our heavenly future is eternity with Christ, as Dominggus so clearly saw. After all, we are much more than just earthly bodies that our enemies may maim and even kill. Your life will go on far after your body is destroyed. Your true future is what happens in eternity, not what happens here on earth. What fears do you have about the future? Can you entrust them to God and face the future without fear?

eXtreme singing

NORTH KOREA: SOON OK LEE

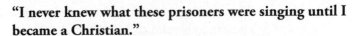

"I never knew what these prisoners were singing until I became a Christian."

Soon Ok Lee was a prisoner in North Korea from 1987 to 1992. She did not become a Christian, however, until she escaped to South Korea. When she first received Christ, she was overwhelmed by her memories of what she had seen and heard in prison.

Day 150

I am greatly encouraged; in all our troubles my joy knows no bounds.

2 Corinthians 7:4

It was the simple things, like the Christians who sang as they were being put to death. At that time, she did not understand and had thought they were crazy. She was not allowed to talk, so she never had the chance to speak with a Christian. She does remember hearing the word, "Amen."

"While I was there, I never saw Christians deny their faith. Not one. When these Christians were silent, the officers would become furious and kick them. At the time, I could not understand why they risked their lives when they could have said, 'I do not believe,' and done what the officers wanted. I even saw many who sang hymns as the kicking and hitting intensified. The officers would call them crazy and take them to the electric-treatment room. I didn't see one come out alive."

It was the singing that stuck with her. Perhaps it was the singing of these precious saints that planted a seed in her spirit and eventually led her to Christ.

Like spies, those who are curious about Christianity zero in on believers so that they can evaluate the truth for themselves. They observe. They watch. They take mental notes. Whenever Christians go through trials, these silent observers often hope to see the believers fall, so that they can assure themselves that Christians are like everyone else after all. However, when Christians smile through trouble, they are stumped. When believers clap instead of cry, they are amazed. When Christ followers sing amid sorrow, they are drawn in by what they cannot explain. If you are going through a trial right now, you have an unprecedented opportunity to witness for Christ. Pray that your joyful example will inspire others.

eXtreme endurance

TURKMENISTAN: SHAGELDY ATAKOV

"Break him morally or destroy him physically!" The Turkmenistan bureaucrats had no more patience for this street preacher.

Day 151

We continually remember before our God and Father your work produced by faith, your labor prompted by love, and your endurance inspired by hope in our Lord Jesus Christ.

1 Thessalonians 1:3

Shageldy Atakov was offered his freedom under President Saparmurat Niyazov's December 23, 2000, amnesty, provided he would swear the oath of allegiance to the president and recite the Muslim creed. Shageldy refused the amnesty again.

Shageldy had previously been threatened by state officials to stop preaching. He was arrested in December 1998 and sentenced to two years in jail, but a prosecutor appealed the verdict as "too lenient." He was then sentenced to two additional years in prison. Shageldy was in such pain from the harsh beatings that he asked his children not to touch him.

In February 2000, his wife and five children had been forcibly taken from their home and exiled to remote Kaakhka where they remained under "village arrest."

When his family visited him in early February 2001, Shageldy said his farewells. His wife noticed that "during the visit he was bruised and battered, his kidneys and liver hurt, and he was suffering from jaundice. He could barely walk and frequently lost consciousness." He did not expect to survive much longer.

Despite this, Shageldy was still not broken. He would not give in, and though release was within his reach, he would not accept it if it meant forsaking his allegiance to Christ.

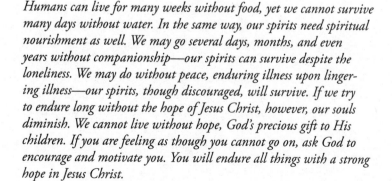

Humans can live for many weeks without food, yet we cannot survive many days without water. In the same way, our spirits need spiritual nourishment as well. We may go several days, months, and even years without companionship—our spirits can survive despite the loneliness. We may do without peace, enduring illness upon lingering illness—our spirits, though discouraged, will survive. If we try to endure long without the hope of Jesus Christ, however, our souls diminish. We cannot live without hope, God's precious gift to His children. If you are feeling as though you cannot go on, ask God to encourage and motivate you. You will endure all things with a strong hope in Jesus Christ.

eXtreme loyalty

LAOS: HEZEKIAH

Day 152

If we are faithless, he will remain faithful, for he cannot disown himself.

2 Timothy 2:13

Shortly after becoming a Christian in 1997, Hezekiah went to what was known locally as the "sanctuary" to receive discipleship and evangelism training. He then returned to his father's house and was immediately approached by thirty-five relatives and villagers demanding to know why he had converted to Christianity. He told them, "Jesus is the only way I can be saved from my sins and have eternal life."

The crowd grew angry, and Hezekiah tried to reason with them. Finally, they grabbed him by the hair and began to punch him in the face until he fell unconscious.

A friend of Hezekiah was able to take him to his house where he remained in bed for four days recuperating from the beatings. Hezekiah has never been able to return to his father's house, but he continues to travel from village to village in Laos carrying the Good News of salvation.

Since this first incident, Hezekiah has been beaten on ten occasions, sometimes preferring death to the continued suffering. He testifies: "As I have matured in my walk with Christ, I have more faith to endure these hardships. The trials I have gone through have served to strengthen my faith, and I see God's faithfulness in delivering me. I thank God I have been able to bring thirty people to the saving knowledge of Jesus."

God's loyalty to His children is not based on reciprocity. If it were, we would all have been abandoned long ago. Instead, God is well aware of our frailties and chooses to love us anyway. We must be careful to read the stories of Christian martyrs in light of God's loyalty to His children. The martyrs would be the first to remind us that their story is not about them. It's about God! Though we read of many believers who willingly endured scourging rather than renouncing Christ, the amazing conclusion is not the extreme loyalty of a person but the extreme faithfulness of the God of glory. Your faithfulness may falter, but His steadfast loyalty to you never ends. Take time to thank God for His loyalty today.

eXtreme surroundings

The young Jewish doctor was so sad. One night, Sabina Wurmbrand tried to offer her some comfort: "God promised Abraham that the Jewish people would have a bright future. They will be like the sand on the seashore and the stars of the sky."

Day 153

The doctor looked up with tears in her eyes and said, "Like the sand on the shore, we are trampled underfoot by these Communist guards. Don't speak to me anymore about your God."

A few days later Sabina became very sick. While she was lying near death in the prison hospital, the prison director came. He said, "We Communists have medicine and hospitals, and we are stronger than your God. In this hospital you are not to mention the name of God." Only Sabina dared to speak about the existence of God. The other women were ecstatic that someone had actually defied the director.

No, in all these things we are more than conquerors through him who loved us.

Romans 8:37

The following day, they forced Sabina to go back to work. God miraculously touched her body, and she was completely healed. The news spread through the prison and did not escape the ears of the sad young doctor.

She approached Sabina late that evening and said, "If your God can restore your body and give you such peace in this pit of hell, then I have to believe He is real. No other power could accomplish this. How must I be saved?"

Whenever we feel like our lives are in a pit, we can be sure people are watching to see how we'll get out of it. Christianity seems to attract interested spectators—especially when we are struggling. People observe our faith at arm's length to determine what God is all about. They watch with keen interest when we experience a crisis. If we live by faith during times of trial, people cannot refute the evidence they see in our lives. What do people see in how you live? What does your reaction to life's circumstances tell others about God? If you feel like your life is in a pit, remember people are watching to see how you will handle it.

Day 154

*In spite of the painful reflections and memories,
I have no time for bitterness. My life is filled
with too much happiness, too many loving,
caring people to allow myself to be devoured by
the cancer of hate. I rejoice. I sing. I laugh.
I celebrate, because I know that my God
reigns supreme over all the forces of evil and
destruction Satan has ever devised. And best
of all—my God reigns supreme in me!*

PASTOR NOBLE ALEXANDER, IMPRISONED IN CUBA FOR
TWENTY-TWO YEARS, *I WILL DIE FREE*

eXtreme request

CHINA: ZHANG RONGLIANG

Day 155

The LORD loves
righteousness and
justice; the earth is
full of his unfailing
love.

Psalm 33:5

Zhang Rongliang is the leader of one of China's largest house-church groups, which has an estimated ten million Chinese believers attending services each week. In 1998, Zhang and other house-church leaders—representing fifteen million underground believers—signed a document entitled the "House Church Confession of Faith" that publicly called on the Communist government to stop harassing unregistered house churches.

A few months after making the document public, Zhang and other signers were arrested and imprisoned. Zhang was later released providing that he "behave" himself for the next seven years. Zhang now travels to minister to his various flocks. Since he is not "behaving" as the government would like, Zhang never sleeps in the same bed more than a few nights in a row.

When Paul wrote in Romans 13 that we are to submit to our governments, he of all people must have known the risks. Yet, although the Romans persecuted him, it was through an appeal to their law that he took the gospel to Rome itself. His request to be tried as a Roman citizen enabled him to advance the gospel to Rome, though it would be his last journey.

Like Paul, Zhang took an extreme risk when he made his formal request. The consequences of his personal risk, however, have enabled many to know Christ.

Like Paul, church leaders in China know that God ordains governments. But they also know that God will not overlook an evil authority's injustices. Tradition holds that the Romans actually beheaded Paul. Similarly, the believers in China suffer great injustices under their current government regime for the sake of Christ. If risking their lives to bring justice to China is necessary, then pastors such as these are willing to die. How strong is our desire to see justice done? How much do we value the right to freely preach God's Word? Pray for believers in China today who inspire us to seek God's justice for their oppressors. Ask God to show you ways you can support their work to advance God's kingdom.

eXtreme prophecy

For the third time, Christ asked Peter, "Simon, son of Jonas, do you love Me?"

Peter was grieved. Three times he had denied Christ; now three times Jesus questioned his love. He responded slowly this time, as if weighing the significance of each word in his heart, "Lord, You know all things. You know that I love You."

Day 156

"Feed My sheep," Jesus repeated a third time. Only this time, He added, "When you were young, you dressed yourself and went wherever you wanted; but when you are old, another will dress you, and take you where you don't want to go." Then Jesus said, "Follow Me."

Nero persecuted Peter when Peter was seventy years old. According to legend, Peter's friends and fellow believers urged him to flee Rome. He refused at first, but eventually he was persuaded to escape. As he approached the city gate to leave, he saw a vision of Jesus walking into the city. He fell to his knees, worshiping Him. "Lord, where are You going?"

Jesus said this to indicate the kind of death by which Peter would glorify God. Then he said, "Follow me!"

"I have come again to be crucified. Follow Me."

Peter turned, and followed where "he didn't want to go." He returned to face Nero. When the authorities arrested him, he requested that he be crucified upside down as he was unworthy to be crucified in the same manner his Lord had been.

John 21:19

The point of this legend is not to say Jesus truly was crucified a second time. Jesus died and was resurrected once and for all. Rather, the legend reminds us that Jesus identifies with our pain and sufferings so much it is as if He is going through them Himself. In Peter's case, the Bible says Jesus' earlier prophecy referred to Peter's crucifixion. Who else but Jesus could relate to Peter's tortuous experience? Jesus is the expert on suffering. He knows what it is all about and wants to come alongside us. If there is pain in your life, Jesus understands. If you are hurting, Jesus has been there too. Let Him assume your burdens and sorrows in prayer today.

eXtreme pastor's wife

ROMANIA: SABINA WURMBRAND

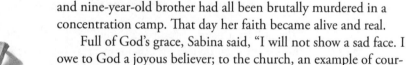

A sharp contrast existed between the beautiful Romanian countryside and the sufferings that Christians and Jews experienced at the hands of invading Nazis and Communists. For Sabina Wurmbrand, the troubles were threefold: she was both a Christian and a Jew and also the wife of a renowned pastor.

Day 157

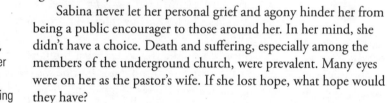

We sent Timothy, who is our brother and God's fellow worker in spreading the gospel of Christ, to strengthen and encourage you in your faith.

1 Thessalonians 3:2

One day she learned that her mother, father, three younger sisters, and nine-year-old brother had all been brutally murdered in a concentration camp. That day her faith became alive and real.

Full of God's grace, Sabina said, "I will not show a sad face. I owe to God a joyous believer; to the church, an example of courage; and to my husband, a serene wife."

Sabina never let her personal grief and agony hinder her from being a public encourager to those around her. In her mind, she didn't have a choice. Death and suffering, especially among the members of the underground church, were prevalent. Many eyes were on her as the pastor's wife. If she lost hope, what hope would they have?

Sabina later spent three years in prison and slave labor camps, where women faced the most humiliating and brutal acts of all prisoners. Yet even in prison, she was known as a friend to all, and she always had a kind word. Before leaving Romania, God gave Sabina her reward. She and her husband, Richard, later brought their family's murderer to Christ!

Pastoring is a partnership between pastors and their mates. One is not complete without the ministry and encouragement of the other. God does not call any Christian to work and live in isolation; He calls us to community. We need other Christians to come alongside us in our ministries and give us wisdom and encouragement from time to time. We are not expected to do it alone, nor should we try. Think about your own sphere of influence. Who is your partner in ministry? Who is praying for you to be an effective witness in your workplace, home, or school? Ask God to lead you to a companion Christian who will encourage you and strengthen you when you need it.

eXtreme strength

Day 158

Fritz felt each crashing blow to his head and prayed for strength. The Muslim attackers surrounded him and took turns beating him in the face. One of the Muslim attackers brandished a large knife thinking this would rid them of the Christian pastor. The first time the blade went into Fritz, all he could do was yell, "Jesus!" He was stabbed repeatedly. And each time, he yelled, "Jesus!" The attackers grew frustrated at the pastor who just wouldn't die!

The radical Muslims proceeded to pull the benches and pulpit from the church and set them on fire. Two of the Muslims grabbed Fritz and heaved him onto the blazing wood. Satisfied with their attack, they ran away. Fritz doesn't remember much after that, but he knows one thing: not a hair on his head was singed.

Always be prepared to give an answer to everyone who asks you to give the reason for the hope that you have.

1 Peter 3:15

Shortly after the attack, Fritz was brought to the largest hospital in that area of Indonesia, but he was refused treatment when they learned he was a Christian. He was brought to another hospital, but the attending doctor said that if he happened to live through the night, he would have permanent brain damage.

After a long recovery, Fritz is now preaching again at a new church. To his amazement, one of the Muslims who attacked Fritz began looking for him, only to ask a single question: "Who is this Jesus?"

Who doesn't enjoy being thought of as the resident "expert"? It may be mechanics, mathematics, tools, carpentry, art, stamp collecting, or sports—everyone can be thought of as an expert in at least one area. We love to field questions on a topic with which we are very familiar. But if someone were to ask, "Who is this Jesus?" would we be as prepared as an "expert" would be? Not every Christian serves as an evangelist, per se. But every Christian can evangelize by sharing the plan of salvation when the opportunity arises. If you were asked that question by a nonbelieving friend, how would you answer? If you're not sure, talk to someone who knows.

eXtreme youth group

RUSSIA: PASTOR SEREBRENNIKOV

Local newspapers described the scene as "savage." It wasn't a murder scene or car wreck; it was a Bible study.

Day 159

You are the light of the world. A city on a hill cannot be hidden. Neither do people light a lamp and put it under a bowl. Instead they put it on its stand, and it gives light to everyone in the house.

Matthew 5:14,15

The story appeared in a Communist Russian newspaper around 1960. It read in part, "Young boys and girls sing spiritual hymns. They receive the ritual baptism and keep the evil, treacherous teaching of love toward the enemy." The story went on to disclose the shocking reality that many young people in the Communist Youth Organization were secretly Christians.

"We must believe our Savior as the first Christians did," Pastor Serebrennikov told his youth group. "For us, the principal law is the Bible. We recognize nothing else. We must hurry to save men from sin, especially the youth."

The pastor was thrown in prison when the Communists discovered a letter written by one of his converts. The teenage girl had written, "I send you blessings from our beloved Lord. How much He loves me!"

Newspaper editorials wondered how Communist students could choose to follow Christ and accused the Communist school of being "powerless" and "deprived of light." They said that Christianity could "snatch away its disciples from under the nose of their indifferent teachers."

It wasn't the teachers' indifference. It was the call of Christ's love as presented by Pastor Serebrennikov and the members of his youth group—Christians who let their light shine in a darkened land.

"This little light of mine, I'm gonna let it shine..." This familiar childhood song has a simple melody with not too many words to remember—it can stick in one's mind for days after it's sung. Young children find the song easy to learn, but it's much more difficult to live, especially as we get older. How many chances do we have in a day to let our lights shine and honor God? One or two? Ten? Twenty? The exact count doesn't matter. What does matter is our response to the events we face every day. Who knows? Your light may be just what others need to find their way home.

eXtreme "sale"

ROMANIA: SABINA WURMBRAND

The repetition was maddening, and Sabina's nerves were stretched to the breaking point. But the officer was unrelenting. "We have methods of making you talk which you won't like. Don't try to be clever with us. It wastes our time."

Day 160

You were bought at a price; do not become slaves of men.

1 Corinthians 7:23

Their questions were aimed at getting her to reveal the names of other Christians—those whom she had nurtured in the faith and encouraged to be strong in the face of persecution. Now it was her turn to be strong, but she didn't think she could bear another one of those interrogation sessions.

The next session was played with a gentler, craftier approach. The interrogator was alone and smiling. "Dear woman, you are only thirty-six years old, with your whole life before you. Just give us the names of the traitors." Sabina remained silent.

He continued, "Let's talk practically. Everyone has his price, so why don't you just name yours? Just tell us what you want. Freedom for you and your husband? A nice home and a church? We would take good care of your family."

Sabina responded with fiery conviction, "Thank you, but I have sold myself already."

"You have?" the interrogator interrupted. "For how much and to whom?"

"The Son of God was tortured and gave His life for me. Through Him I can reach heaven. Can you pay a higher price than that?"

We call it "buyer's remorse." It's the feeling that the product isn't worth the cost we paid. There is also "seller's remorse"—the feeling that the price received doesn't equal the value of the product. All too often we feel the pain of "being bought" by someone or something whenever we are tempted to compromise our values. After the deal is done, we feel like suckers. Fools. We feel cheap, having betrayed our own self-worth. However, Christ paid the ultimate price in order to win our affections. If everyone has a price, He named ours for us, once and for all. His purchase of blood makes us invaluable in His sight. You are already bought and paid for, so don't sell yourself short. Remind yourself of that today.

Day 161

A church that does not remember its persecuted brethren is no church at all.

A LUTHERAN PASTOR WHO ENDURED HORRIFIC TORTURE
TO PROTECT MEMBERS OF THE UNDERGROUND CHURCH

eXtreme tools

The smoke of the train wreck was thick as cries of agony came from the sea of passengers whose bleeding, broken bodies lay amid the ruined cars. Among the wounded and dying walked a surgeon who was unharmed in the collision. His luggage, though, was lost in the confusion, and he cried out, "My tools! My tools! If only I had my tools!"

Day 162

With medical instruments, the man could have saved many lives. With his bare hands, he stood virtually helpless, watching as many died.

Today's persecuted church is like that surgeon. They have the knowledge and the willingness to save many lives caught in the wreckage of communism or Christless Islam. What they lack are the tools.

"Hear the cries of your brothers and sisters in captive nations!" wrote Pastor Richard Wurmbrand when he first came to the United States. "They do not ask for escape; they do not ask for safety or an easy life. They ask only for the tools to counteract the poisoning of their youth—the next generation—with atheism. They ask for Bibles. How can they spread the Word of God if they do not have it?"

Christians in restricted nations cannot provide these tools for themselves. They count on Christians in free nations to help. "Give us the tools we need," one Christian told us, "and we will pay the price for using them!"

How, then, can they call on the one they have not believed in? And how can they believe in the one of whom they have not heard? And how can they hear without someone preaching to them?

Romans 10:14

Chalk for a teacher, needles for a nurse, patience for a parent, and a tractor for a farmer. Every person, regardless of calling, uses tools. It may be as complicated as a computer or as primitive as a hammer, but our lives change drastically with those tools. As Christians, we know our spiritual tools because we read about them in God's Word, the Bible. But what about those who never read about the tools of compassion, forgiveness, love, sharing, and all the gifts and talents that God offers? You cannot keep these spiritual truths to yourself, hiding them as a miser hoards gold. Willingly share your tools freely with others in need.

eXtreme travels

VIETNAM: YOUNG CHURCH PLANTER

Each clickety-clack of the train wheels bounced the Vietnamese Christian woman's frail body painfully on the hard wooden seat. But she was on a mission.

Day 163

She needed spiritual food for the Christians she led in North Vietnam. Three congregations of people were praying that their leader would be successful and bring back precious copies of the Bible.

Her work back home was tiring. She was the only mature Christian in the area, and she had planted the three churches from nothing, winning one soul at a time through her personal witness. She had no car or even a bicycle. She walked or paddled a small wooden boat to her church meetings.

She had faced police threats and harassment and her Buddhist parents' dismay because of her faith. Now she rode the train across eight hundred miles for three consecutive days, hoping to find one believer who could help. Finally she reached Ho Chi Minh City. There she met visiting western Christians who gave her Bibles for the Christians in the North. They also gave her a bicycle to help her minister to the three congregations. Before leaving, they prayed together, asking God's blessing on her travel and her ministry.

Be diligent in these matters; give yourself wholly to them, so that everyone may see your progress.

1 Timothy 4:15

"How old are you?" one of them asked, just as she was about to leave.

The woman smoothed strands of black hair away from her face and whispered, "I'm twenty-two."

Child prodigies have special abilities beyond their years. We may know of someone who finished college at age fifteen or wrote a symphony before age twelve or who excelled at a sport by age sixteen. Often our response is jealousy; we wish we could do something great in our youth and gain recognition for it too. The Vietnamese Christian woman did just that, but she probably didn't have any special abilities above those of her peers. She did, however, have a desire to follow Jesus and to bring Him to the people of her country. Christ calls you to be diligent for Him as well. Sharing God's love is simple enough that it requires no special abilities—just your availability.

eXtreme instruction

FRANCE: FRANZ RAVENNAS AND MARTIN GUILLABERT

Day 164

For I am convinced
that neither death
nor life, neither
angels nor demons,
neither the present
nor the future, nor
any powers, neither
height nor depth, nor
anything else in all
creation, will be able
to separate us from
the love of God that
is in Christ Jesus our
Lord.

Romans 8:38,39

"On hearing the death sentence, you will receive it as the invitation of the King of glory, who invited you to his wedding feast."

The instructions were difficult but clear. The French authors Franz Ravennas and Martin Guillabert wrote an instruction manual for Christians facing the threat of death. Their "publishing office" was their jail cell during the French Revolution. They saw their cell as the "ante-chamber to paradise."

"When they have finished reading your sentence," the manual continues, "you will say with many martyrs who have gone before you, 'Thank God.' Sing joyful songs. When they bind your hands, say the words of St. Paul: 'I am ready not only to be bound, but also to die for the name of Jesus Christ.'

"On the way to being shot, speak to the guards from Scripture about the delight of suffering and dying for Christ. 'Who shall separate us from the love of Christ?' (Romans 8:35).

"When you encounter the executioner, remember the words of the great martyr Ignatius: 'When will the happy moment come when I will be slaughtered for my Savior? How long must I wait?' Remember to also say a prayer for the persecutors."

Ravennas and Guillabert were beheaded. Their words are too much to imagine for most Christians in free nations, but they are followed, even today, in restricted nations.

Every day we live should come with a warning: Watch out! At any given moment, tragedy is a distinct possibility. Whether we are riding in a vehicle, crossing a street, or just going about our daily work, we are not safe from an accident, a disease, or a purposeful act of violence. While we can't live protected from the evils of this world, we can live with the promise that God gives us: Nothing, absolutely nothing, can cut us off from the love we have in Jesus. Although you may never die for your faith, you may face rejection and other painful persecutions. God's love will instruct you and help you face all that comes your way today.

eXtreme trials

IRAN: A BEATEN BELIEVER

"We are the clay, he is the potter."

One believer stood at the window, watching the midnight streets for movement that could signal the police closing in on the worshipers. The Christians were meeting secretly in the southern part of Iran. The foreign visitor added to the danger, for Iranian police would be furious to know Christians were sharing fellowship with an outsider.

Yet, O LORD, you are our Father. We are the clay, you are the potter; we are all the work of your hand.

Isaiah 64:8

One believer had recently been released from police custody, and the bruises on his body told about the treatment he had received. Although the police watched him closely and knew of his Christian work, he continued, ministering as much as he could when he wasn't under arrest.

He spoke with passion and urged the gathered believers to grow more like Christ, regardless of the cost. All of them knew that the cost would be high, for all of them knew Christians who had been arrested, beaten, or murdered. Others had simply disappeared.

The wonderful service was long and worshipful. Afterward, the amazed foreign guest asked the speaker about his prison experiences and the suffering he had endured. "How can you," he asked, "keep such a spirit of hope and cheerfulness in the midst of these troubles?"

"These trials are just 'tools' in God's hands," said the Iranian believer. "Who am I to criticize the tools that God uses to make me more holy?"

Humans have a fascination with the future. For centuries we have consulted astrologers and others claiming to know our futures. We've written books and made movies based on the concept of time travel. We want to know what lies ahead of us on our journeys through life. Just as the clay cannot ask the potter what it will be, however, so we cannot ask our Maker what we will be. But we can trust that God will create something beautiful and holy with our lives. We know by faith that we are the products of God's hands. In what ways do you need to trust that God, the Master Potter, is making you into a work of art?

eXtreme love for the cross

ROME: ANDREW

"If you do not denounce this Jesus, you will die on the cross," Governor Aegaeas fumed. This Christian had caused him personal embarrassment in the eyes of Rome by spreading Christianity throughout the governor's Greek province and even to his own wife.

Day 166

Let us fix our eyes on Jesus, the author and perfecter of our faith, who for the joy set before him endured the cross, scorning its shame, and sat down at the right hand of the throne of God.

Hebrews 12:2

"Had I feared the death of the cross, I should not have preached the majesty and glory of the cross of Christ," Andrew replied.

"Then you shall have it! Crucify him!"

As Andrew approached the X-shaped cross, he joyfully proclaimed, "O beloved cross! I rejoice to see you erected here. I come to you with a peaceful conscience and with cheerfulness, desiring that I, who am a disciple of Him who hung on the cross, may be crucified. The nearer I come to the cross, the nearer I come to God."

Andrew hung, bound to the cross for three days, preaching and exhorting the people before him, "Remain steadfast in the Word and doctrine which you have received, instructing one another, that you may dwell with God in eternity, and receive the fruit of His promises."

Andrew declared, "O Lord Jesus Christ! Don't let Your servant who hangs here on a tree for Your name's sake be released to live among men again; receive me into Your kingdom." Then, having finished his plea, he gave up his spirit to God.

Porcelain. Sterling silver. Twenty-four karat gold. Even platinum. The cross comes in a number of designs today. Jewelry. Wall hangings. Even rearview mirror décor. The ubiquitous cross. For all its popularity, however, how many Christians have stopped to consider what it means to display the cross? For one, the cross represents an instrument of torture—imagine having a gallows or electric chair on display in your home! The cross reminds us that Christ died a painful death. Beyond that, it represents a bridge that spans over the sin that once separated God and His people. Jesus brought us back to God through the cross. Right now, consider what meaning the cross holds for you.

eXtreme rescue

THE NETHERLANDS: DIRK WILLEMS

In the sixteenth-century Netherlands, Dirk Willems had been labeled an "Anabaptist" during the rule of Spanish Catholics and imprisoned. Now he was running for his life.

Day 167

Trust in the LORD with all your heart and lean not on your own understanding.

Proverbs 3:5

He had escaped out the tiny window and lowered himself on a rope made of old rags. Landing on the frozen pond along the side of the prison wall, he stepped gingerly on the ice, wondering if he would fall through. But the months of starvation endured in prison now served him well. He barely weighed one hundred pounds.

Before he reached the other side of the pond, a scream broke the night silence. "Halt immediately!" yelled the guard coming out the window Dirk had climbed through only moments ago. Dirk was too close to freedom. He kept going.

The guard yelled again as he set foot on the ice. Quickly he began to chase after Dirk, but on his third step there was a crack. A splash followed as the guard fell through the ice. His screams changed to shrieks of cold and terror. "Help me, please! Help me!"

Dirk paused, looking toward freedom. Then he turned and quickly made his way back to the prison pond. He lay on his stomach and stretched his arm to rescue the nearly frozen guard. In sarcastic gratitude, the guard grabbed Dirk and ordered him back to his cell.

Despite his heroism, Dirk was burned at the stake for his faith.

Committed Christians don't live according to common sense. They do the unthinkable with full knowledge of the consequences. They do the impossible as if it were commonplace. Believers live according to a higher calling. Their actions and reactions are so unnatural that they are often misunderstood. For some, Dirk's extreme rescue seems an unnatural choice. Even, perhaps, a bit foolish. Dirk, however, believed he was simply following the basics of the Bible. He put another's needs above his own. When we make sacrifices, we may not always make sense to the world, but we know we are making progress from a heavenly perspective. Do you most often live according to common sense? Or are you committed to following God's commands at any cost?

Day 168

I hate the Communist system, but I love the men. I hate the sin, but I love the sinner. I love the Communists with all of my heart. Communists can kill Christians, but they cannot kill their love toward even those who kill them. I have not the slightest bitterness or resentment against the Communists or my torturers.

FORMER PRISONER OF FAITH UNDER COMMUNISM

eXtreme security

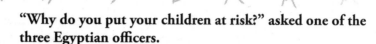

"Why do you put your children at risk?" asked one of the three Egyptian officers.

"Ahmed" had been arrested many times for sharing his faith and for giving out Christian literature. But he saw each interrogation as a chance to witness for Christ.

Day 169

"The security of my children does not come from me," he told the officers calmly. "It comes from God."

"Why aren't you willing to obey the government?" asked the lead officer.

"I won't stop sharing about Jesus, because He is the Way of Truth," Ahmed said. "Jesus has changed my heart."

The officers questioned him about Christian literature that had been secretly printed. They also asked about specific Christians and their activities. Both times, Ahmed remained silent.

"I told them nothing," he said later. "I would not be a traitor to the Body of Christ." When they asked him to spy on other Christians and report back to police, he told them, "That's not my job."

Put on the full armor of God so that you can take your stand against the devil's schemes.

On another occasion, Ahmed was caught and questioned by the police in Turkey for carrying in bags full of Christian literature. "If you don't answer our questions and help us, we will lock you up for causing trouble for the Turkish government," the police assured him.

Ephesians 6:11

"Jesus doesn't tell us to cause trouble for governments," Ahmed replied. "He wants us to witness about His love and forgiveness."

Troublemakers. They are the children in class who cannot stop talking. They are the bullies in the school lunchroom who steal others' lunch money. They are the gossips in the office maligning others and spreading rumors like disease. Christians are not called to be troublemakers. In fact, Jesus calls us to be peacemakers. This rule has one exception, however: we must be troublemakers to Satan and his schemes. We cannot afford to be overlooked by the devil as merely harmless for the kingdom. Prayer is our most effective weapon. How often do your prayers disrupt Satan's work? Get busy today by praying in Jesus' name against your adversary's plans.

eXtreme obedience

CHINA: A PASTOR AND HIS MOTHER

The pastor had been questioned and beaten often, but today the guard took him to a room to talk. He said, "I'm curious about your beliefs and ask you to tell me the Ten Commandments."

Shocked, the pastor began to share the Commandments. When he got to "Honor your father and mother," the officer interrupted him. "Stop there. You Christians believe that God chose 'Honor your father and mother' as a very important commandment. Please look in the corner."

The pastor turned to see an elderly woman chained and bruised beneath a pile of rags. She was the pastor's own mother.

The guard inquired. "Look how much your mother has suffered. If you tell the secrets of the underground church, you and your mother can go free. If she dies from our torture, you will have failed to keep the commandment to honor her, and her blood shall be on your head."

The pastor looked at his mother who was starting to regain consciousness. "Dear Mother, what should I do?"

Lovingly she replied, "Since you were a small boy, I have taught you to love Christ and His church. Do not betray God. I am ready to die for the holy name."

The pastor looked back at the guard and said with renewed courage, "You were very right, Captain. First of all, a man must obey his mother."

But rejoice that you participate in the sufferings of Christ, so that you may be overjoyed when his glory is revealed.

1 Peter 4:13

"Why is there so much suffering in the world?" skeptics often ask when they wish to discount Christianity. They cannot reconcile a loving God who permits innocent suffering. In fact, they may try to persuade Christians who undergo suffering that their trials somehow prove God's plans have gone awry. Is suffering truly part of God's plan? In answer to that question, look at Jesus' life on earth. His suffering on the cross was the heartbeat of God's plan—resulting in our salvation and His glory. When you suffer according to God's plan, you are walking where Jesus walked: to the cross, to the grave, and—ultimately—to heaven. Will you trust that God knows what He is doing even in your pain?

eXtreme examples

UNITED STATES: SOPHIA'S MOTHER

"In 1996, our daughter Sophia had a long seizure causing permanent brain damage. She suffered badly for months, crying incessantly for two or three days at a time and writhing in pain. She did not know us or respond to us.

Day 171

You show that you are a letter from Christ, the result of our ministry, written not with ink but with the Spirit of the living God, not on tablets of stone but on tablets of human hearts.

2 Corinthians 3:3

"One nurse could not understand why we were not angry with God for allowing this to happen. I tried to help her see that we are His servants and cannot deny the tremendous gift that God had given us in His Son. Four months after her seizure, Sophia died.

"The day she died, I saw a picture from a *Voice of the Martyrs* article of a Sudanese sister whose breasts had been cut off sitting next to her infant. Her persecutors tortured her by doing this horrible thing, forcing her to watch her child die of starvation. Thousands of miles away from where she was, I knew her pain, and I wept, thinking, I will not allow myself to wallow in self-pity.

"That woman and others like her did not have the benefit of medical care, fellowship, and love from brethren that we had. Yet they have endured so much, and I, by the grace of God, can also endure it.

"I need these living epistles of the Lord Jesus Christ to express the reality that Jesus lives and this world is not my home."

While God's presence is always near through the person of the Holy Spirit, we often need those spiritual encouragers with skin on them to help us in our faith. Martyrs and other believers throughout the centuries are real people whose real examples of courage inspire us to believe that maybe, just maybe, we will be able to respond likewise. While we may not share in their exact adversities, we can adopt the spirit of their tenacity and bravery for our daily lives. If you have been inspired by an extreme story of faith, share it with others. Pass along the example. Teach others to draw strength from those who have gone before, living their faith as examples to all.

eXtreme refusal

RUSSIA: SERGHEY MECHEN

"Christianity is not a teaching that one can get from books or sermons," preached Serghey Mechen, leader of the Maroseyka Church in Moscow. "Jesus said, 'I am the truth.' Truth is a specific kind of life that you attain by following Christ's example."

Day 172

And the God of all grace, who called you to his eternal glory in Christ, after you have suffered a little while, will himself restore you and make you strong, firm, and steadfast.

1 Peter 5:10

It was 1923, and the new Communist government of Russia had launched the so-called "Living Church," which was nothing more than socialism disguised as Christianity. Pastor Serghey flatly refused to read the prescribed prayers or preach the watered-down idea of God that the Communists approved. He continued preaching the truth to his flock, knowing he might suffer for it.

Serghey was imprisoned for five years, and the Communists closed his church. But his time in prison only prepared Serghey more fully for ministry. Immediately upon his release, he resumed his work with the underground church. He faithfully ministered long hours each day until his former pastor, a man who had turned his back on God, betrayed him. The government rewarded that pastor with a job as a professor.

Serghey had often read Jesus' words that "a good shepherd gives his life for his sheep." He resolved to never betray his brethren. For his steadfast Christian activities, Serghey Mechen was executed by a firing squad in 1941. His life has passed, but his message remains: "The truth does not change to benefit one's needs."

God does not come in a box. He comes in all His glory and fullness, or He is not God at all. Some may be quick to say they are not opposed to God, as long as it is the right god they want preached. As if they were in a spiritual cafeteria, they pick and choose what they like and enjoy about the idea of God and dismiss the rest like leftovers. God's character and nature do not change with humanity's whims, however. We may try to fashion God into another form, but we will ultimately fail. Refuse anyone who dismisses the full character and nature of God at any point. Can you recognize heresy when you see it?

eXtreme serenity

ROMANIA: A PASTOR AND HIS FAMILY

The pastor, his wife, and their six small children had just read Psalm 23 while eating breakfast. Suddenly, the police burst into the family's home to search the house and arrest him.

Day 173

You will keep in perfect peace him whose mind is steadfast, because he trusts in you.

Isaiah 26:3

The police asked him, "Don't you have anything to say? Have you no sorrow or regret?" The pastor said carefully, "You are the answer to what we prayed today. We just read in Psalm 23 that God prepares a table before us in the presence of our enemies. We had a table but no enemies. Now you have come. If you would like anything that is on the table, I would like to share it with you. You were sent by God."

"How could you say such stupid things? We will take you to prison, and you will die there. You will never see your children again."

With continued ease, the pastor replied, "We also read about that today: 'Though I pass through valley of the shadow of death, I will not fear.'"

The officer shouted, "Everyone fears death! I know because I have seen it on their faces."

"A shadow of a dog can't bite you, and a shadow of death can't kill you. You can kill us or put us in prison, but nothing bad can happen to us. We're in Christ, and if we die, He will take us to His world."

Peace. It's becoming as valuable as blue-chip stock in today's economy of unrest and violence. Fortunately, all believers are shareholders in God's gift through Jesus Christ. But many people lack this peace. Some take prescriptions and worry to no end, trying to receive peace apart from God. Whatever good feeling they may find is only temporary at best. Then it's back to worry and unrest. In contrast, God's peace enables us to succeed with serenity in our sufferings. No trial can unnerve your trust in Him. Like the gentle pastor in this story, though calamity may strike without warning, you will be prepared with God's perfect peace.

eXtreme thoughts

ROMANIA: PRINCE VLADIMIR

Day 174

"Move it, Prince!" laughed the guard, grabbing the man's arm. "Let's see how you like your new accommodations." The guards shoved Prince Vladimir from the royal house of Ghica into the harsh prison cell. In one corner, he could see prisoners taking clothes and blankets from a thin, dead prisoner. In the back he could hear the screams of a prisoner being tortured.

And the peace of God, which transcends all understanding, will guard your hearts and your minds in Christ Jesus.

Philippians 4:7

This place was a long way from the life of luxury he had known at home. Yet Prince Vladimir survived the dehumanizing conditions in prison by holding on to his faith in Christ who comforted him and guided him. A cellmate of Vladimir once said, "Nowhere have I heard purer prayers and more thoughts of eternal value than in Communist prisons."

Vladimir's eternal thoughts from this time were published in a powerful book. He wrote, "Blessed are those who spread joy that arises out of their own suffering. He who denies himself for others clothes himself with Christ. Seek one who pushes you away. May my joys never come through the suffering of others. May my suffering bring some joy to others."

Who would dream that such "pure prayers and thoughts of eternal value" would come from a dethroned prince who survived the dungeons of Communist cruelty?

Negative thoughts can affect us profoundly. If we focus our minds on our sufferings, we can grow bitter and resentful as a result. If we choose to think positively in the midst of a crisis, however, then we can lift ourselves above our circumstances. Not only can we save ourselves from discouragement and despair, but we can also help others. Vladimir experienced joy in his sufferings. Are you prone to negativity when you are going through trials? Remember, you cannot control what happens in life. But you can control your attitude. Refuse to be negative. Ask God to give you a positive perspective on your trials, and open your eyes to help others.

Day 175

Uneasy is the heart until it rests in thee.

St. Augustine

eXtreme saint

ROME: ST. NICHOLAS

"Don't do it," Nicholas yelled as he saw the executioner lift his sword to kill another prisoner. **"He's done nothing to deserve this."** The man was about to be executed for his faith in Jesus Christ. Nicholas bravely grabbed the executioner's sword before it penetrated the prisoner's flesh.

Day 176

Love the LORD, all his saints! The LORD preserves the faithful.

Psalm 31:23

"Have it your way, Nicholas...I have many others to kill today." The executioner spat as he walked away and resumed his duties elsewhere.

Nicholas boldly spoke up for Christ at a difficult time in history. In the year 303, Emperor Diocletian began one of the most brutal persecutions of Christians. So many Christians were killed that the executioners were exhausted and took turns at their work.

Nicholas was branded with hot irons. He survived terrible beatings from the guards. And he endured other torture as well—simply for refusing to deny that Jesus is the Son of God. How could he deny the one who was so real to him? Nicholas remained resolute in the midst of great injustice.

After being released from prison, he spent the rest of his life establishing orphanages and protecting poor children. He was committed to advancing the gospel of Christ in creative ways. Once, he even threw money wrapped in a stocking through the window of a home of three very poor girls so they would not be sold to a house of prostitution.

Many years after his death, Nicholas was affectionately called St. Nicholas. For many children, the night before Christmas is the most magical night of the year as they await a visit from Santa Claus, a caricature of St. Nicholas. The real life story behind St. Nicholas is much more heroic and loving than most children could even dream. Think about your own life's story. Do people know the truth about your faith in Jesus Christ? Or do they merely know you as an affectionate and moral person? Although Santa Claus is not real, St. Nicholas was and you must be too. You may not feel like a saint, but the world needs real examples of resolute Christians. What will you do today to live your faith in a real way?

eXtreme willingness

"This isn't how I envisioned us having our first baby," said the young woman between contractions. "Are you sure this is clean enough?" she asked her husband, Joseph.

"I don't know, honey," he said, concerned. "But it's what we've got. We know God's going to protect this baby. He must have some plan in us having it *here*."

Day 177

As another painful contraction came, her husband advised, "Try to breathe through it," and wiped her face with a damp rag. "Hang on . . . should be just a few more minutes."

She said through gritted teeth, "I wanted to have the baby in my own house. I wanted my mother to be there to help me."

"I'm here to help you," Joseph said, "so we'll just have to get along by ourselves. And we both know God's here, too." Then he weakly joked, "If we need more help, we've always got the cows and the sheep next door."

"I am the Lord's servant," Mary answered. "May it be to me as you have said."

Luke 1:38

The contraction passed, and Mary smiled at her husband. At the next contraction, Mary began to push. Soon, her Son entered the world. They named Him Jesus, just as the angel instructed.

We sometimes forget the hardship that Joseph and Mary endured to deliver the King of kings: a stable for a delivery room, exile into Egypt, poverty, and scandal. Yet they endured everything willingly out of love for God.

As we read the Bible, we may think that believing God's promises would be easier if He packaged them with some definitive sign, like an angelic messenger. Yet even Mary, who received such a sign, had her doubts. When the angel Gabriel announced to Mary that she would give birth to God's Son, it probably sounded like the unthinkable. She asked Gabriel, "How will this be . . . since I am a virgin?" Despite her concerns, Mary chose to willingly believe God's promise and obey Him. Her simple willingness brought God's plan of salvation to the world. Is God calling you to willingness despite your doubts? Like Mary, your willingness to obey could have an eternal impact in God's kingdom.

eXtreme poetry

ROMANIA: DUMITRU BACU

Dumitru Bacu was a Christian prisoner during the 1950s and 1960s. Like so many others, his crime was simply being a Christian. Dumitru used his twenty years in prison to compose poetry of love to God. The poems were carefully written in small bars of soap or tapped through the walls in Morse code so that others could learn and pass them from cell to cell.

Day 178

I have learned to be content whatever the circumstances.

Philippians 4:11

"The pains which weakened our bodies were not able to master our hearts," Bacu said after his release. "Instead of hate, we cultivated love, understanding, and wisdom."

Here is one of his poems, composed in solitary confinement in a cell infested with rats, bedbugs, and lice:

Jesus appeared in my cell last night;
He was tall; He was sad, but oh He was light.
The moonbeams I treasured grew suddenly dim
As, startled and happy, I looked upon Him.
He came and He stood by the mat where I tossed
And silently showed what His sufferings cost.
The scars were all there, in His hands and His feet,
And a wound in His side where His heart did beat.
He smiled, and was gone. And I fell on the stone
And cried out, "Dear Jesus, don't leave me alone."
Clutching the bars, I was pierced through the palms:
Blessed gift, blessed scars.

A dingy prison cell and the loss of basic freedoms aren't usually the stuff of poetic inspiration. Dumitru was able to turn his sufferings into opportunities to praise God and impact other people's lives for Christ. His sufferings paled to him when he considered what Christ had suffered on his behalf. Experiencing what Dumitru faced, many believers would feel frustrated or insulted, not inspired. Some would doubt that God cared about them at all. Composing lines of poetic praise to God would be about the farthest thing from their minds. Yet Dumitru focused on Christ instead of his cell, and he was filled with praise. How do you react in times of suffering? When you are called to suffer, will you see obstacles to your happiness or opportunities to praise and serve God?

eXtreme advocate

ROMANIA: ANUTZA MOISE

After the Soviet Communists took over Romania, they hunted Germans as Nazi sympathizers. Anutza Moise decided to provide a hiding place to the very men who had hated her for being a Jew and a Christian. When she offered to help hide these men from the Communists, they couldn't believe that her offer was genuine.

Day 179

Love your enemies, do good to those who hate you.

Luke 6:27

"Do you not remember that we were the very ones who sent you to prison?" one of them asked.

"Of course I remember," said Anutza. "But I am a Christian, and God does not permit me to hold a grudge. I have forgiven you, and now I have the chance to help you. Jesus loves you, so I will love you also."

Her love amazed them, and many were won to Christ by her example. She, along with Richard and Sabina Wurmbrand and others, raised children whose Jewish parents had been exterminated in Nazi death camps.

Later, Anutza migrated to Norway, where she was active in a ministry to Jewish believers. In this ministry, she raised $10,000 to pay a ransom for her former pastor, Richard Wurmbrand, gaining his release from Romania. Anutza also handled the travel arrangements to get the Wurmbrands and their son, Mihai, to the West. Without Anutza's love and advocacy on his behalf, an influential pastor and founder of The Voice of the Martyrs might have died in a Communist prison.

When God calls us to follow Him and we respond, it means following Him everywhere and doing whatever He asks. Because Anutza took this calling seriously, she acted with love and forgiveness toward her enemies. The task of sheltering her former oppressors must have seemed monumental, but Anutza was able to do it. She obediently chose forgiveness over bitterness and revenge, and she followed Christ's example of love. What has God told you to do? Don't miss the opportunity to do eternally significant work.

eXtreme longing

IRAN: A PERSECUTED PASTOR

"Sometimes I miss those days of persecution!"

The words came from an Iranian pastor who had escaped to the West. In Iran, arrest and police harassment were common experiences. He had even lost his home and job because of his faith. Now he was free to live and worship wherever he wished. How could he long for the days of persecution?

Day 180

For our light and momentary troubles are achieving for us an eternal glory that far outweighs them all.

2 Corinthians 4:17

"Sometimes I miss those days," he said, "because I was so alive. I felt every day that Jesus was with me."

The pastor had planted a church near the front lines of the Iran–Iraq war. He earned money by driving a taxi and grew his church by sharing Christ with his passengers. In two years, he had won souls from nine language groups. Many soldiers worshiped with them each week, and he had baptized fifteen Muslim converts.

The pastor and his wife counted on God for everything. When the bombs of war fell around them, they prayed for his protection. When there wasn't enough money, they prayed for his provision. And each day God came through for them.

Their ministry was rewarded. Ten members of his church have gone on to become pastors. Even now, the pastor can see fruit from the time of ministry at the front lines.

If you've never been in love, you cannot understand what it is to be heartbroken. If you have never lost a loved one, you cannot truly relate to those who mourn. You cannot understand a longing for something you have never experienced. Those who have been persecuted for their faith describe a peculiar longing. They long not for the persecution as much as they long for the sense of fellowship their persecution brought them. They don't miss the torture as much as they miss what the torture taught them. The end result far outweighs the suffering. If you want to experience a deeper walk with Jesus, you must be willing to obediently sacrifice for Him. That is also a type of suffering.

eXtreme declaration

RUSSIA: PETER SIEMENS

Peter Siemens lay on the grimy floor of a Russian prison after being unconscious for three days. He had been arrested for sharing the gospel with children. His fellow prisoners had horribly beaten him in return for being promised parole by the guards. As they attacked him, Peter remained silent.

Day 181

A word aptly spoken is like apples of gold in settings of silver.

Proverbs 25:11

Seeing that he was conscious, one of the prisoners asked, "Why didn't you scream as we beat you?"

"I wondered if you were beating me just for your own sport, without the approval of the guards," Peter answered through bleeding lips. "If so, and I had yelled, you would have been punished for prison misconduct. I did not want you to suffer, because Jesus loves you, and I do, too."

Peter's elegant declaration won the hearts of the hardened criminals in his cell. They sent word through the prison grapevine that no one should touch him, regardless of where he was transferred or what incentives the guards offered.

Prisoners waiting to be executed at the prison heard Peter's story and sent word asking for his help. Peter responded, and through sympathetic guards, he shared with them the story of Jesus' love. Because of Peter's ministry, some of them may have trusted Christ before their execution. His living example of Christ's love brought a significant opportunity to others. Those who would have never heard otherwise received the gospel message.

The spoken word can be powerful. A well-timed word of counsel, love, or encouragement can go miles when someone is in need. But what about when someone is spiritually needy? Peter Siemens' words were motivated by his love for Christ. That love enabled him to courageously speak of Christ's love to his enemies at a time when they needed to hear it most. Peter was obedient to God's leading, and God used Peter's words to change many of his fellow prisoners' eternal destinies. Did God use someone's words to lead you to Jesus? When God calls you to tell someone else about Jesus, will you obey Him at that time? Consider the eternal difference your example and words can make.

Day 182

Persecution does not take us away from our home. Persecution helps send us along the way to our true "home."

PASTOR JOSEPH COLAW

eXtreme disappointment

"The teenager never came back."

The famous evangelist spoke from behind prison bars. A powerful preacher, known throughout Eastern Europe, he was telling how he could not find peace. This man had led thousands to Christ, so the other Christian prisoners could not understand his feeling of failure.

Day 183

As long as it is day, we must do the work of him who sent me. Night is coming, when no one can work.

John 9:4

"I had preached at an evangelistic meeting," he explained. "I had poured out my heart, and, at the end, two hundred people had come forward to accept Christ. I was thrilled, but I was also exhausted. As I was leaving, one young man came to me. 'Pastor, I need to talk to you,' he said. I told him that I was too tired, and could he maybe come back in the morning. He never came back. The Communists arrested me later that evening. I was interrogated nonstop, day and night for five days. I answered all of their questions. I answered because I feared the tortures, the beatings I would receive if I did not answer. Out of fear of the Communists, I could speak for five days and nights without stopping.

"Out of love toward God, however, I could not speak five minutes more to that teenaged boy looking for the way of life. How will I stand before God and account for bringing only two hundred to Christ that day when it could have been two hundred and one?"

We may choose to overlook opportunities that God puts before us to share Christ with others, thinking that we'll get to it later or that we'll have a better time. But we may never get another chance. When we choose to ignore a divinely given opportunity, we, like the evangelist, may find that the moment was fleeting—a once-in-a-lifetime gift. Tragically, it may be the only time a person asks to hear about God's gift of eternal life through His Son, Jesus. In heaven, God may ask you why you did not share the gospel with someone when you had the opportunity to do so. How would you answer?

eXtreme gift

CHINA: A YOUNG DAUGHTER

"I want to talk to you about an unusual gift," said the Chinese father to his beautiful, black-haired daughter. She smiled with anticipation. She loved it when her wise father shared special lessons about God. He loved Christ, and everyone who knew him was touched with his kindness and compassion.

Day 184

He opened a worn Bible and began, "This gift is found in Philippians 1:29. It says, 'For it has been granted to you on behalf of Christ not only to believe on him, but also to suffer for him.' Something that is given to us is a 'gift.' The two gifts in the verse are belief and suffering. Suffering that results from our belief in God is a precious gift, the value of which will be fully realized only in heaven."

The daughter smiled. "Thank you, Papa," she said as she reached up to hug him. "I understand."

The young girl grew up to be the wife of Pastor Li Dexian, who has been arrested over twenty times and nearly beaten to death for his faith. She carries on the work with him, persevering because she learned at a young age that godly suffering is a gift. Pastor Li and his wife have won countless souls to Christ in Communist China, and they continue to work under a constant threat of arrest.

Consider it pure joy, my brothers, whenever you face trials of many kinds.

James 1:2

The gifts of belief and suffering are a package deal. Not only are they impossible to separate, each gift also strengthens the other. If we have been given the gift of belief in Christ, we will follow Christ. Following Christ means taking risks, going against popular trends, being misunderstood, and even enduring physical and emotional pain. Belief often leads to suffering. As we experience the same kinds of suffering that Jesus lived, we come to know Him in a richer and deeper way. The cycle begins again because suffering strengthens our belief. Don't expect to be able to filter suffering out of your life without reducing your belief in Christ.

eXtreme author

INDIA: WILLIAM CAREY

Day 185

"They just can't do this," exclaimed William. "Can't you see how wrong it is?"

"Look, most of the people in this town think it's the right thing to do," replied the exasperated government official. "It's part of their religion."

William questioned, "How is tying a living woman to her dead husband and burning them together the right thing to do?"

With this, the official threw up his hands. "William," he answered, "one man alone can't change this. Just give it up and go back to tending your flock."

When his denomination said that "God alone" would convert heathens in pagan countries, William ignored them and embarked on one of the most successful missionary journeys in church history. In addition, he taught himself several languages and published a book that became the source for the modern missionary movement. He also translated the New Testament into thirty-four languages and the Old Testament into eight.

William Carey fought for years against the practice in India of burning wives alive with their dead husbands. Eventually, despite government opposition, he succeeded in getting the burnings banned. Carey spent his life as an innovator for Christ, facing hardship to make a difference. And he was known for encouraging others to "Expect great things from God; attempt great things for God" (based on Isaiah 54:2,3). William Carey did just that.

Then Jesus came to them and said, "All authority in heaven and on earth has been given to me. Therefore go and make disciples of all nations."

Matthew 28:18,19

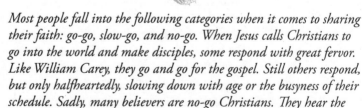

Most people fall into the following categories when it comes to sharing their faith: go-go, slow-go, and no-go. When Jesus calls Christians to go into the world and make disciples, some respond with great fervor. Like William Carey, they go and go for the gospel. Still others respond, but only halfheartedly, slowing down with age or the busyness of their schedule. Sadly, many believers are no-go Christians. They hear the command, but they figure that someone else will do it. Which category best describes your response to Jesus' call to evangelism? Ask God to renew a desire to share your faith with others. If you are expecting great things from His answer, then be prepared to attempt great things in His name.

eXtreme martyrs of old

ROME: CHRYSANTHES

"Son, you can't believe this Jesus is real," said Chrysanthes' father.

"I know it's true, Father," replied Chrysanthes. "I believe that Jesus came into the world to save sinners like you and me. He is the light of the world. There is no hope in the idols you adore."

As punishment, his father locked Chrysanthes into a dark cellar for days, but he could still hear his son singing praise to God. To turn Chrysanthes from the faith, his father also tried surrounding him with worldly delights and girls, but Chrysanthes held strong. Then his father brought Daria, an idolatrous woman of uncommon beauty, into his home to make him forget Christ. Instead, Chrysanthes brought her to salvation, and she was baptized.

Later, Chrysanthes and Daria married and enjoyed a wonderful and miraculous ministry bringing others to Christ. When Roman guards tried to bind them for witnessing, the ropes fell off their hands. The governor ordered soldiers to tie Chrysanthes to a pillar and beat him with rods, but the blows left no trace on his body. As a result, the soldiers and the governor fell at his feet confessing to God's power.

In a land that worshiped idols, Chrysanthes stood out because he trusted in the living God, not in stones or woodcarvings. Because of his endurance, scores of pagans came to faith.

Day 186

But you, O LORD, sit enthroned forever; your renown endures through all generations.

Psalm 102:12

The gospel of Christ is nothing new. It has been changing lives for centuries and will continue to do so until Christ returns. The stories of old are the stories of today. The Christian martyr in hand-sewn robes and sandals shares the same heart with the modern, blue-jean-clad believer who e-mails his testimony. No generation gap separates those who left a legacy of faith and those who carry on their legacy today. Where do you fit in the story line? Are you willing to align your testimony with the saints of old? Live fully for Christ today and leave a legacy for tomorrow. You can help transform a home, a workplace, a community, or even an entire country for Christ.

eXtreme discipleship

JERUSALEM: JAMES, THE SON OF ZEBEDEE

History teaches us that the man who was to kill James refused to do so. King Herod beheaded them both. Perhaps it happened like this.

Day 187

I will show you my faith by what I do.

James 2:18

The execution was to take place symbolically on the same Friday of Passover, roughly fourteen years after Jesus had been crucified. James, the son of Zebedee, was escorted into the execution room. A number of soldiers were already in the room. The light from the oil lamps reflected off bloodstains on the floor. How many followers of Jesus had gone before him in this very room?

James looked into the eyes of his guard, but the guard turned away, his heart deeply troubled. Many times James had spoken to him about Jesus through the small slit in the heavy prison door, and the guard's heart seemed to be opening. Now his "friend" had become his executioner.

James willingly knelt down. When the sword reached its height, it perceptibly shook with uncertainty, and then it was hurled to the ground beside James, doing him no harm. "I cannot!" the executioner cried. "I will not kill him! What he says about Jesus is true, and I cannot kill His servant James."

At Herod's gesture, soldiers came forward and took the executioner, bound his hands behind him, and forced him on the floor beside James.

Kneeling together, they were both beheaded.

Mentoring is a popular topic in both secular and spiritual realms. It seems more and more people are taking note of the unique power of a personal relationship between two people. One has something to learn; the other has something to teach. One has something to gain; the other has something to give. Following the example of someone else who is following after Christ is the spiritual definition of mentoring. One believer shows another how to practically live out the Christian faith. Who would you say is a mentor in your life? What Christlike qualities have you seen in that person's life that you will pursue?

eXtreme definition of prayer

CHINA: A SOLDIER IN THE RED GUARD

This interesting letter was smuggled out of Communist China:

Day 188

Therefore let everyone who is godly pray to you.

Psalm 32:6

"I am a teenager and a soldier in the Red Guard. I did not believe in any God, in any heaven, in any hell, in any Savior, in anything at all. One day I accidentally tuned into your transmission on the radio. At first I was tempted to turn it off. Good Communists do not believe in God. But I found the program interesting, so I tuned in again and again. Now I believe in Christ. But I have two questions.

"The first one: Does God accept anybody from Communist China? In your broadcast you speak about the church, but I am in China where we have almost no churches. Can God accept somebody without a church?"

This young soldier did not know how many unofficial churches existed in China or that all those who love Christ are the church.

Then he asked his second question: "Would you please teach me to pray? You start every radio program with a prayer and you end with a prayer. I would like to pray, but I don't know how."

The soldier had never been in a church, but he said that he imagined prayer meant "to speak the whole day so that after everything you say, you might be able to add 'Amen.'"

What a beautiful definition of prayer.

Prayer is not natural. In fact, it doesn't come to anyone naturally because it is a supernatural experience. God gives us a spiritual desire to communicate with Him. Like mathematics or language, prayer is a learned skill. The more we practice prayer, the more natural it becomes. The young believer in this story defined prayer as affecting every aspect of life, thus making one's whole life a prayer to God. How are you growing in your own experience with prayer? Are you out of practice? Starting today, ask God to give you a supernatural desire to speak with Him and make prayer a natural part of every day. Then start practicing. May your life be a prayer.

Day 189

Before prison we heard about God.
But in prison we experienced God.

PASTOR SZE, A CHINESE HOUSE-CHURCH LEADER WHO WAS
IMPRISONED FOR HIS FAITH. HE SURVIVED FAMINE, ILLNESS, AND AN
EXPLOSION IN THE COAL MINE WHERE HE WAS FORCED TO WORK.

eXtreme contentment

The straightjackets were torturous for Anna Chertokova. She hated having her hands covered and tied close to her body. To the attendants, she was nothing more than an animal, not worthy of consideration.

Day 190

I have learned to be content whatever the circumstances.

Philippians 4:11

Anna spent ten years in an insane asylum in Russia. She was not even slightly insane. A judge had sent her there because she was a Christian. Her refusal to deny Christ was, to the judge, crazy.

Surrounded by the mentally ill, Anna sometimes questioned her own sanity. In the long nights she would cry out to God in her mind, even as those around her cried out in their anger or terror. Yet she never became angry. The faith that she refused to deny in court, she also refused to deny in the asylum. To those who were able to understand, Anna even tried to be a witness and an example of Christ's love.

"I greet you all with love in our Lord Jesus Christ," Anna wrote from inside the asylum. "I pray to God that He will make us beautiful and perfect in Christ and that He will take charge of all our affairs. I firmly believe that God who created everybody's heart and who examines all the affairs of mortal men will judge my dispute with the idolatry of atheism and will execute His judgment and justice."

Christians may sometimes find themselves in crazy situations that try their patience and test their character. A difficult living arrangement. Confounding office politics. A rebellious child. Can we remain confident in God, no matter our circumstances? We can if we know the secret of contentment. The Bible teaches us that our inner sense of contentment must rule when facing outward circumstances. Our attitude takes its cues from God, not our situation. Otherwise, we risk becoming as confused as our circumstances. Take a lesson from Anna. Instead of anger, resentment, or turmoil, ask God to teach you the secret of being content despite your circumstances.

eXtreme job

ROMANIA: DR. KARLO

The application process was long and cumbersome. The background checks were extensive, and Dr. Karlo's application was almost derailed over rumors of his Christian ties. But Dr. Karlo made it through the arduous process and became a doctor for the Secret Police. He avoided telling them that he was a Christian.

Day 191

I have become all things to all men so that by all possible means I might save some.

1 Corinthians 9:22

Dr. Karlo's own family rejected him because they thought he had become a Communist. One by one, his church family and all those he had been close to turned their backs on him. None of them knew his mission: to find the pastor.

In his role as a Secret Police doctor, he could come and go at the prison without questions. He had access to every cell, so—finally—he found the pastor locked away.

Karlo got word to other Christians, who then got word to the outside world. They had been told that he was dead, but now they had proof that Pastor Richard Wurmbrand was alive. During talks between Khrushchev and Eisenhower in 1956, Christians around the world clamored for Wurmbrand's release. Eventually he was freed for a ransom of $10,000.

"If it had not been for this doctor," Wurmbrand later wrote, "who joined the Secret Police specifically to find me, I would never have been released. I would have remained in prison—or in a prison grave."

Undercover agents are the stars of the big screen. Their missions involve one adventure after another in service to headquarters' commands. In the same way, extreme believers in restricted nations lead adventurous lives. Their stories make an eternal difference for many. They dare not advertise their mission, but they are always prepared to make the most of every opportunity to share the Good News of Christ. Regardless of geography or life situation, God calls each of us to be His spiritual agent, reporting to heavenly headquarters. We are on mission to share God's message of love and forgiveness every day. God gives no guarantee of safety or security with this job assignment, but He promises eternal rewards.

eXtreme martyrdom

ROME: POLYCARP

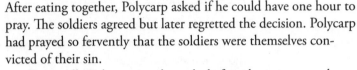

Polycarp had been a student of the apostle John, but was on the run late in his life. While traveling, a child recognized him and immediately informed the soldiers. When they found Polycarp eating, he offered to share his food with the arresting soldiers.

Day 192

We ought always to thank God for you, brothers, and rightly so, because your faith is growing more and more.

2 Thessalonians 1:3

After eating together, Polycarp asked if he could have one hour to pray. The soldiers agreed but later regretted the decision. Polycarp had prayed so fervently that the soldiers were themselves convicted of their sin.

Eventually Polycarp was brought before the governor, who sentenced him to be burned in the marketplace. The governor gave him the opportunity to save his life if he denied Jesus. Polycarp refused, stating, "For eighty-six years I have served him. How then should I blaspheme my King who has saved me?"

They secured Polycarp to a stake and lit the wood around him. The flames rose up around the courageous believer but, miraculously, did not burn a hair on his body. The governor was furious. He ordered a soldier to pierce the Christian's side. They succeeded in killing Polycarp, but were unable to kill his faith and triumphant spirit.

Polycarp's last recorded prayer was this: "I praise You for making me worthy to be received among the number of the martyrs this day and this hour, so that I share in the cup of Christ for the resurrection of my soul."

Polycarp gives new meaning to the phrase "active retirement." A seasoned saint in his late eighties, Polycarp lived long enough not to care how his opposition felt about his faith in Christ. On the other end of the spectrum, young zealots often take on the enemy without knowing any better. Most believers fall somewhere between the two. We miss the zeal from our youthful commitment, yet we haven't lived long enough to dismiss the opinions others have of our faith. Thankfully, Jesus takes us as we are and not as we should be. Determine to give Him every ounce of commitment you can give Him today and let Him grow you toward greater faith tomorrow.

eXtreme servant

"Repeat these verses!" Zeba was ordered.

"I will not repeat the verses. I am a Christian. I will always be a Christian."

Day 193

With her family in poverty, Zeba was forced to work as a servant for a wealthy Muslim family. While she was working, the head of the household tried to teach her about Islam and coerce her to memorize verses from the Koran. On three occasions Zeba refused, stating, "I am a Christian." Each time she refused, she was beaten.

Zeba's employers then had her arrested, falsely accusing her of stealing from the family. After securing her daughter's release, Zeba's mother visited the Muslim family to take up her daughter's defense. She was not welcomed.

Instead, whoever wants to become great among you must be your servant.

Matthew 20:26

One of the family members screamed, "You are an infidel! Both you and you daughter are infidels and do not deserve to live." They threw gasoline on Zeba's mother and lit a match. Zeba never saw her mother again. Despite the tragedy, Zeba continued her walk with Christ and was baptized.

Today in Pakistan, a sewing school has been established so young Christian girls like Zeba will no longer have to seek employment as servants to help feed their families. Despite her pain, Zeba holds no grudges, and she dreams of sharing her faith with others in her country. She wants to become a Bible teacher.

God's kingdom is right side up only when it is upside down. His hierarchy of importance is upside down compared with how the world structures people in society. Instead of the talented, beautiful, and wealthy at the top of the list, humble servants make the heavenly headlines. Zeba is nothing in the world's eyes, yet she is doing great work for the kingdom. A servant may not be especially talented, but a servant is available to work. A servant may not be worth much to others, but a servant is invaluable in God's service. What does it mean to live contrary to the rest of the world? If you surrender to God as a servant, you will know the feeling firsthand. Are you willing to humble yourself to the role of a servant and do whatever is necessary to spread God's Good News?

eXtreme turnaround

CHINA: CHANG SHEN

Before his conversion, Chang Shen had been known as a gambler, womanizer, and thief. When he was stricken blind in midlife, neighbors said it was the judgment of the gods for his evildoings.

Day 194

You were taught, with regard to your former way of life, to put off your old self, which is being corrupted by its deceitful desires; to be made new in the attitude of your minds; and to put on the new self, created to be like God in true righteousness and holiness.

Ephesians 4:22–24

In 1886, Chang traveled hundreds of miles to a missionary hospital where people were receiving sight. His eyesight was partially restored, and he also heard about Christ for the first time. "Never had we a patient who received the gospel with such joy," reported the doctor.

When Chang asked to be baptized, missionary James Webster replied, "Go home and tell your neighbors that you have changed. If you are still following Jesus when I visit you later, then I will baptize you." Five months later, Webster arrived and found hundreds of believers. He baptized the new evangelist with great joy.

Later, a clumsy, native doctor robbed Chang of the partial eyesight he had, but Chang continued his travels to different villages. Though some spat on him and rejected him, he still won hundreds more to Christ.

When the Boxer Rebellion arose, Christians led Chang to a cave in the mountains for safety. The Boxers rounded up fifty Christians for execution in a nearby town but promised to spare them all if Chang came forward. When news reached Chang, he said, "I'll gladly die for them."

Chang was beheaded three days later, and the remaining local Christians were spared.

The great exchange is the message of the great gospel. Jesus offers the opportunity to exchange our old life for a new one. Look how He changed Chang, from someone living for self to a person sold out completely for Christ. No matter how much ruin we have caused in our former life, we can be restored to a right relationship with God. This is why our personal testimony is such a powerful witness. A changed life presents strong evidence for the fact of salvation. We don't talk like we used to talk. We don't walk like we used to walk. Who needs to hear about the difference Christ has made in your life?

eXtreme burden

COLOMBIA: JUAN

Neither drugs nor civil war can stop the spread of the gospel in Colombia.

Day 195

For my yoke is easy and my burden is light.

Matthew 11:30

Juan and his wife, Maria, are missionaries among the indigenous people north of Cali, Colombia. Cali is controlled by the Revolutionary Armed Forces of Colombia (FARC), a leftist guerrilla group. Many Colombian pastors and missionaries have faced opposition from FARC and have fled the area. When Juan met with a group of fifty FARC guerrillas three years ago, however, twenty of them received Christ. As he says, "We exchange pistols for epistles."

Now, the National Liberation Army has been attacking Christian churches in the region. Recently, more than twenty churches were shut down, and many pastors fled for their lives. Guerrillas often come and demand all the tithes and offerings or take the pastor's life. Now Juan is the only pastor left in the area, and he receives no outside aid.

Still, Juan and his wife made a decision to stay and continue ministering to the people. They say, "If we are to die because we preach the Word of God, we would rather die than leave the church."

Juan does not condemn those who have left, nor does he talk about the difficulties they have faced. He prefers to share what God is doing and his burden for ministry. His mind is preoccupied, not with danger, but with reaching Colombia's people for Christ.

Jesus describes an image of a pack animal burdened with a load. The animal does not struggle against the weight of the burden, however, for it is hardly heavy at all. Being burdened with the gospel is not the same as being weighed down with earthly concerns. The burden of the gospel simply means an awareness of others' spiritual needs. Juan has a "burden," but his burden is light. Following Christ's example, we must be burdened for lost people. This load is light because we are always giving it away. We are not supposed to keep the Good News to ourselves. Have you been rejected when you share Christ? Perhaps you have considered giving in to the opposition. Let Jesus' burden for the lost motivate you to persevere in sharing the gospel.

Day 196

If we Christians don't continue to share the gospel and push the envelope, the envelope will close in on us. If we maintain a "silent witness," there will be no witness, and Christianity will die in America.

RAY THORNE, MISSIONARY TO THE PERSECUTED CHURCH

eXtreme evangelist

CHINA: PASTOR LI DEXIAN

"I will preach until I die."

Pastor Li Dexian had preached just a few minutes when Public Security Bureau officers stormed into the house. They dragged Pastor Li outside and beat him, as well as others in the Chinese congregation.

Day 197

At the police station, the evangelist was beaten again until he vomited blood. The officers beat his face with his own Bible, leaving him bleeding and barely conscious on the concrete floor of the cell.

When he was released seven hours later, he resumed his ministry. The next time he delivered a message to that church, seven PSB officers came in, shouting accusations against the evangelist. When they saw a visiting Westerner with him, they left but returned fifteen minutes later with reinforcements. Li was beaten with rods and kicked as he held his Bible to protect his ribs.

If you continue in your faith, established and firm, not moved from the hope held out in the gospel.

Colossians 1:23

"Why must you beat him?" shouted some of the foreigners. "What about the 'freedom of religion' you claim in China?"

The PSB took the foreigners to the local police station, as well as the woman who owned the home where the meeting took place. It was her son who had told the PSB about the meeting.

Since the attack, the large meetings in the village have ceased, but the church has not stopped. Now they gather in more than forty smaller meetings, and new people find Christ each week.

Like droplets of mercury, when the opposition tries to keep the church within its grasp, it only divides into smaller and smaller units. Churches within restricted nations may never experience the Western culture of the megachurch with forty-acre campuses; however, their attendance continues to grow. In fact, one Christian church in Korea far exceeds the attendance of several Western megachurches combined. Yet, like the strategy in China, the Korean congregation is made up of thousands of smaller house meetings or "cells." What we may perceive as obstacles to evangelism are merely opportunities in disguise. When you come up against opposition, do you give up too easily? Or can you persevere and find another way for the gospel message to advance?

eXtreme force

"If Abu wanted to be a Christian, he'd have to do it somewhere else. We surrounded his house, ready to force him out and burn it.

"As we got closer, we could hear him talking. *Had he gathered others to help him?* we wondered. Then we could hear that he was praying for the entire village and asking Jesus to forgive us for what we were about to do! This made us even angrier, so twenty-five of us rushed toward his house to apprehend him. But there was an invisible force that would not let any of us enter his house, and we were frightened away.

"When I got home, I could not sleep. I kept thinking about Abu's prayer. Finally at three in the morning, I went back to Abu's house. I asked him to tell me about Jesus. After three hours of talking with Abu, I asked Jesus to forgive me, and I surrendered my life to Him. I rushed to my house and shared what happened to me with my wife, and she also became a Christian, along with my children."

Within days, Idris Miah, the Bangladeshi believer who told this story, faced a test. He was fired from his job, and his children were forced out of school. Yet he says that he still has joy, for he has Jesus in his life.

Day 198

Answer me when I call to you, O my righteous God. Give me relief from my distress.

Psalm 4:1

Often we can't choose our life context, but we can choose our attitude and response. We can always make those choices, despite the circumstances. So when, like Abu, we stand at the brink of disaster, will we choose a prayerful, Christlike response, or will we give in to panic and distress? It is impossible for others, despite their best efforts, to make us angry or stressed. We make those choices ourselves. In the same way, we can choose to imitate Christ in our response to opposition. Who knows what will come of it? Ask God for help today to choose the proper response to any trying situation.

eXtreme "slave"

VIRGIN ISLANDS: LEONARD DOBER

Leonard Dober wondered if Jesus had thought the cross too much; then he remembered Jesus' prayer in the garden ended, "Not My will, but Yours, Father." Leonard's task seemed impossible, but he was pursuing God's will and not his own.

Day 199

If we are out of our mind, it is for the sake of God; if we are in our right mind, it is for you.

2 Corinthians 5:13

Leonard Dober determined that God's call to him was to reach slaves in the Virgin Islands. He planned to reach these men and women by selling himself as a slave and working alongside others each day while sharing Jesus' love with them. The thought of being a slave frightened and sickened him. He dreaded the treatment he would receive. *But Christ was willing to die on the cross for me,* he thought. *No price is too high to serve Him.*

It wasn't the slave masters who were Dober's harshest persecutors, but rather fellow Christians. They questioned his call to minister to slaves and ridiculed him as a fool for his plan. But Dober would not be dissuaded. He arrived in the Virgin Islands late in the 1730s.

When he became a servant in the governor's house, he feared that this position was too far removed from the slaves to whom he had come to minister. So he left and moved from the governor's house to a mud hut where he could work one-on-one with slaves.

In just three years, Dober's ministry included more than thirteen thousand new converts.

Jesus freaks. That's what the world calls those whose faith seems a bit radical. Odd. Extreme. Dober was an eighteenth century "Jesus freak"—a free man who chose to live as a slave in order to win others to Jesus. He was willing to do whatever it took to squeeze the last ounce of devotion from his heart in service to Christ. For Dober, that meant a specific plan that made sense to no one but him. Have you been written off because of your freakish refusal to go along with the majority rule? If God has called you to do something radical for Him in your family, church, or community, you must obey. Let others call you crazy, but may Jesus find you committed.

eXtreme worship

He heard the decree from his window: "For the next thirty days, anyone who prays to anyone other than the king will be thrown to the lions."

Daniel pushed the shutters open. On the rooftop across the way stood two of the king's advisors, who hated him, glaring intensely. He nodded cordially as he met their eyes, and they nodded back, as cunning smiles spread across their faces.

Daniel went to every window in his chamber and swung it wide open. At each there seemed to be observers. Then he went to the center of the room, where all could see him, knelt, and began worshiping God.

The king was dejected when the guards brought Daniel before him. The king had been tricked. His decree could not be revoked, though he had sought all day to find a way to free Daniel, whom he considered to be a good man.

"Take him," King Darius said to the guards. Then he looked in Daniel's eyes and said, "May your God, whom you serve continually, rescue you!" (Daniel 6:16). The soldiers took Daniel to the den, with the king following close behind. Daniel did not say a word, but bowed to the king and walked in among the lions. The doorway was sealed with a large boulder.

Daniel went to the center of the den, knelt, and began worshiping God.

Extreme worship is not a manner of praise. It's not a specific method or a particular tradition. It's not determined by debating organ music versus contemporary praise. In fact, it has little to do with how we praise God at all. Extreme worship is defined by when and where we worship. When we are drawn to worship during our most stressful times, we practice extreme worship. When we are drawn to sing praise where the opposition is strongest, we practice extreme worship. Like Daniel, we must not allow our circumstances to dictate when and where we worship God. We must be prepared to live out our faith anytime, any place. Are you willing to serve God in extreme worship today?

Day 200

The king said to Daniel, "May your God, whom you serve continually, rescue you!"

Daniel 6:16

eXtreme refusal

NORTH KOREA: A BIBLE OWNER

"They begged and begged me, but I couldn't give it to them," said the man. "I know Christians are supposed to share, but I just couldn't part with it." He sadly held out his hand so that his listener could see his prized possession.

Day 201

For I delight in your commands because I love them.

Psalm 119:47

"I really wanted to, but I couldn't. You see, people in North Korea told me that they have been praying for fifty years to get a Bible. But I didn't give them mine because I had been praying for twenty years, and I had just gotten it from a pastor in South Korea."

He sighed deeply as his mind went to the needy believers in North Korea desperately praying for one copy of the Bible. He hugged his Bible to his chest. He had escaped the Communist prison state and was now living freely in South Korea.

Bibles in North Korea are rare. Because of the opposition from the Communists, believers consider them more precious than gold. One man was beaten to death with an iron rod along the Chinese border when he was caught bringing Bibles into North Korea. Sadly, cases like this are reported over and over.

"I cannot forget those people," he said with a sigh. "I cannot forget the look of envy on their faces when I showed them my Bible. I feel so bad for them."

They serve as coasters for drinks or a handy spot to rest the remote control. Their sturdy covers help compose a letter on hotel stationery or catch the ashes falling from a cigarette. They listlessly adorn the coffee table, next to the caramel candy dish and the TV Guide. Although this book remains a best-seller year after year, fewer people seem to be reading it very much. It is the Bible. The Bible is abused and neglected outside of those places where its true value is known all too well. How differently we might treat our Bibles if we had to pray twenty years to get one! What can you do to revive your passion for God's precious Word?

eXtreme sight

Liuba Ganevskaya had been beaten repeatedly in the Russian prison. But when she looked up at her torturer, holding the whip above her back, she smiled.

"Why do you smile?" he asked, stunned.

"I don't see you as a mirror would reveal you right now," Liuba said. "I see you as you surely have been—a beautiful, innocent child. We are the same age. We might have been playmates."

Day 202

God opened Liuba's eyes to see the man differently. She saw his exhaustion; he was as tired of beating her as she was of being beaten. He was frustrated that he wasn't able to make her reveal the activities of other believers.

"He is so much like you," God said into Liuba's heart. "You are both caught in the same drama of life. You and your torturers pass through the same veil of tears."

Seeing the man through God's eyes, Liuba's attitude changed. She continued talking to him. "I see you, too, as I hope you will be. A persecutor worse than you once lived—Saul of Tarsus—and he became an apostle and a saint." She asked the calmed man what burden weighed on him so much that it drove him to the madness of beating a person who had not harmed him.

I, the LORD, have called you in righteousness . . . to open eyes that are blind.

Isaiah 42:6,7

Through her loving concern, Liuba ushered her torturer into Christ's kingdom.

Earthly eyesight is often hindered by a variety of ailments: astigmatism, nearsightedness, glaucoma, and others. Just as our eyesight benefits from corrective lenses, the eyes of our heart can profit from spiritual intervention. Left to our own devices, we see only the bad in others and not the good. But God grants spiritual vision to those who want to see life from heaven's perspective. We can begin to see an intolerant boss, or someone who insults us, as a wounded individual who needs love. We can see behind the intimidating mask of a rebellious teenager to the frightened girl or boy who is crying out for acceptance. Do you see others with heaven's eyes? What difference would spiritual eyesight make in your life?

Day 203

I would rather be hung than betray my Lord.

SALEEMA, A NINETEEN-YEAR-OLD CHRISTIAN IN PAKISTAN
WHO HAS BEEN SEVERELY PERSECUTED FOR HER FAITH

eXtreme honor

ROMANIA: VALERIU GAFENCU

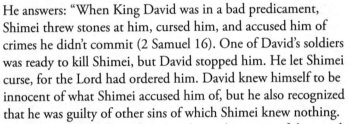

Valeriu Gafencu and his family had lost their father and had suffered greatly at the hands of Communist torturers. Yet he had nothing bad to say about the Communists who had brought so much pain to his family. How could he put up with so much and not speak out against his torturers?

Day 204

Do not judge, and you will not be judged. Do not condemn, and you will not be condemned. Forgive, and you will be forgiven.

Luke 6:37

He answers: "When King David was in a bad predicament, Shimei threw stones at him, cursed him, and accused him of crimes he didn't commit (2 Samuel 16). One of David's soldiers was ready to kill Shimei, but David stopped him. He let Shimei curse, for the Lord had ordered him. David knew himself to be innocent of what Shimei accused him of, but he also recognized that he was guilty of other sins of which Shimei knew nothing.

"The Communists call us bandits and enemies of the people, which we're not. But we all are guilty of not being exemplary saints growing more like Christ. Our reply to the Communists' misdeeds should not be hatred but inner renewal. Beams of holiness gushing from us will destroy the evil."

Gafencu's witness in prison brought many to Christ. And until the day he died, he refused to say one bad word against those who caused him pain.

Does an enemy deserve to be honored? Perhaps it is difficult to think along those lines. We can learn, however, from the persecuted church that God can use even our enemies to bring us closer to God. In that sense, we can honor the role our enemies play in our lives. If we revile our enemies, we may be showing contempt for God's greater plan. If you are busy cursing your enemies for the way they treat you, stop and think why God has allowed the situation in your life. Are you making it easier or harder for God to teach you something through this? If so, you'll surely face it again until you learn.

eXtreme rumor

CHINA: CHINESE BELIEVERS

"We have heard a rumor that people in the West are saying there is no persecution of Christians in China," began the letter from a group of Chinese believers.

"More than one hundred brothers are imprisoned here, and many young Christians under eighteen are under strong pressure from the police. Some were thrown in manure pits; others were beaten with electric-stun batons; some were beaten so much they could not stand and could only crawl.

Day 205

Remember those in prison as if you were their fellow prisoners, and those who are mistreated as if you yourselves were suffering.

Hebrews 13:3

"A few could not endure this. They revealed the names and addresses of their fellow workers to the police. They were sentenced, whereas those who said nothing were eventually released because of insufficient proof.

"Persecution is normal for us. In many cases, we are released after interrogation. Then we return to our original area to preach.

"Some teenagers want to dedicate themselves to God for full-time Christian service. Turned out of their homes, they are willing to spend their entire lives in this dangerous wandering fashion as evangelists. We see this with fear and trembling, fearing that after preaching the gospel ourselves, we may be castaways.

"We have paid a great price for the gospel—much blood and sweat, many tears shed, many lives sacrificed, and much braving of wind and rain."

Rumors that the persecution of Christians in China has ended are surely false. In fact, these rumors may be tools that the enemy uses to suppress the prayers and support that these persecuted believers need. Often we feel that if we tell ourselves that something isn't so, then maybe it really isn't. If we shield ourselves to the accounts of persecutions and the stories of sheer survival, then we may begin to believe oppression doesn't exist. We cannot hide or deny the truth long enough for it to change, however. Our brothers and sisters are being persecuted today in restricted nations. Knowing this, what is your response? Will you pray? Serve? Give? Spend some time thinking and praying about your reaction.

eXtreme answer

"Are you a Christian?" Three times the question was asked. Three times the answer was, "Yes." Three Christians were martyred. The Roman ruler Urbicus had no tolerance for Christians in AD 150.

Day 206

You are the salt of the earth. But if the salt loses its salti- ness, how can it be made salty again?

Matthew 5:13

Ptolemaeus had been accused of teaching that salvation comes through faith in Jesus Christ alone. He hated the deceit and ungodliness of the day. Therefore when Urbicus asked if he was a Christian, he could not lie. He had to stand for righteousness and boldly answer, "Yes." For this he was put in chains and beaten many times.

Again he was brought before Urbicus. Again he was only asked one question: "Are you a Christian?"

Pain and suffering could not change reality. "Yes," Ptolemaeus answered again. This time he was sentenced to death.

Hearing of Ptolemaeus' arrest, an elderly man approached Urbicus and pleaded for his life. "Why would you execute such a fine teacher? What benefit does it serve you or the emperor? He has broken no laws. He has only confessed to being a Christian."

Intrigued by the man's defense, he asked a single question. "Are you also a Christian?"

The elderly man courageously stood his ground, "Yes, I am."

"Then you may join the teacher."

If this was not enough, another man came forward with the same protest. Again the question was asked, "Are you a Christian?"

The three children of God were executed for answering, "Yes."

The question is simple enough: "Are you a Christian?" It's direct. It's personal. It's a yes/no point of truth. Then what is difficult about the answer? The problem is not that Christians don't know how to answer. The real problem is that others aren't asking us the question often enough. We don't live in such a distinct way that anyone thinks to ask what is different about our lives. We must admit far too few people are asking us the question asked of Ptolemaeus. That is the real problem. When is the last time your lifestyle piqued the interest of your coworker, friend, or neighbor—enough for them to inquire about your faith? You know the answer; now live so that others will ask the question.

eXtreme smile

ROMANIA: MILAN HAIMOVICI

The cold, dark prison cell was crowded with Romanian Christians who were determined to bring the light of Jesus into the darkness. One of these prisoners was a Jewish believer named Milan Haimovici.

Day 207

Be joyful in hope, patient in affliction, faithful in prayer.

Romans 12:12

One day, Milan began a discussion with another cellmate who was a great scientist but a godless man. Milan was not of the same intellectual and cultural level as this professor, but he told him about Jesus. The professor scorned him, "You are such a liar. Jesus lived two thousand years ago. How can you say that you walk and talk with Him?"

Milan replied, "It is true that He died two thousand years ago, but He is also resurrected and is living even now."

Then the professor challenged Milan, "Well, you say that He talks with you. What is the expression on His face?"

Milan answered, "Sometimes He smiles at me."

"Such a lie," the professor laughed. "Show me how He smiles."

Milan graciously conceded. He was shorn and only skin and bones, with dark circles around his eyes. He was missing teeth and was wearing a prisoner's uniform, but such a beautiful smile appeared on his lips. His dirty face shone. There was so much peace, so much contentment, and so much joy on his face.

The godless professor bowed his head and admitted, "Sir, you have seen Jesus."

A smile is a natural human expression of confidence, peace, and contentment. A smile during pain and suffering and even agony can give supernatural evidence of God. If Jesus Christ, God's own Son, is really living in our hearts, then some of us need to inform our faces of the good news! In church, we sometimes sing hymns like funeral dirges— our thoughts a thousand miles away from our words. What does your face reveal about your relationship with Jesus? Are you a witness to others who pass you by on the street? Do you attest to Christ's contentment in your heart? Or is your brow furrowed with worry and your lips constantly pursed? Ask God to help you be aware of your silent message and to fill you with His joy.

eXtreme challenge

Day 208

The Lord Jesus Christ used a particular strategy when He fed five thousand people who had followed Him on foot from the surrounding towns. It was near evening, and the disciples came to Him, asking Jesus to send the crowd away for the night. Jesus had a different plan, however. He had the people sit in orderly rows on the grass. After Jesus took the food and gave thanks, the disciples started at one end of the front row and went all along the row giving everyone a helping.

A preacher and writer, J. Oswald Smith, asks an unusual question at this point: "Did the disciples turn right around and start back along that front row again, asking everyone to take a second helping?

For God so loved the world that he gave his one and only Son, that whoever believes in him shall not perish but have eternal life.

John 3:16

"No! Had they done that, those in the back rows would have been rising up and protesting most vigorously. They would have been saying, 'Come back here. Give us a helping. Why should those people in the front rows have a second helping before we have had a first?'

"And they would have been right. We talk about the second coming of Christ. Many haven't heard about the first coming yet. *Why should anyone hear the gospel twice before everyone has heard it once?* Not one individual in that entire company of five thousand got a second helping until everyone had had a first helping."

Many Christians fear going to countries where no missionaries have stepped foot. It is far easier to remain in familiar territory. Yet Jesus commanded believers to go into "all the world" and find new locations where Christ's name has never been proclaimed. Smith's realistic interpretation of the feeding of the five thousand challenges our methodology when it comes to evangelism. Why are most of the personnel and financial budgets designed and directed toward those who have already heard the gospel? In fact, many of those nations are in danger of being overchurched, while other people groups lack a single Bible translated into their own language. Can your support help balance the scales? Can your life make a difference in tomorrow's evangelistic effort?

eXtreme hostage

ENGLAND: BILL AND JOHN

Bill and John were near the docks in southern England when they saw the Romanian flag hanging from the stern of a ship. It was during the years of Romania's hard-line Communist rule.

Day 209

With little conversation, they recognized the mission field before them, untied their cases of Bibles and went aboard. They stepped into the mess room where the ship's entire thirty-five-man company was gathered. Bill and John explained why they had come and began to pull out the Romanian Bibles. The crew immediately gave the two their undivided attention. Most of them had never before heard about God and His Son, Jesus.

Consequently, faith comes from hearing the message, and the message is heard through the word of Christ.

Romans 10:17

When Bill and John discovered that they didn't have enough Romanian Bibles, two burly seamen grabbed Bill by the arms and gently but firmly sat him in a chair. They explained apologetically in broken English that Bill would stay there until John came back with Bibles for all of them.

A hostage for Bibles—John didn't know whether to laugh or cry, but it was the only way the Romanians could make sure that John would return. In a Communist country full of broken promises, they didn't trust anyone.

John rushed to the office and packed his case full of Romanian Bibles. Within an hour, he was back in the mess room, where the crew gratefully received the Bibles and released their "hostage."

Get the word out. That's what Jesus said to do about His gospel message. However we can, wherever we go, whatever we do, we must be about the business of spreading the word about Christ. Our commitment may take us to the docks or simply to the breakfast table of our unbelieving neighbors next door. Either way, we must be prepared to share God's Word with those who are spiritually perishing. Are you driven to get the word out about Christ? Are you conscious of the limited time you may have to complete your mission? Don't waste another moment, thinking someone else will do your part. What can you do today to spread the Good News?

Day 210

We pray for the government of Sudan but thank God for it, too. Thanks to its policies and its war against Christians—the terror, the threats, the imprisonment—look at how the church has grown. Look at what God has allowed us to do here in the middle of this! Look at how many are turning to Christ.

A Sudanese Christian

eXtreme printer

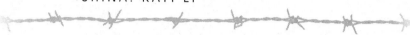

The visitors secretly and quietly arrived at the home of the elderly Chinese woman. They were escorted behind a curtain and then crawled over one hundred yards through a long, dark tunnel that opened up into two small cave-like rooms.

Day 211

Being confident of this, that he who began a good work in you will carry it on to completion until the day of Christ Jesus.

Philippians 1:6

In one of the rooms, a nineteen-year-old Christian girl named Kati Li operated a small, primitive press. For months at a time, Kati would work in this cave, printing illegal books and other Christian material. If discovered, she would no longer be able to show her true identity in public.

But as the secret press produced more books and tracts, the Public Security Bureau (PSB) became suspicious and began to question the villagers. Those who knew of the press were unwilling to cooperate.

Finally, angered by the lack of cooperation, the PSB began to use dynamite and blow up each house in the village until they finally arrived at the old woman's home. The cave was discovered and the printing press confiscated. However, the workers had escaped beforehand, unharmed.

To this day, Kati Li and the other workers remain in hiding. If found, they would be immediately imprisoned and possibly executed. They will never be able to see their friends and family members again. But Kati's work and testimony live on through the books and tracts she produced. To this day they are read by thousands of Chinese Christians.

It may be interrupted. It may be diverted. It may even be temporarily suspended. But God's kingdom is constantly advancing forward. It can never be stopped. Christ set the kingdom in motion when He gave the Great Commission to His disciples. Since that day, those who are being added to the kingdom have continued to grow full force despite enemy opposition. Certainly, many have attempted to stop the gospel altogether, but they have failed. Have you experienced an interruption to your ministry? Have you been concerned that your part is over due to unforeseen circumstances? Remember, God is not finished with you yet. Your impact for the gospel will continue as long as you remain faithful to Him.

eXtreme "riches"

SOUTHEAST ASIA: HMONG CHRISTIANS

"They stabbed one believer through the mouth with a long knife and poured boiling water down the throat of another who was caught with a Bible. An entire family had been drowned."

Day 212

These have come so that your faith—of greater worth than gold, which perishes even though refined by fire—may be proved genuine and may result in praise, glory and honor when Jesus Christ is revealed.

1 Peter 1:7

Believers in the Hmong tribe of Southeast Asia agreed to give their testimony on videotape. They wanted to encourage Christians in the West.

One Hmong Christian shared: "The Communist authorities feel threatened because so many Hmong people have become Christians. They beat the Christians to try to force them to return to their worship of evil spirits."

"The local police forbade us to become Christians. They threatened to put us in jail and even kill us," a woman added. "But if we have to die for Christ's sake, we are willing."

These believers are willing to put themselves in even greater danger to let the world know they are standing strong in the face of persecution. The Hmong tribe is the largest of Southeast Asia and is experiencing the greatest growth of Christianity. It is also one of the most persecuted people groups.

Another woman said, "I thank God that we have remained strong. I do believe that the persecution is just a test of our faith in Christ. It brings out the true riches. It brings out the silver and the gold. Just pray that we will be faithful to the end."

Steel is strengthened through a tempering process—heated to extreme temperatures, pounded into form, and cooled. Then the process is repeated again and again, heating and pounding the impurities away and then cooling so that the metal can bond. A similar tempering process strengthens our faith. When we are heated by hatred from others, pounded upon by persecution, and then cooled by the gentle reassurance of God's presence, our impurities are driven out and our faith strengthened. Have you recognized the tempering process in your life? Don't resist any part of it. Learn from your brothers and sisters in the Hmong tribe. Your enemies don't realize you will be stronger as a result of their hatred.

eXtreme limitation

EASTERN EUROPE: MIHAI

Mihai's Volkswagen van slowly inched its way closer to the border checkpoint. He anxiously whispered a short prayer, "Dear Jesus, please protect Your Word from being found and confiscated by the border guards."

Day 213

But we have this treasure in jars of clay to show that this all-surpassing power is from God and not from us.

2 Corinthians 4:7

The guards sternly and methodically ordered Mihai out of the van and began their list of questions: "What brings you to our country? Will you be visiting anyone here? If so, who? Do you have any guns?"

Mihai carefully answered each question, but his heart beat with great intensity as, out of the corner of his eye, he caught one of the guards looking under every seat in his van. Mihai started to get weary from standing so long. Satisfied with Mihai's answers, the guards finally allowed him to enter their country, his precious goods successfully hidden from their view.

For years, this courageous young courier had smuggled gospel literature into Communist nations in Eastern Europe, his secret cargo never being discovered. Mihai was an ordinary man whose extraordinary vision was quite a challenge. He had no legs—they had been amputated almost to his hips—but he was determined not to let this handicap get in his way.

Like the apostle Paul, Mihai knew that Christ's power would be perfected in his physical weakness. After being fitted with metal limbs, he would stuff the literature into the hollow of each leg and then eagerly begin his journeys.

God is an equal-opportunity employer when it comes to His service. Rather than a limitation, Mihai saw his physical imperfection as a great way to join God in a creative work. Every liability can be an opportunity for a unique ministry. For example, one who comes from the tragedy of a divorced family can minister to those in similar situations in a way that others cannot. What have you long considered to be drawbacks regarding your own usefulness in God's kingdom? Think about them from God's perspective. Then offer them to God and see how He can use them to His glory and your gain.

eXtreme treasure

Day 214

It was Sunday, and the congregation of Grace Sonmin Church in Dushanbe, Tajikistan, had gathered for their weekly worship service. Even though their country was now free from oppressive Communist rule, radical Muslims still blatantly opposed the church. The oppression had simply changed hands from one terrorist authority to another.

Just as the visiting pastor wrapped up his sermon, a loud explosion in the back of the church rumbled the building. A bomb. In one moment, the believers went from worshiping God to frantically running for their lives. They tried to flee into the hallway, but another bomb exploded along their escape route. Bodies and blood were strewn everywhere in the church that was once called a "sanctuary."

An elderly woman lay on the floor, unable to move. The Bible she had been studying moments ago in a worship service fell next to her, stained with her blood. It was opened to a page where she had circled three verses sometime before the attack on her church. "But we have this treasure in jars of clay to show that this all-surpassing power is from God and not from us. We are hard pressed on every side, but not crushed; perplexed, but not in despair; persecuted, but not abandoned; struck down, but not destroyed" (2 Corinthians 4:7–9).

We always carry around in our body the death of Jesus, so that the life of Jesus may also be revealed in our body. For we who are alive are always being given over to death for Jesus' sake, so that his life may be revealed in our mortal body.

2 Corinthians 4:10,11

The radical Muslims considered the innocent Christians expendable for the sake of their cause. But the believers' deaths gleamed like jewels as a testimony to God's faithfulness. The enemy may have broken the elderly woman's body—her "jar of clay"—but her inner treasure was revealed as her spirit ascended to heaven shortly after the attack. We are more aware than ever before that death may come unexpectedly at the hands of our enemy. Yet you do not have to fear death. After all, the worst our enemy can do to us is to kill our mortal bodies. Your physical body is not the real "you." Be comforted today, knowing the treasure of your soul cannot be touched.

eXtreme beginnings

UNITED STATES: RICHARD AND SABINA WURMBRAND

Day 215

Be wise in the way you act toward outsiders, make the most of every opportunity.

Colossians 4:5

On a beautiful autumn day in 1967, the couple sat before their old typewriter on the tiny kitchen table in their new home—the United States. It wasn't that long ago that Pastor Richard Wurmbrand had sat in a cold, dark Romanian prison cell for his work in the underground church. His wife, Sabina, had been sentenced to forced labor in a prison camp.

The couple now pondered the message that God had given them. They wanted to share the trials and triumphs facing persecuted Christians in Communist countries worldwide. The couple had been threatened by the Romanian secret police not to speak against communism, but the intimidation could not stop them. They were compelled to raise the voice of Christ's suffering body—a voice that had been overlooked and forgotten by many in the free world.

The words flowed easily onto the pages, and before long they had their first edition of *The Voice of the Martyrs* newsletter. They began with only one hundred dollars and a few hundred names and addresses from Christians who were interested in how they could help.

The vision that was birthed in a solitary prison cell has now grown into a worldwide organization dedicated to serving the persecuted church. Millions of subsequent *The Voice of the Martyrs* newsletters have been distributed around the globe in more than a dozen languages.

Start somewhere. That's where good ideas in God's service always begin—somewhere. Serving Christ means it doesn't matter where you start or when or how—as long as you start. Many keep delaying their dreams instead of beginning somewhere. We tell ourselves we will serve Christ someday: when the kids are grown up and out of the house; when we finally get the bills paid off and are able to tithe. Each time we say that we will start serving Christ after we finish something else, we have missed the point of our calling. What is God calling you to do? Not when is He calling you to do it—what is it He wants done? What are you doing now to begin fulfilling His call?

eXtreme son

GREECE: TIMOTHY

Though Timothy was young, Paul encouraged him to be an example to all. Timothy proved he could live up to these instructions.

But as for you, continue in what you have learned and have become convinced of, because you know those from whom you learned it.

2 Timothy 3:14

Timothy was from Lystra, one of the cities Paul had visited on his first missionary journey. Timothy's father was Greek, and his mother and grandmother were Jewish Christians who greatly influenced young Timothy. In fact, the Bible points out they were Timothy's examples in the faith. Paul must have noticed Timothy's potential to become a strong believer himself. When Paul came through on his second journey with Silas and Luke, Timothy joined them and journeyed into Macedonia.

Paul considered Timothy his son in the faith. When the church in Ephesus needed a pastor, Paul left Timothy there to teach and encourage the believers in that city. Timothy shared Paul's life and ministry. He may have even been with Paul the day he was beheaded in Rome, as Paul had asked for him to come for a final visit.

After Paul's death, Timothy returned to Ephesus to lead the church there. He continued to condemn the worship of idols that made many in the city of Ephesus rich. When Domitian ratified the second great Roman persecution of Christians, the idolaters became emboldened. Timothy was stoned to death around AD 98—faithful until the end, as Paul had taught him to be.

No one is expected nor encouraged to live the Christian life alone. In fact, it is impossible to do so. In the same way that Paul mentored Timothy, we need someone to show us the way and believe in our potential to make a difference for Christ. We grow by watching others who lead by example in our church, our community, our families, and our schools. As we begin to assume our own roles of influence, we need fans on the sidelines, cheering us on toward greater commitment. Who is your example in the faith? Who is responsible for teaching you how to live for Christ? It may be a close family member, friend, or pastor. Thank God for their influence in your life.

Day 217

I've come to believe that God, in His wisdom, allows martyrdom in every generation in part because, without them, the reality of Christ's death for us becomes increasingly blurry… As we look at [the martyrs], the mist that sometimes enshrouds first-century Golgotha is burned away, and we see… the Lord nailed to the cross.

MARK GALLI

eXtreme faces

ROMANIA: AN IMPRISONED PASTOR

Day 218

You will rejoice,
and no one will take
away your joy.

John 16:22

"It is amazing how you can see Jesus in the face of other believers. Their faces shine, and it was quite an achievement for the glory of God to shine on the face of a Christian in Communist jails. We did not wash—I had not washed for three years—but the glory of God shone even from behind the crust of dirt. And they always had triumphant smiles on their faces," wrote an imprisoned pastor.

"I know of other Christians who were released from Communist prisons, such as I was. Like them, I was stopped several times on the street by passersby asking, 'Sir, what is it in you? You look like such a happy man. What is the source of your happiness?' I told them that it came from many years in Communist jails suffering for my Savior.

"They could not understand this because they could not think beyond the difficulties of their own lives. They had not learned to walk in the Spirit and to experience the presence of God. Many would think, 'If only you knew what a life I have—a husband who batters me, a wife who nags, and children who break my heart.' There are many material difficulties and tempests in your soul. But what of them? How are they to compare with the joy of knowing Jesus?"

What Jesus gives, no one can take away. He gives us joy in the presence of the Holy Spirit within us. And though our circumstances may grow dim and dark, our joy still shines. Even the darkest dirt from three years in a Communist prison cannot disguise Christian joy. We are not necessarily happy for our affliction. We are not glad for our sorrow. Yet we remain joyful because of Christ's presence within our sorrow. Have you lost your sense of joy? You realize no one can take your joy from you. If it is missing from your life, it is because you willingly gave it up on account of your circumstances. Ask God to restore your joy in Him today.

eXtreme healing

Day 219

Asif's leg was broken when a car hit him on a Pakistani street. In the midst of pain, he felt a hand on his leg. He looked up to hear a woman praying for Jesus to heal him. Asif began to get angry because he was Muslim. Then a strange energy began running through his body. His leg straightened, and the bone came back into place. He eventually walked home from the accident.

My ears had heard of you but now my eyes have seen you.

Job 42:5

Hungry to know more about this Jesus who had healed him, he read about Jesus' other miracles in the Bible that the woman gave him. Asif took his questions to the *mulvi* (religious leader) at his mosque. "Why are you talking about Jesus?" the mulvi sneered. "How could I *not* have an interest in Him?" Asif asked. "He healed me."

The mulvi and others at the mosque locked Asif in a room and forced him to drink poison, thinking that if he died before trusting in Christ, he would still make it to paradise. However, Asif woke up and called out to Jesus.

Suddenly a bright light filled the dusty room. Asif pledged, "This life is for you. As long as I am on earth, I will work for you."

Since this time, Asif's family has disowned him, and he has been beaten repeatedly because he refuses to stop telling people about his new friend, Jesus Christ.

Sometimes we have to experience God's power before we'll believe it. In fact, many nonbelievers would rather debate religion from a distance than have to deal with a personal spiritual encounter. No one can dispute personal experience. The individual is the sole expert on the issue. To encounter God is to experience His power and feel His presence. The Bible provides many examples of nonbelievers who encountered God's power. Some responded with worship. Others resisted His power and suffered the consequences. Either way, a person is never the same after an experience with God. It is as if God is saying to a decidedly doubtful heart, "I am real. Deal with it." How has God shown you that He is real? With whom can you share your experience?

eXtreme balloons

NORTH KOREA: KOREAN FAMILIES

"Grandma, look at what I found!" The young North Korean girl was so excited. She was holding something she had never seen before. The grandmother looked at it with her failing eyes but could not make out the details. So she called the girl's mother. "Please come tell me what this child has found."

Day 220

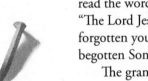

All scripture is God-breathed and is useful for teaching, rebuking, correction and training in righteousness, so that the man of God may be thoroughly equipped for every good work.

2 Timothy 3:16,17

The elderly woman's daughter entered the room and took the item from her mother's wrinkled hand. Her daughter began to read the words printed on the well-constructed plastic balloon. "The Lord Jesus loves you. Your brothers and sisters have not forgotten you. For God so loved the world that He gave His only begotten Son."

The grandmother exclaimed, "It's Scripture! They've sent us Bible verses on a balloon! Please keep reading."

The plastic balloon held words of encouragement for the three generations of North Koreans. It contained a message from Christians in the West and over six hundred Bible verses taking the reader from the creation, to the cross, to the second coming of Jesus Christ. In the last decade, over one hundred thousand of these "Scripture balloons" have been floated into North Korea.

The ministry of The Voice of the Martyrs found a unique way to reach these oppressed people with the Word of God and the gospel. It says in Psalm 19:1, "The heavens declare the glory of God; the skies proclaim the work of his hands."

Like the balloons in this story, God longs to float encouraging Scriptures across our minds and hearts just when we need them most. However, He cannot bring to mind Scriptures that were never there in the first place. Ironically, though we live in a free society, we often act as if we were in a restricted nation like North Korea without access to God's Word. Our Bible reading is sporadic and seldom—as if we did not have a copy of Scripture at all. Perhaps it is time to ask God to "float" His Word across the borders of your closed mind. Carve time in your schedule for Bible reading each day, and ask Him to renew a desire for His Word.

eXtreme trust

"I prayed day and night asking my Jesus, 'You are my everything. I don't have a father, brother, or sister... Please send me an angel. Who can release me from this bondage?'" Azra Bibi said. **"After seven months, God answered my prayers."**

Day 221

The God we serve... will rescue us from your hand, O king. But even if he does not, we want you to know, O king, that we will not serve your gods or worship the image of gold you have set up.

Daniel 3:17,18

Twenty-year-old Azra Bibi was born into the only Christian family employed at the Malik Saleem brick kiln. She learned to love and worship the Lord from her mother, who worked many backbreaking hours making bricks, earning just $1.14 a day. "The kiln owner wouldn't allow us to go to church," Azra said. They snuck away to attend church and hear about the miracles of Jesus whenever they could.

One day Azra and her mother were beaten by some Muslim women who called them "dogs." Some men dragged Azra and her mother to the office of the kiln owner, who was furious. He said vile things to them and locked them in a room. Late that night he took Azra's mother out of the room. Ten days later, her mother's friend told Azra, "Your mother is not in this world now. The kiln owner violated her, chopped up her body and burned it in the kiln." The kiln owner's assistant, a seventy-year-old man named Muhammad Akram, made advances toward Azra and violated her. He tried to force her to marry him and convert to Islam.

A group of believers eventually secured Azra's release by paying her $1,100 debt to the owner. "What a moment," she said. "I cried before my Lord... I also wept... because I missed my mother." One of the Christian brothers took her into his home and provided her with food, clothing, and basic necessities. Azra is now rebuilding her life.

Trust is something that is hard to maintain, especially when you experience the kind of situation that Azra did. Even though she knew the possible consequences of remaining true to her faith, she did not deny Christ, nor did she despair. She continued to rely on the Lord, pouring out her heart to Him in prayer. We do not often face circumstances this extreme, but we have the same duty to trust God no matter what happens. What are the circumstances God is asking you to trust Him with, regardless of the outcome?

eXtreme certainty

ROME: JUSTIN

"If you are scourged or beheaded as a criminal, do you believe you will still ascend to heaven?" asked Rusticus, the city official.

"I believe that if I endure these things I shall have what Jesus promised me," Justin said. "For I know His gift of life stays with all who remain in Him, even until the end of the world."

Day 222

"Do you think then that you will receive some reward there?"

"I do not think it; I know it. I am certain of it."

Rusticus sat back with impatience. "You must agree to offer a sacrifice to the gods."

Justin stood unmoved. "No right-thinking person slanders communion with God by going to the godless."

Rusticus had had enough. "Unless you obey, you will be mercilessly executed."

Do not be afraid of those who kill the body but cannot kill the soul. Rather, be afraid of the One who can destroy both soul and body in hell.

Matthew 10:28

"I know if I die for His testimony that I need not fear. I count dying for such a reason to be our salvation and confidence before Christ," Justin answered.

The other believers who stood with Justin said, "Do what you will, for we are Christians and do not sacrifice to idols."

Rusticus pronounced the sentence on the Christians who refused his demands. "These people, who have refused to sacrifice to the gods and do not obey the dictates of the emperor, shall be scourged and beheaded according to the law."

When Justin said to his executioners, "You may kill us, but you cannot do us any real harm," were they the words of a madman? Was he confused as he contemplated the certainty of his own death? No, he was certain of only one thing: Jesus Christ's gift of eternal life. As he contemplated the end of his earthly existence, Justin could almost see the beauty of his heavenly home. Are you more frightened of losing your life on earth than you are certain about your eternal life in heaven? Death is not a time for doubts. Settle the issue while you are still alive and well. Receive God's gift of eternal life by placing your trust in Jesus Christ.

eXtreme author

ENGLAND: JOHN FOXE

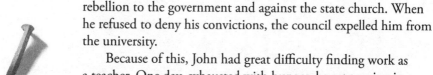

John Foxe, a young teacher at Magdelen College, pleaded in prayer, "They call themselves Your priests and ministers, but they worship themselves and their political power. Help them realize that there is no need for another mediator between God and man but Christ Jesus and His Word."

Day 223

Someone overheard John and immediately reported him to the college administration. They accused him of holding beliefs in rebellion to the government and against the state church. When he refused to deny his convictions, the council expelled him from the university.

Because of this, John had great difficulty finding work as a teacher. One day, exhausted with hunger, he sat praying in a church. A man John had never met suddenly appeared and thrust a sum of money into his hand. "Cheer up," he said. "In a few days new work will present itself to you." A few days later he was hired as a tutor.

For we also have had the gospel preached to us, just as they did; but the message they heard was of no value to them, because those who heard did not combine it with faith.

Hebrews 4:2

Under the reign of Henry VIII, Christians like John were tolerated. When Mary I came to power, however, she executed any who defied the religious edicts of the state. Three hundred people died during her five-year reign. John and his pregnant wife fled England to Belgium, barely escaping being apprehended.

In defense of those who died for their faith, John wrote *Foxe's Book of Martyrs*.

It is one thing to read about persecution, yet quite another to experience it. In the same way, many people read about the lives of committed Christians and admire their courage from afar. Yet they have no firsthand experience of faith to call their own. While they extol the martyrs' courage, they cannot relate to its source: a personal relationship with Jesus Christ. They may read the gospel message, yet they do not respond in faith. Martyrs lived and died calling others, even their oppressors, to faith in Christ. Could they be calling you toward Christian commitment even now as you read their stories? Don't merely extol their faith when you are invited to experience it firsthand.

Day 224

Jail is no hindrance to a useful Christian life.

PASTOR RICHARD WURMBRAND

eXtreme penalty

ENGLAND: JOHN WYCLIFFE

On a cold English morning in 1428, men traipsed irreverently through the graveyard. One of them, finely dressed in religious robes, said, "Here it is. Dig it up. Let's get this over with."

Day 225

But we also rejoice in our sufferings, because we know that suffering produces perseverance; perseverance, character; and character, hope.

Romans 5:3,4

When the shovels finally hit something solid, the man in fine clothes stood by, idly watching, and said, "Open it."

"But, sir, he's been in there fifty years!" replied one of the diggers. "There can't be much left!"

The religious leader shuddered and then shrugged off his irritation. "Then pull the whole thing out. We'll burn it all."

What could have angered this man so much? Why dig up the man's body fifty years after his death to ceremoniously burn him as a heretic?

Around 1376, John Wycliffe had published the doctrine of "dominion as founded in grace." This highly controversial message states, "The gospel alone is sufficient to rule the lives of Christians everywhere."

Wycliffe had also begun translating the Latin Vulgate Bible into English and distributing it secretly in pamphlets and books. He continued this work until his death in 1384, one hundred thirty-three years before the Reformation.

"Dump the ashes in the river," the man ordered as the fire died down. "That should be the last we hear of John Wycliffe and his teachings." One hundred more years would pass before it was legal to read an English Bible.

The religious officials tried their best to do away with the "last" of John Wycliffe. Instead, it appears that every bit of ash from John's burnt body carried a new thirst for God's Word across Europe. Their efforts not only missed their target, but they actually aided the cause of Christ. Likewise, we may often see our enemy, Satan, going to great lengths to dispose of Christianity. Yet his attempts result in a backfire at best. God allows persecution to inspire believers and drive them toward greater commitment. Are you allowing personal persecution to play out according to God's plan? You may soon see that opposition makes you stronger and that your persecutor's curses bring God's blessings.

eXtreme martyrdom—part one

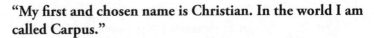

ROME: CARPUS

"My first and chosen name is Christian. In the world I am called Carpus."

"You know the emperor's decrees," the proconsul stated. "You must worship the all-powerful gods of Rome. Therefore, I advise you to come forward and sacrifice to them."

Day 226

"I am a Christian. I honor Christ, the Son of God, who came not long ago to save us and has delivered us from the madness of the devil. I will not sacrifice to such idols. They represent ghosts at best, demons in truth. It is impossible for me to offer sacrifices to them."

"You must sacrifice; Caesar has commanded it."

"The living do not sacrifice to the dead."

"Do you believe that the gods are dead?"

"They were never men, nor did they ever live that they could die. Those who worship them are caught in a grave delusion."

For the message of the cross is foolishness to those who are perishing, but to us who are being saved it is the power of God.

1 Corinthians 1:18

"I have let you talk too much nonsense and now have let you blaspheme the gods and his majesty the emperor. You must stop this now, or it will be too late. You will sacrifice or you will die!"

"I cannot sacrifice. I have never sacrificed to idols and will not start now."

The proconsul ordered him to be hung up and have his skin flayed with tools of torture, as he cried out, "I am a Christian! I am a Christian! I am a Christian!"

Like the proconsul in this story, the message of the cross seems foolish to those who do not understand it. And that which they do not understand they feel they must oppose. Perhaps they fear what they can't understand. Perhaps their pride keeps them from humbly accepting God's gospel by faith. For whatever reason, they would rather perish than trust in the message of the cross. We must realize those who argue against Chri..... often do so because they are unable to accept the truth by faith. Are you praying for those who come against the gospel? As you pray for those who persecute others, ask the Holy Spirit to help them understand the message of the cross.

eXtreme martyrdom—part two

ROME: PAPYLUS

The proconsul turned his attention to Papylus, not far from where Carpus hung bleeding. "Do you have any children?" the proconsul asked.

"Oh, yes, through God I have many children."

One in the surrounding crowd shouted, "He means he has children by his Christian faith."

Day 227

Hearing this, the proconsul grew even angrier. "Why are you lying to me, saying that you have children?" he shouted.

"I am telling you the truth. In every district and city I have children in God."

The proconsul's anger was not appeased. "You will sacrifice or suffer the same fate as Carpus! What do you say now?"

Papylus answered steadily, "I have served God since I was young. I have never sacrificed to idols. I am a Christian. There is nothing I can say which is greater or more wonderful than that I am a Christian."

When I came to you, brothers, I did not come with eloquence or superior wisdom as I proclaimed to you the testimony about God.

The proconsul ordered him hung beside Carpus and flayed with iron instruments of torture. Papylus did not utter a sound, but as a courageous fighter he endured the treatment.

1 Corinthians 2:1

When the proconsul saw their outstanding steadfastness, he ordered Carpus and Papylus burned alive. They both descended on their own into the amphitheater, satisfied that they would soon be freed from this world. Papylus was nailed to the stake. When the flames leaped up he prayed quietly and gave up his soul.

Christians often worry about what they are to say when called upon to defend their faith. When the opportunity comes, we prod ourselves like a college student mentally rehearsing questions for a midterm exam. "What if they ask me to defend the Trinity?" "What do I say if they ask about the fate of those who never heard the gospel?" "And how do I defend the virgin birth?" In truth, we can find no better, more truthful, words than our own testimony of faith in Christ. "There is nothing I can say which is greater or more wonderful than that I am a Christian." All the rehearsing will not convince a nonbeliever more than your willingness to sincerely share your love for Jesus.

eXtreme martyrdom—part three

ROME: AGATHONICA

Carpus was nailed to the stake, and as the flames took hold of him, he joyfully prayed, "Praise be to thee, O Lord, Jesus Christ, Son of God, that thou didst deem me, a sinner, also worthy to die a martyr as you did!" Then he gave up his soul to heaven.

Day 228

Revive us, and we will call on your name.

Psalm 80:18

As Carpus prayed, Agathonica saw the glory of God roll out before him. The heavens opened up to reveal the wedding feast of the Lamb of God, with sumptuous tables spread out before her and Jesus Himself standing at its head. Her heart leapt, and she recognized a call from heaven.

She sprang to her feet and shouted, "This meal has also been prepared for me. I must receive the meal of glory."

A cry came from the stands, "Have pity on your child, your son!"

"He has God to take care of him," Agathonica responded, "for God is the provider for all. As for me, I will go and be with Him."

She jumped into the amphitheater, threw off her outer robe, and jubilantly allowed herself to be nailed to the stake.

Those standing by burst into tears. They cried, "This sentence is cruel and unjust!"

In the flames, she cried out, "Lord, Lord, Lord, help me, for I flee unto thee!" Then she gave up her soul and joined her Lord. It was the year AD 165.

Chain reaction. It's that unexpected effect one life has on another—something inexplicable and unplanned. It began with Carpus, who showed the way of courage to Papylus, as both were tortured for their faith. Then an observer, inspired by the incredible results of their martyrdom, flung herself toward faith by willingly dying at the stake. Today, we see the chain reaction of faith in church revivals and on college campuses. We see it in villages, townships, and communities across several continents where one life spurs another, and yet another, on to greater commitment. How long has it been since you experienced a chain reaction of commitment in your church or community? Pray for revival to start with you—the most important link in the chain.

eXtreme fugitive

CHINA: LO LIEU

Lo Lieu cautiously walked down the crowded street in China, looking over her shoulder to make sure she wasn't being followed or recognized. She passed another poster showing her face and listing the reward of almost six hundred dollars for her arrest.

Day 229

So then, each of us will give an account of himself to God.

Romans 14:12

When Lieu was just seventeen, she left home to be God's servant. She founded a fellowship organization that helped to establish unregistered house churches—illegal in the eyes of the Communist government. Her work put her in contact with foreign Christians who would smuggle Bibles into the country.

Almost ten years into Lieu's ministry, the police arrested her. She endured intense questioning. One time she was beaten so badly that she lapsed into a coma for several hours. But Lieu refused to give the authorities information on the believers with whom she worked and their activities.

Months later, she was released after revealing nothing to the police about her work, but she was still under surveillance. A few years later, she and five others were arrested, and all her belongings were confiscated. This time she was sentenced to three years in a labor camp.

Lieu was released after serving her sentence, but she is still a target of the police. Despite the threat of arrest, Lieu continues to live as a fugitive for Christ, committing the "crime" of loving Jesus and sharing that love with others.

Think about this: If there was a warrant out for the arrest of all committed Christians, who would turn you in to the authorities? Would your gracious spirit and appreciative greeting each week as you shopped tip off the local grocer to your identity? Would fellow parents in the carpool line know to identify you as a potential believer by the courteous way you patiently wait your turn? Would others in your workplace debate whether or not to turn you in, as they had concrete evidence of your faith in Christ? Would your own family wrestle with the decision to phone the police? Or would they convince themselves that your attitude and actions did not actually match the description of "committed Christian"? What do you think? What should you do?

eXtreme fruit

PAKISTAN: SAFEENA

Safeena is a quiet, lovely girl. Growing up in Pakistan, she learned that as a woman and a Christian, her opportunities in life would be limited and meager.

So, when she got the job cooking and cleaning for a wealthy Muslim family, she was overjoyed that she could earn some money and help her impoverished family.

Day 230

By their fruit you will recognize them. Do people pick grapes from thornbushes, or figs from thistles? Likewise every good tree bears good fruit, but a bad tree bears bad fruit.

Matthew 7:16,17

Eventually Safeena's beauty and gentle demeanor attracted her employers' son. He approached his parents about taking her as his wife, but Safeena was a Christian. They pressured her to convert to Islam, but Safeena bravely and steadfastly refused to renounce her Lord. After weeks of pressure, she wanted to leave, but she knew her family desperately needed the money.

Finally, the young man gave up trying to convince Safeena to be his wife and made a harsh decision. He viciously dragged Safeena to one of the bedrooms and took her by force.

Safeena was shattered. She immediately quit her job, but before she could bring charges, the family turned on her and told police that she was stealing. Safeena was immediately arrested and suffered further abuse in jail.

Safeena does not regret taking a stand for Christ but still struggles with the shame of what happened to her. She is courageously holding on to the promises of God for physical and emotional healing amid her struggle to forgive her perpetrator.

We learn a lot about a religion from examining the results in the lives of its followers. This is a story about a family who followed the wrong god down the wrong path. This family's religion pressured them toward manipulation, sexual immorality, lying, and injustice. In contrast, Safeena's God, the God of love, led her to be industrious, sacrificial, and steadfast. One day, God will help Safeena come to a place of forgiveness for those who wronged her. Be careful when you hear others say that all religions are basically the same. We are called to be fruit inspectors—carefully examining the fruit of people's lives to reveal their motives. Don't be fooled by what you read about any religion. Look closely at the results in the lives of its followers.

Day 231

The harder the devil strikes, the more we will enjoy his defeat. Let him come!

A Christian in Sudan

eXtreme safehouses

BANGLADESH: ANDREW

Andrew's ministry in Bangladesh saw 749 Muslim converts baptized. Additionally, the ministry was involved in distributing more than 3,000 Bibles and New Testaments and over 137,000 gospel tracts.

Day 232

Then he said to his disciples, "The harvest is plentiful but the workers are few. Ask the Lord of the harvest, therefore, to send out workers into his harvest field."

Matthew 9:37,38

But Andrew saw the dangers of many Muslim converts and established a sanctuary that serves as a safehouse. Christian families or individuals from all over the country arrive at the secret sanctuary, but not for rest and safety. The new Christians are taught in discipleship and evangelism from sunrise to sunset.

After graduating from the program, they are sent out to another village where they were not previously known. This becomes their new mission field! These Christians arrive at the compound to escape from danger, only to be trained for an even more dangerous situation. And they know that they are not alone; hundreds of their brothers and sisters have gone out before them to take the gospel of Jesus Christ throughout Bangladesh.

Andrew's work is not without risk. He has been arrested and held repeatedly by the police and beaten by radical Muslims who fear his outreaches. His family and home have also been continually threatened.

Andrew's ministry is to provide safehouses for Muslim converts, but his ministry is hardly safe. It is a daily risk to his family and those involved in his ministry; however, his students receive eternal life and graduate to give others the same opportunity.

Imagine a farmer attempting to harvest a large crop alone. No matter how diligently the farmer worked, he would not have enough time in the season to complete the task. Jesus compared lost people to a field ready to be harvested. That job requires too much work for one person to do alone. Consequently, we are called to employ a similar strategy to Andrew's method in the Bangladesh safehouses. We must tell others how to tell others about Christ. It is not enough to win converts to Christianity. We must win disciples who, in turn, learn to be disciple-makers. Are you the farmer struggling alone? Or are you showing others how to work the field?

eXtreme perseverance

Pastor Roman Abramov and his wife worked diligently for three years to plant a church in Ismailly, Azerbaijan. But within a year of moving to the village, officials arrested them in an attempt to force them out of town.

Day 233

Perseverance must finish its work so that you may be mature and complete, not lacking anything.

James 1:4

The church is down to ten members most weeks, but they continue to share the gospel of Jesus Christ. Due to pressure from local officials on potential landlords, the Abramovs had trouble renting a house, so they managed to build one in which they could both live and hold meetings according to the law.

When the Abramovs began to hold church meetings in their new home, the regular attendance climbed slowly. Then last December, *mullahs* (Muslim religious leaders) came to their house and told them that they had no right to hold Christian services.

Pastor Abramov defended his church and invited the mullahs to the services. One accepted the invitation and has since returned. Another mullah accused the Christians of stomping on a copy of the Koran, however, and petitioned the regional government to close the church. Local authorities then started visiting the homes of church members, harassing and questioning them and sentencing some to ten days in prison.

Despite the condemnation and the fear of many parishioners, Pastor Abramov prayerfully believes that revival will come. His home remains open to all who would come and attend their meetings.

Some things we wish we could do without. Trials are one of them. Why does life often seem to be one problem after another? Yet the Bible teaches us that life is not supposed to be trouble-free. As children, we would often give up if a task became too hard. We quit in the face of difficulty. As we matured, however, we learned to persevere —to hang in there and see it through. In the same way, as we mature in our faith, we learn the value of perseverance. Are you still immature, becoming easily discouraged and tempted to give up? Tell God you're ready to "grow up."

eXtreme shave

UNITED STATES: PARK GILLESPIE

People are often willing to give a great deal to help persecuted brothers and sisters around the world. Seventh grade science and social studies teacher Park Gillespie may be the first to give his hair!

Day 234

When he saw the crowds, he had compassion on them.

Matthew 9:36

After hearing Christian workers talk to his class about Sudan, Park's students caught a vision for helping refugees who were being persecuted for their faith. The students' fervent compassion surprised even their teachers.

What started out as a drive for the seventh graders to collect blankets for the suffering Sudanese soon spread to the entire school and eventually to the community. Gillespie contacted WBTV in Charlotte, North Carolina, and told them about what the kids were doing to alleviate suffering in Sudan.

Blankets had already begun to fill the classrooms, but the question of shipping costs had not yet been addressed. When the reporter from WBTV came for the story, Gillespie mentioned that he would shave his head if people would help with the bill. Shortly after the story aired, funds began to pour in.

Thus, out of his love for people he had never even met, Gillespie shaved his head. The entire school body was gathered for the shaving and the reporter from WBTV filmed the event. Americans often feel as though they can do little to help persecuted Christians in other countries.

Park Gillespie proved otherwise.

Park Gillespie and his students teach us the process of how compassion moves to creativity, to commitment, and—ultimately—to cost. Park and his students were glad to pay the cost—even down to the last hair on his head! Compassion is a natural response to suffering, but it is not enough by itself. We must activate our compassion with creative solutions to problems. Next, we must commit to putting our solutions in motion and be willing to pay their cost. Where are you in the process? Have you put your compassion to work with some creative thinking? Have you made a commitment to help make a difference? Are you ready to now pay the cost?

eXtreme death

PAKISTAN: AYUB MASIH

"This cell cannot stop me from loving my Lord, Jesus Christ," wrote Ayub Masih. **He has now served more than five years in prison because of false accusations.**

Day 235

For the wages of sin is death, but the gift of God is eternal life in Christ Jesus our Lord.

Romans 6:23

Christians in Pakistan are often falsely accused of blasphemy against Mohammed, the founder of Islam. According to Muslim law, blasphemy is a crime that carries a penalty of death. Ayub was talking casually to a Muslim friend with whom he had often discussed and joked about controversial issues. The conversation turned to the book *The Satanic Verses*, a controversial book against Islam. They were overheard, and under the pressure of others, Ayub's "friend" filed a complaint against him.

Ayub was arrested and sentenced to death for blaspheming Mohammed. Shortly after that, his village was raided, and all twelve Christian families living there were chased from their homes. Ayub pleaded innocent to the charges and appealed the court's judgment. He has prayerfully waited five years in jail for a response from the courts.

He believed that, even upon his release from prison, his life would still be in danger, and he would bring danger to others in his family or community. He was right. An attempt was made on his life, and an Islamic *mullah* (religious leader) offered a reward of ten thousand dollars to anyone who would kill Ayub.

In Muslim nations today, even speaking on a religious subject considered to be contrary to Islam can mean death. Ironically, Muslim worshipers face a death penalty themselves. The Bible teaches that the penalty for sin is spiritual death. Apart from Christ, everyone faces eternal death. Thankfully, however, Christ has paid the death penalty for all who believe, even Muslims. Jesus Christ took our place at the hand of the executioner by being crucified on a cross. His death enables us to have eternal life with God in heaven. Thank God today that your death sentence has been commuted and that you have been pardoned. And pray for those in Muslim nations who may kill Christians on earth, but without Christ, face their own eternal death.

eXtreme logic

SUDAN: A CHRISTIAN PRISONER

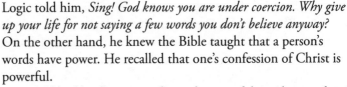

"Chant this song [a Muslim creed], or you will die," cried the Northern Sudanese soldier. The captive Christian could see the hate in his eyes and wondered how many lives he had taken. The soldier pressed a large knife to the Christian's throat.

Day 236

I have been crucified with Christ and I no longer live, but Christ lives in me.

Galatians 2:20

Logic told him, *Sing! God knows you are under coercion. Why give up your life for not saying a few words you don't believe anyway?* On the other hand, he knew the Bible taught that a person's words have power. He recalled that one's confession of Christ is powerful.

Would a blasphemous confession be powerful, too? he wondered. *Even if I didn't mean it?* The questions seemed to battle against each other in his mind. His logic fought against his love for Christ.

Christians in Sudan often face such choices, and they have seen many of their friends and family members killed for believing in Christ. The martyrs chose not to chant a Muslim creed, not wanting to pollute their spirits with blasphemous songs and risk breaking God's heart.

Their defense against the logical arguments is that the Christ living within them could not sing such a song. Therefore, they had to face the consequences. This same Christ living in them who would not chant along also did not fear a death threat. These believers considered themselves already dead in Christ—the Christ in them could not really be harmed.

Each day we tune in to the crosstalk between logic and faith. Logic tells us to go along. Faith tells us to go against the grain of popularity. When we listen to logic, we may put our own convictions aside in order to do another person's bidding. How often do we sing another's song to avoid confrontation? It may be a job that requires deceptive practices. Logic tells you to keep your mouth shut to keep your job. If you sense that you may have listened a bit too long to the voice of reason, ask God to help you tune in to Him instead. Ask Him for the faith you need to wisely speak the right thing at the wrong logical moment.

eXtreme smugglers

UKRAINE: UNDERGROUND CHRISTIANS

The Russian border guard was walking a routine patrol. With the end of World War II, borders were zealously guarded for any suspicious activities. Two threats were paramount: Soviet citizens trying to escape and smugglers trying to bring in illegal items such as Bibles.

Day 237

I am sending you out like sheep among wolves. Therefore be as shrewd as snakes and as innocent as doves.

Matthew 10:16

This particular guard had been assigned to the border between the Ukrainian Soviet Socialist Republic and Romania. He walked slowly in the peaceful cold, running his flashlight back and forth over the freshly fallen snow.

Suddenly his reverie was broken as his light struck some indentations in the snow. Footprints! Headed into Romania! He raised his whistle to his lips and sounded a long, steady, shrill alarm.

Soon other guards surrounded him. "This way! This way!" he jumped and shouted, pointing to the four sets of footprints. "They can't be far! Perhaps we can catch them before they reach Romania!" The group headed out as quickly as they could into the night.

At the sound, four Romanian Christians froze in the darkness. They listened intently, as the guards' shouts and the barking slowly got farther and farther away. They turned and smiled to one another. At the nod of their leader, they continued their journey, carefully walking *backwards* into Ukraine, carrying their precious cargo of Bibles to their brothers and sisters in the underground church.

The Bible says that our spiritual adversary uses cunning attempts to thwart Christianity. In contrast, we who carry the gospel of peace seem like innocent wolf bait. Jesus instructs us to recognize the dangers of being sheep among wolves, however, and to plan accordingly. We must use precise strategy and clever tactics to outwit and outmaneuver the opposition. Satan has power, but God is all-powerful. He will enable you to gain the victory over your enemies. Your job is to ask for wisdom and courage to fulfill God's victory plans. Are you up against a particular problem? Have you prayed and asked God for wisdom as you are planning your next move? Trust Him to know how to outwit your enemy—He's been doing it for millennia.

Day 238

*Since Christ is no longer on the earth,
He wants His body, the church, to reveal
His suffering in its suffering. Since we are His
body, our sufferings are His sufferings.*

JOHN PIPER, *DESIRING GOD*

eXtreme impulse

VIETNAM: LINH DAO

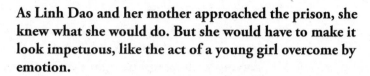

As Linh Dao and her mother approached the prison, she knew what she would do. But she would have to make it look impetuous, like the act of a young girl overcome by emotion.

Day 239

Linh's father is an underground pastor in Vietnam. A year earlier, when she was ten, four police officers burst into her family's home and ransacked it, searching for Bibles that she had hidden in her school knapsack. Her father was arrested and sentenced to reeducation through hard labor.

As they reached the chain-link fence separating them from Linh's father, Linh saw her opportunity. She quickly squeezed through a gap in the fence, darted to her father, and hugged him tightly. The guards watched her, surprised, but left her alone. After all, what harm could a little girl do?

Give me an undivided heart, that I may fear your name.

Psalm 86:11

Linh's family was able to smuggle their father a small pen with which he wrote Scriptures and sermons on cigarette paper. These "cigarette sermons" were circulated from cell to cell and brought many prisoners to Christ.

Linh Dao is now an impetuous teenager who does not worry about the risk before doing what is right. Her desire is to follow in the footsteps of her father and be a preacher of the gospel. She knows firsthand the dangers of sharing her faith in Communist Vietnam and remains "impulsive" to obey Christ rather than man.

One of the reasons believers are not more impulsive in their witness for Christ is that they hear two voices when they should hear only one. Impulsive obedience can never arise from divided attention. We hear God's voice in our hearts immediately telling us what we should do in a certain situation. "Say it now. Share your faith." Yet we simultaneously hear our own voice presenting all sorts of excuses. "Not now. Later. What are you doing?" God offers us an undivided heart that listens to His voice alone. When we mature in our faith, we learn that obedience comes more naturally—as impulsive as a reflex. To which voice will you listen today?

eXtreme power

BANGLADESH: ABDULLAH

Since Abdullah trusted in Jesus, his family had tried very hard to change his mind. After all, his father was a respected man in their village and in all of Bangladesh, having built a mosque right next to their property.

Day 240

But you will receive power when the Holy Spirit comes on you.

Acts 1:8

When talking didn't convince Abdullah to return to Islam, they resorted to beating him. When beating didn't work, they called others in to beat him more severely. Nothing worked; Abdullah tenaciously hung on to his faith in Christ. Finally, in exasperation, his mother stopped feeding him, putting only ashes on his plate. Abdullah prayed for God's strength, and he stood strong.

As a last resort, the family called on the *mullah* (an Islamic religious leader) to come and hold an Islamic ceremony to rid the boy of the "devil" that had taken over his life. The mullah came to their home and recited Muslim prayers over Abdullah. He chanted. He laid hands on the boy. He danced and he yelled. The Spirit inside Abdullah stood fast. After five hours, the mullah gave up, exhausted.

"Abdullah's Spirit is more powerful than my spirit," he told the boy's father as he left. Abdullah couldn't be turned away, and he couldn't be stopped from sharing that powerful Spirit with others. In a few short months, he had led twenty-seven Muslims to faith in Jesus, who infused them all with the Spirit of Christ!

In an attempt to creatively deal with a potential energy crisis, modern engineers are attempting to design cars that run entirely on battery power. The hitch is that the cars must have access to a power source to recharge their batteries. As it is, the concept is relatively new, so that the stations with the auxiliary power chargers are fairly sparse. Without a power source, the car is helpless. In the same way, Christians who attempt to be effective witnesses apart from the power of the Holy Spirit are equally helpless. Along with learning the Word of God, we must rely on the Holy Spirit for wisdom, protection, and power in our witness. Are you trying to do things in your own strength for Jesus instead of allowing His power to flow through you?

eXtreme love for God's Word

In the sixteenth century, King Philip II took a hard line against those who would try to interpret Scripture for themselves. Anyone found studying the Bible during this time was hanged, burned at the stake, drowned, torn in pieces, or buried alive.

Day 241

Open my eyes that I may see wonderful things in your law.

Psalm 119:18

The inquisitors from the king were sent to inspect the house of the mayor of Brugge to see if any Bible studies were taking place there. In their search, they discovered a Bible. All present denied knowing anything about it. Then a young maidservant came in. When asked about the Bible, she declared, "I am reading it!"

The mayor sought to defend her saying, "Oh, no, she doesn't know how to read."

But the maidservant did not wish to be defended by a lie. "It is true, this book is mine. I am reading from it, and it is more precious to me than anything!"

She was sentenced to die by suffocation, sealed in the city wall. Just before her execution, she was asked by an official, "So young and beautiful and yet to die?"

She replied, "My Savior died for me. I will also die for Him."

When finally only one brick remained to complete the wall, she was told again, "Repent! Just say a single word of repentance!"

Instead she voiced her sole desire to be with Jesus and added, "O Lord, forgive my killers!"

To some it is simply a book—a best-seller for years running, at that. To others it is merely a family tradition—given at weddings, births, and funerals. To still others, it is God's holy and inspired Word. These believers cling to the words as if they were letters from a lover, pouring over them again and again. What do they see in the truth of God's Word? What makes them willing to risk death to read it? Ask God for the answer. If its truths remain a mystery to you, ask God to open your eyes to see His words more clearly. Without His help, the words will remain marks on a page. But God can bring them to life.

eXtreme witness

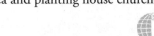

"What happened?" asked the North Korean mother as her son walked through the front door with a look of shock.

"I was with my friend today when two police officers stopped us. They knocked my friend down and accused him of being a Christian. My friend did not try to defend himself. Even with a gun pointed directly at him, his face remained peaceful.

Day 242

For you have been born again, not of perishable seed, but of imperishable, through the living and enduring word of God.

1 Peter 1:23

"He looked straight into my eyes and without speaking a word, I knew what he was saying. He wanted me to believe the same thing he did. And then he just said, 'Bless them.' He was executed right in front of me because he was a Christian. I do not even know what a Christian is. I don't understand any of this."

After he shared his story, his mother held his head in her hands and simply said, "I understand." She then began to share with him the truth about Christ—her Savior. She taught her son about Jesus' miraculous birth, and the opportunity for salvation that came through His death on a cross.

Though it pained her that she had never dared to tell her son because she worried for his safety, she was thankful that God was giving them a second chance. "As those bullets hit your friend's heart, God planted a seed of hope in yours."

Today this young man is active smuggling Bibles into North Korea and planting house churches.

The boy's mother gave him physical life when he was born into her family, but she passed on the opportunity to help him receive eternal life through the gospel, by being born again. Physical life fades away, but God's gift of eternal life lasts forever. When we share God's Word with others, God offers them everlasting life. Have you missed an opportunity to share the plan of salvation with those you love? Ask God to give you a second chance as He gave to the mother of this young boy. Don't wait for tragedy to strike before you take the opportunity.

eXtreme hymn

NORTH KOREA: ELIZABETH PRENTISS

"I feel so empty," Elizabeth Prentiss wept. The loss of two children seemed overwhelming. Even though she had experienced great pain in her life from losing the use of her legs, her faith in Christ had always kept her smiling with a unique ability to encourage others.

Day 243

This time the grief was too much to bear. "God, please minister to my broken spirit."

God answered her prayer. One afternoon, moved beyond her deepest sorrow, she penned the words to this familiar, inspiring hymn:

> *More love to thee, O Christ, more love to thee!*
> *Hear thou the prayer I make on bended knee.*
> *This is my earnest plea: More love, O Christ, to thee...*
> *Once earthly joy I craved, sought peace and rest;*
> *Now thee alone I seek, give what is best...*
> *Let sorrow do its work, send grief and pain;*
> *Sweet are thy messengers, sweet their refrain*
> *When they can sing with me: More love, O Christ, to thee...*

Rather, as servants of God we commend ourselves in every way:...sorrowful, yet always rejoicing.

2 Corinthians 6:4,10

Elizabeth never knew the comfort and impact her song would make on modern-day Christians. In North Korea when the late Communist leader Kim Il Sung discovered thirty Christians living underground, he had them brought out for public execution. The last words sung by the Christians as they faced death were the words of her song, "More Love to Thee."

Jesus does not begrudge us sorrow. He realizes that sometimes we simply must cry. But He loves us too much to let us drown in our sorrowful tears. He allows sorrow to last long enough to do its work in our lives, growing us into His likeness. Then, just when we think we can't take it anymore, we see our lives take a turn for the better. The day will come when we will feel stronger. The burden will seem lighter. Like the North Korean Christians awaiting execution, we will finally know what it is like to rejoice even while we are suffering. Have you experienced the full work of sorrow? Has it brought more love to Christ?

eXtreme storage

ROMANIA: PASTOR RICHARD WURMBRAND

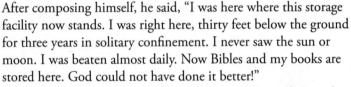

Pastor Richard Wurmbrand opened the heavy steel door and stepped into the large concrete room. He looked around at the books piled on the floor. With a wide smile and a tear in his eye, he picked one up and showed it to his friend. It was a children's Bible in the Romanian language.

Day 244

After composing himself, he said, "I was here where this storage facility now stands. I was right here, thirty feet below the ground for three years in solitary confinement. I never saw the sun or moon. I was beaten almost daily. Now Bibles and my books are stored here. God could not have done it better!"

When communism fell in Romania in 1989, workers with The Voice of the Martyrs were able to buy a bookstore and large printing press from the fallen Communists for pennies on the dollar. They printed thousands of Richard Wurmbrand's books and Bibles and needed a temporary place to store them. The new mayor of Bucharest offered the storage facility under Ceaucescu's palace—the exact place Richard had spent years in prison praying for a ministry to his homeland of Romania!

When Richard was in prison, the guards told him he would never be released or accomplish another useful task for God. Today, their place of torture has become a place of ministry!

And we know that in all things God works for the good of those who love him, who have been called according to his purpose.

Romans 8:28

Vanilla, butter, sugar, flour, and cocoa headline the list of ingredients for a perfect chocolate cake. Mixing all these ingredients together makes a sweet dessert. But if we take any one of these individual ingredients alone—like vanilla—the taste is not so sweet, but even bitter. In the same way, God is a master chef, mixing together the ingredients in our lives to make a sweet offering to Him. An individual experience by itself may be bitter; yet mixed together with the whole, our lives turn out to be a divine creation. Are you experiencing a bitter trial right now? Wait to see how God will use that experience and bring other events into the mix. Trust Him, wait, and see.

Day 245

You can only help others in proportion to what you yourself have suffered. The greater the price, the more you can help others. The lesser the price, the less you can help others. As you go through the fiery trials, the testings, the afflictions, the persecutions, the conflicts— as you let the Holy Spirit work the dying of Jesus in you—life will flow out to others, even the life of Christ.

WATCHMAN NEE,
IMPRISONED FOR HIS FAITH IN CHINA

eXtreme allegiance

The twelve students stood with their pastor along the fence. On the other side was a large ditch, beyond which was an opening to a manmade cave. A large lion paced back and forth in front of the cave's opening.

Day 246

Now it is God who makes both us and you stand firm in Christ.

2 Corinthians 1:21

Their pastor said, "Your forefathers were thrown before such wild beasts for their faith. Know that you also will have to suffer. You will not be thrown before lions, but you will have to suffer at the hands of men who would be much worse than these animals. Decide here and now whether you wish to pledge allegiance to Christ."

The students looked at each other. Before them stood their pastor, Richard Wurmbrand, a man who had spent fourteen years in prison for his work in the underground church. This was the pastor's last week in Romania, for he and his family had been ransomed from their homeland and would be leaving within a few days.

Richard didn't know if his Sunday school students would suffer under the brutal hand of atheistic Communists, but he wanted to implant a faith that would survive the harshest trials. So he had brought the students to the local zoo to see the lions.

Although young, the students fully understood what their pastor meant. With tears, they answered resolutely, "We pledge our allegiance to Christ."

Richard's lesson to the young people was timely. Though they may not have fully understood the implications of martyrdom until later and may never have had to face it themselves, that illustration helped them make an important decision. They secured their allegiance to Christ ahead of time. Advance decision-making is the key to success during opposition. We must have already established who has our allegiance long before it is tested. The moment of greatest pressure is not the time to weigh our options and decide our convictions. It is the time to put our predetermined convictions into action. Have you established your convictions in advance of temptation so that no boss, spouse, family, government, or other authority can change your mind?

eXtreme testimony

ARMENIA: BARTHOLOMEW

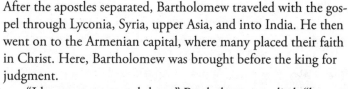

King Astyages raged at him. "You have perverted my own brother, my wife, and some of my children! You have disturbed the worship of our gods! The priests of Ashtaroth cry for your blood! If you do not stop preaching this Jesus and sacrifice to our gods, you shall die a most painful death!"

Day 247

They overcame him by the blood of the Lamb and by the word of their testimony; they did not love their lives so much as to shrink from death.

Revelation 12:11

After the apostles separated, Bartholomew traveled with the gospel through Lyconia, Syria, upper Asia, and into India. He then went on to the Armenian capital, where many placed their faith in Christ. Here, Bartholomew was brought before the king for judgment.

"I have not perverted them," Bartholomew replied, "but converted them to the truth. I shall not sacrifice to your false gods. I have only preached the worship of the one true God, and I would rather seal this testimony with my own blood than suffer the least shipwreck of my faith or conscience!"

The king was incensed. In order to silence Bartholomew, he ordered him beaten with rods and tortured. Still Bartholomew urged others to hold to the truth. Then he was hung upside down on a cross and flayed alive with knives. Still he called all to come to the one true God and His Son, Jesus Christ. Finally, the king ordered Bartholomew's head cut off with an axe, silencing his cry but preserving his witness and sealing his fate in Jesus Christ.

Perhaps some who hear the stories of the martyrs read about their lives with a sense of defeat. After all, like Bartholomew, they died in the end at the hand of their enemies. Jesus was not spared a similar conclusion. Those who refute His resurrection think of Him as a wonderful teacher whose ministry was tragically cut short by His premature death. Is death really a sign of Satan's victory? Not in Jesus' case. In fact, Jesus' death was God's ultimate victory over sin. In the case of Christian martyrs, the testimony and witness provided through their courageous deaths brought many more to faith than their lives ever could. It is possible to honor God with your death as well as your life.

eXtreme statements

ROME: THE APOSTLE PAUL

Paul wrote to Timothy, "Fight the good fight of the faith. Take hold of the eternal life to which you were called" (1 Timothy 6:12). He was familiar with the fight.

Day 248

However, I consider my life worth nothing to me, if only I may finish the race and complete the task the Lord Jesus has given me—the task of testifying to the gospel of God's grace.

Acts 20:24

Paul described some of his experiences to the Corinthians: "In great endurance; in troubles, hardships and distresses; in beatings, imprisonments and riots; in hard work, sleepless nights and hunger... dying, and yet we live on; beaten, and yet not killed; sorrowful, yet always rejoicing; poor, yet making many rich; having nothing, and yet possessing everything" (2 Corinthians 6:4,5,9,10).

While in jail with a death sentence, Paul wrote to the Philippians, "For to me, to live is Christ and to die is gain. If I am to go on living in the body, this will mean fruitful labor for me... I am torn between the two: I desire to depart and be with Christ, which is better by far; but it is more necessary for you that I remain in the body. Convinced of this, I know that I will remain, and I will continue with all of you for your progress and joy in the faith" (Philippians 1:21–25).

Some years later, however, he wrote Timothy, "I have fought the good fight, I have finished the race, I have kept the faith" (2 Timothy 4:7). In Rome at the age of sixty-four, Paul was beheaded by the order of Emperor Nero and went to be with Christ.

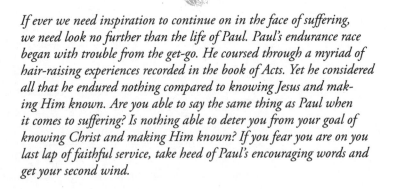

If ever we need inspiration to continue on in the face of suffering, we need look no further than the life of Paul. Paul's endurance race began with trouble from the get-go. He coursed through a myriad of hair-raising experiences recorded in the book of Acts. Yet he considered all that he endured nothing compared to knowing Jesus and making Him known. Are you able to say the same thing as Paul when it comes to suffering? Is nothing able to deter you from your goal of knowing Christ and making Him known? If you fear you are on you last lap of faithful service, take heed of Paul's encouraging words and get your second wind.

eXtreme "baptist"

JUDEA: JOHN THE BAPTIST

Day 249

John the Baptist never failed to speak for righteousness. When King Herod Antipas put away his own wife to take the wife of his brother, John called his hand. He told Herod he would disobey God's laws if he did so. Herod grew to hate John for his rebuke, but he also feared John because the people regarded him as a prophet. Herod wanted to kill John, but he dared not lay a hand on him and risk the public backlash. Under pressure from his new wife, Herodias, however, he did the next best thing to killing him—he put him in jail.

He must become greater; I must become less.

John 3:30

While in prison, John sent messengers to Jesus to verify that Jesus was the awaited One of whom he had prophesied. At Jesus' assurance that He was, in fact, that One, John rested in the knowledge that his life's mission was complete. The Messiah had come. John knew what happened to him now was of little consequence. All that mattered was Jesus.

At King Herod's birthday, Queen Herodias sent her daughter to dance before him. When Herod made an impetuous oath to give the girl whatever she wanted, she shrewdly asked for John's head on a platter. Herod, embarrassed in front of his guests, did not have the courage to refuse this outrageous request, so he had John beheaded.

Many admire their bravery and extol their courage, but martyrs did not live and die in order to be admired. It is possible to revere their stories so much that we lose sight of their lives' purpose. Those who were killed for their faith died in order to exalt Jesus, not to eclipse Him. One's response to their lives should be a greater reverence for the Lord, not awe for flesh and blood. Your greater sense of commitment is not about what will bring you accolades. Your devotion is not about what will write your name into the Christian hall of fame. Your commitment must bring glory to Jesus and Him alone.

eXtreme record keeper

COMMUNIST PRISON: FLORICA

Florica was skeptical and resisted hope. For weeks now, they had seen women leaving the prison. No one knew where they were being taken as the names were called out and the women gathered in the prison yard. Maybe they really were being released.

And so, when she heard her name called, she resigned herself to accept God's will, no matter what it was.

The major behind the desk said, "In this place, you must know that I am more powerful than God. At least, up to this point your God has not made any interventions on your behalf. But have you really accepted this? I mean, you must realize by now that in a Communist society, a god is not needed! And you shouldn't need one either. If you are ever released from here, you will see for yourself the amazing achievements we have made in the last few years, and this is just the beginning!"

... so that every mouth may be silenced and the whole world held accountable to God.

Romans 3:19

Florica looked at the documents on his desk and responded, "I see that you are powerful. And I'm sure you have documents there about me that I've never seen that can decide my fate. But God keeps records, too. Neither one of us would have life without Him. So whether He keeps me here or sets me free, I'll accept that as best for me."

Three days later, Florica was released.

When children are in school they quickly learn the power of the chalkboard. In a child's perspective, having one's name written on the board by the teacher is the ultimate accountability for rebellious students. As children, we longed for those who were causing us trouble to get their name written up. We were sure punishment would be swift and certain. Have we lost a bit of that childlike trust? Are we so jaded by the proliferation of evil in today's world that we no longer believe God is still "taking names"? The Bible teaches us that the whole world is accountable to God. So, don't lose heart when you see evil seemingly going unpunished. God will ultimately bring everyone to justice.

eXtreme revolutionaries

ROME: EARLY CHRISTIANS

The early Christians were spiritual revolutionaries. In a society that worshiped idols and called those who refused "atheists," Christians were a radical force that threatened Rome's continuity. They went against the majority rule and so became a perceived threat to the Roman authority. They were hated so much that their deaths were not only numerous, but they were carried out with horrendous flair.

Day 251

Take hold of the eternal life to which you were called when you made your good confession in the presence of many witnesses.

1 Timothy 6:12

Early Christians were revolutionaries who proclaimed the last judgment and the coming transformation of the world through Christ's return so that many could be saved. They promoted Jesus Christ as a higher authority than the Roman emperor. Therefore, Roman emperors sent out decrees stating that any professing Christians were sentenced to die with no further legal proceedings. No due process was provided for these "rebels" who dared to challenge the emperor's rule. Roman imperialism sponsored ten extreme periods of persecution, each worse than the one before it.

The revolutionaries became known by the term *martyr*. It was adopted for those witnesses who bore their testimony before judges and emperors with the steadfastness of well-disciplined soldiers. They were termed martyrs, or *confessors*, even if they did not die under scrutiny. They simply would not change their minds. Martyrdom signifies being a *witness* of one's faith in Christ, despite exacting circumstances. Every witness for Christ is a modern-day revolutionary.

The martyrs in history were, as we are today, soldiers in a spiritual war. This battle began when Jesus routed the powers of evil by dying on the cross. In His death, He disarmed hell and its demons. Martyrs carry on His battle, however, fighting not with physical weapons but spiritual ones. Their weapon of choice is their confession. They march into enemy territory, such as the restricted nations, and fearlessly proclaim Christ's victory over Satan. Their prized possession is not their lives, but their testimony. This is why they are willing to trade their lives in order to maintain their beliefs. Where will you take up the battle? Are you willing to wield the weapon of your confession?

The Commission

Day 252

I asked the Lord to help my neighbor,
And carry the gospel to distant lands,
And to comfort the sick, but He said to me,
"If you love Me, be My hands."

I asked the Lord to go to the dying,
And the orphan in the street,
And visit the prisoner, but He said to me,
"If you love Me, be My feet."

I asked the Lord to look to the poor,
And watch over each babe that cries,
And see each man's need, but He said to me,
"If you love Me, be My eyes."

I said to the Lord, I want to serve you,
But I don't know where to start.
To love is the answer, He said to me.
"If you love Me, be My heart."

G. Shirie Westfall

eXtreme resilience

PATMOS: THE APOSTLE JOHN

What do you do with someone who is boiled in oil but doesn't die?

Day 253

I, John, your brother and companion in the suffering and kingdom and patient endurance that are ours in Jesus, was on the island of Patmos because of the word of God and the testimony of Jesus.

Revelation 1:9

It is said that Roman emperor Domitian commanded that the apostle John be boiled to death in oil, but John only continued to preach from within the pot. Another time, John was forced to drink poison, but, as promised in Mark 16:18, it did not hurt him. Thus John, the head of the church in Ephesus at the time, was banished to Patmos in AD 97.

John survived all of this because God had not finished with him yet. A "revelation" was still to come.

While he was in a cave on the island of Patmos, John received a vision. This vision became the book of Revelation—the book that would serve as the driving force for evangelism in the church age. It prophesied the events that surround the return of Christ. John wrote of Christ's second coming and looked forward to His arrival. Even today his writings inspire believers to anticipate the glorious return of Christ.

Two years after John's exile, the emperor Domitian died, and John returned to the church in Ephesus. The youngest of the disciples lived also to be the oldest, dying in peace in Ephesus at the age of eighty after over half a century of resilient service to Jesus' church.

It's impossible to retire from God's service. Just ask John. At a time when the average age of death was much younger, John lived on to be eighty years old, faithfully serving all the while. Perhaps you have been struggling with your own usefulness in God's service. Perhaps you feel too old and find yourself thinking God could use someone younger in your place. Or perhaps you are young and single and wonder if a married couple might be more what God has in mind. Instead of letting you quit on your own excuses, God wants to build into you a spiritual resilience that is not readily discouraged. Start asking today for God to reveal your next steps in service to Him.

eXtreme disobedience

JERICHO: RAHAB

Day 254

There is no authority except that which God has established.

Romans 13:1

When Joshua sent two spies to view the land of Jericho, they hid in the house of Rahab the harlot. Rahab's house was built along the wall of Jericho, a wall constructed to prevent illegal passage of unwelcome visitors. When the king heard the Israeli spies were in town, he immediately sent word to Rahab. He instructed her to bring forth the spies, who had entered her home.

Rahab disobeyed the command of her king and hid the spies, even lying to protect their whereabouts. Later that evening, she secretly smuggled the spies out of the city by lowering them with a long chord through her window and down the wall.

Rahab had heard of the mighty works of the God of Israel, believing Him to be the God of heaven and earth, and she was prepared to help His people. She disobeyed her pagan authorities and even placed her life in danger. As a result, her life was spared.

A similar act of smuggling is found in Acts 9:25. Soon after Paul's conversion, he spent several days with the disciples in Damascus, preaching and teaching in the synagogues. The Jews were so baffled by the change in Paul that they considered him a threat. The disciples lowered him down a wall to clear the city gates and spare his life from the Jews who were conspiring to kill him.

Some Christians believe that disobeying the governing authorities in restricted nations warrants persecution. Are Chinese Christians who refuse to register with the official church deserving of the beatings they endure? In Islamic nations, do Muslims who convert to Christianity deserve to be stoned to death? While certain passages may be interpreted differently, all Christians agree that we cannot allow government to force us to disobey God's laws. Of course, this does not permit Christians to exercise personal vendettas against the state. Disobedience is only warranted when we are forced to decide between loyalty to Christ and loyalty to the governing laws. Where do you stand on the issue? Study the Scriptures and decide for yourself.

eXtreme deception

NORTH KOREA: AN ELDERLY WOMAN

And no wonder, for Satan himself masquerades as an angel of light. It is not surprising, then, if his servants masquerade as servants of righteousness.

2 Corinthians 11:14,15

"One day the teacher told us that we would play a special game. She whispered to us about a special book that our parents may have hidden in our homes. We were to wait until our parents went to sleep, search for this book, and secretly bring it to school the following day for a special surprise. I went home and immediately began searching for the book.

"The next day I was one of fourteen children who brought the black book, a Bible, to class. We were awarded bright red scarves, and the other students clapped as the teacher paraded us around the room.

"I ran home that afternoon because I was so excited to tell my mother how I had won the red scarf. She wasn't in the house or the barn. I waited, but neither she nor my father came home, and I began to get scared. I was hungry and it was becoming dark. I began to feel sick inside, and I fell asleep in a chair.

"The next day police officers came and informed me that I was now in the care of the government. I never saw my parents again."

An elderly woman from North Korea relayed this story. She never heard from her parents and is still struggling to find forgiveness. She is only one of many who have gone through such trials.

Contrary to a popular caricature, the devil does not appear in a red suit, poised with a pitchfork. We would easily recognize such an obvious overture to evil. However, like the child in this story, we often come across him in a different light. The enemy's representatives are often impressive people in high places. Consider the influence of a smooth-talking business partner. Or imagine the power a university professor wields in the name of academia. As the child in this story discovered, the enemy plays dirty. We must put away naiveté and be on guard against the enemy wherever we come across him and his representatives. Are you easy prey for the enemy? Or will he find you alert and on guard?

eXtreme prisoner

VIETNAM: TO DINH TRUNG

To Dinh Trung has put hundreds of miles on his bicycle, traveling bumpy dirt roads to minister to the K'Ho tribe. This is one of sixty tribes in Vietnam that the government forbids visitors to evangelize. As he entered the village on April 4, 1995, police suddenly pulled him off his bicycle and started to beat him. They videotaped him and ridiculed him in front of the villagers.

Day 256

I, Paul, the prisoner of Christ Jesus for the sake of you Gentiles . . .

Ephesians 3:1

He was taken to prison and held for six months before his trial. When he sang a children's song called "Love the Lord Day and Night," he was sentenced to spend even more time in prison.

Eventually, due to pressure on the government from Christian aid organizations, Trung was offered release six months early. But, although he had a faithful wife and two small children waiting for him, the evangelist wasn't ready to leave! He saw this as another divine opportunity to preach to the lost. What could they do to him? He was already in prison!

Through Trung's efforts in the prison near Quang Ngai, many came to Christ. After hearing of the numerous Christians praying and petitioning on his behalf, how could he pass up this opportunity to set an example by forsaking his life for the kingdom of God? Trung refused his early release and chose to remain in prison and continue his work as an evangelist.

Trung was once a prisoner of the state and subjected to cruelty and torture. However, when he chose to remain in prison for the duration of his sentence, he became a prisoner of Jesus Christ. The state tried to break him. His new master—Jesus—restored him. The state tried to silence his message. Jesus took his message to every prison cell, making Trung twice the evangelist he was before his sentence. Trung reminds us what it is like to enjoy freedom under Christ's rule even in the midst of feeling enslaved to this life's worry and woe. You may feel like you are a prisoner to a similarly depressing situation. Let Jesus set you free by allowing Him to become the true Master of your life.

eXtreme pastor

Pastor Luke shared difficult good-byes with each of his five children and his wife before he trudged out of the refugee camp and back toward his ministry in Southern Sudan. It would be three months before he saw his family again, for his ministry is in one of the areas most affected by the civil war and the Islamic government's attacks.

Day 257

Who shall separate us from the love of Christ?

Romans 8:35

Pastor Luke's congregation has no church building because many buildings have been destroyed in almost two decades of Sudan's civil war. They meet each week in the shade of a large tree into which a cross has been carved. Members sit on the ground or stand during the services while Pastor Luke stands near the carved cross and preaches.

If Pastor Luke stayed with his family, he would have time with them each day. Of course, aid workers would continue to provide food to the displaced Sudanese, tending to their physical needs. However, God called Luke to tend to the people's spiritual needs. Who would take his place if he did not go?

Luke ministers in a region that previously had no functioning church. He is obeying God's command to be salt and light in a war-torn area. It is difficult—sometimes agonizing—for Pastor Luke to leave his family. Yet God has rewarded his sacrifice with a vibrant and growing "tree church."

God's work sometimes separates us from the ones we love. Jesus Himself left all He had ever known in His hometown and family when He was thirty years old to begin His ministry. If we are to follow God's plans for our lives, that road will often take us away from the familiar and toward the unknown. While our journey may separate us from loved ones, home, comfort, and security, we are never separated from the love of Christ. His love is our constant companion, and thus we are never really alone. Are you lonesome for home? Family? Friends? If you are confident that you are following God's will for your life, then you must stick to the task. Christ will be your constant companion.

eXtreme TV preacher

The first time Brother K'Be's children saw him on Vietnamese television, they were excited. Their excitement disappeared when they heard the announcer say that their father was a criminal. They claimed he was guilty of many "crimes" against the Vietnamese government.

Day 258

This is my gospel, for which I am suffering even to the point of being chained like a criminal. But God's word is not chained.

2 Timothy 2:8,9

Brother K'Be's "crimes" were preaching the gospel at unregistered house-church meetings. The government put his face on TV to shame him and to warn others to watch out for him. They also played police interviews with him on TV and radio, but this only helped to spread the gospel message further. It gave him a platform to reach many others for Christ. Those who saw him on TV asked about his faith, and he was able to tell them about Christ.

He explained, "They put my face on TV so people can identify me. My neighbors say, 'Why leave your family?' I tell them that God will take care of that. I must go. The harvest is ready, and there are few workers."

Seeing that the public shame was not deterring K'Be's ministry, police have threatened to arrest him the next time he is caught preaching. "My wife rejoices that our names are in the Book of Life and that my face is a witness on television. The police are helping to spread the gospel. They can close the church, but not our witness."

Believers may be nailed to a stake, chained in a prison cell, or locked in stockades. Believers may even die. Yet the gospel lives on. K'Be reminds us that the gospel is not about a church building, a meeting, or any one believer. A church building can be closed. A meeting may be disbanded. A believer can be imprisoned or killed. Is your understanding of Christianity tied to a certain pastor or church building or activity? Would your faith still thrive (as it does in restricted nations) if all of these outward forms were taken away? God's Word would yet remain, despite these restrictions. Would you still find a way, like K'Be did, to live out your faith?

Day 259

You can't kill a Christian.
You can only change his address.

PASTOR DUKE DOWNS

eXtreme physician

In Communist Romania, every prison had a doctor who would often be present during the interrogation sessions and direct the torturer in the best methods of inducing pain without causing death. But some doctors took their oath seriously and despised what the Communists were doing.

Day 260

I will go to the king, even though it is against the law. And if I perish, I perish.

Esther 4:16

One such doctor was a beautiful Christian woman named Margareta Pescaru. All medical personnel were frisked when entering the prison, but Dr. Pescaru, at great risk to herself, was able to smuggle medicine in repeatedly. Her selfless efforts saved many lives.

Once she was assigned to a prison hospital that was especially designed for tuberculosis patients. During this time, the Communists assigned men as "reeducators" to use whatever means necessary to convince a person to denounce everything they believed and pledge complete allegiance to communism.

These reeducators were ruthless, and many Christians died under their torture. When Dr. Pescaru heard the news that they had arrived at the prison hospital to begin their destructive work on the tuberculosis patients, she did the unthinkable. She went to the top officials of all the prisons and pled the case of the helpless prisoners. No one knows how, but Dr. Pescaru gained favor with the officials.

For a time in Romanian communism, the torture of innocents by the "reeducators" was stopped, thanks to her bold efforts.

Try. *It's the difference between advancing and remaining still.* Trying. *It's what Christians are committed to doing when they are focused on the gospel of Christ.* Tried. *Saying one at least tried is the only way believers agree to meet failure. It's true—we just never know what will happen unless we try it. Perhaps we too quickly dismiss the creative ideas that come to us concerning advancing the gospel message at work, at home, or in our community. We think they'll never work. We convince ourselves that the opposition would be too strong. But we won't know for sure unless we try it. Are you willing to try obeying Christ at any cost, starting today?*

eXtreme wallpaper

KOREA: ROBERT J. THOMAS

Robert J. Thomas and his wife left to be the first missionaries to Korea in July 1863. His wife died soon after their arrival. In 1866, having evangelized for a few months in Korea and having learned the language, Thomas rode the American ship, the *General Sherman*, along the Taedong River to the location of the present-day capital of North Korea. The *Sherman* became grounded on a sandbar. Korean soldiers on shore were suspicious and scared, and they boarded the ship, waving long, flashing knives.

Day 261

I planted the seed, Apollos watered it, but God made it grow. So neither he who plants nor he who waters is anything, but only God, who makes things grow.

1 Corinthians 3:6,7

When Thomas saw that he was going to be killed, he held out the Korean Bible to them saying, "Jesus, Jesus." His head was cut off.

Twenty-five years after Thomas's death, someone discovered a little guest house in this area with some strange wallpaper. The paper had Korean characters printed on it. The owner of the house explained that he had pasted the pages of this book on the wall to preserve the writing. The owner and many of the guests would come in and stay to "read the walls." This was the Bible that Thomas had given to his murderers.

Even though Communists rule that area today, the church lives. The work of Robert J. Thomas—called the "temporary missionary"—continues in North Korea, where now God's Word is not only pasted on their walls, but also hidden in their hearts.

Imagine planting a garden in the spring, only to move in the summer. All the time and effort spent planting and weeding and watering the seeds for the tomatoes, peppers, and melons seems wasted. The same can be said of our witness for Christ. Here, the stakes are higher than a basket of tomatoes. Without the benefit of seeing the fruit of our labors, it can be painful to trust that our hard work will be appreciated and respected. Remember, God is the one who makes all things grow. We can trust that God will continue the work we have begun— even when He moves us on. What gardens do you need to leave for someone else to grow?

eXtreme endurance

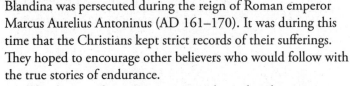

Blandina was a servant who was so filled with God's power that those who took turns torturing her day and night finally gave up. In fact, her torture seemed to make Blandina's faith stronger. She boldly proclaimed her faith, saying, "I am a Christian; we will not be ashamed."

Day 262

So that you may have great endurance and patience, . . . giving thanks to the Father, who has qualified you to share in the inheritance of the saints in the kingdom of light.

Colossians 1:11,12

Blandina was persecuted during the reign of Roman emperor Marcus Aurelius Antoninus (AD 161–170). It was during this time that the Christians kept strict records of their sufferings. They hoped to encourage other believers who would follow with the true stories of endurance.

Blandina was hung on a post, yet she endured, serving to encourage those who witnessed her torture. Having survived this scenario, she was then put into an arena with lions along with a fifteen-year-old Christian boy named Ponticus, who was encouraged by her example. Blandina did not show despair before the animals but was "rejoicing and exulting at her departure as if invited to a wedding supper."

Twice Blandina was thrown before starving lions that would not touch her. Thus, she returned to prison unharmed. She was eventually "torn by the lions, scourged, put into a net and tossed about by a wild bull, and placed naked into a red-hot metal chair." Yet she lived and encouraged all near her to remain steadfast in their faith. Blandina was eventually killed with a sword after her torturers were unable to make her deny her faith.

Although unrelated to Christian witness, there are situations we can't seem to escape that are painfully challenging. Raising a difficult child at home. Laboring beside a contentious coworker. Enduring a stressful living arrangement. There are times when we think we can no longer bear the strain and we are tempted to just give up. No matter what the circumstances, God gives us the endurance and the strength to do whatever He calls us to do. God asked Blandina to endure torture. He may prod us to seek help in our parenting, confront our coworker, or undertake some other seemingly impossible task. Injecting the name of Jesus, we can be His witness. Regardless of our scenario, God is with us, giving us patience and even joy. In what areas do you need this extreme endurance that comes only from our gracious God?

eXtreme thief-part one

RUSSIA: NIKOLAI KHAMARA

Nikolai Khamara was arrested for robbery and imprisoned for ten years. Khamara watched the Christians and wondered what kind of beings they were. They were men, but they would show joy despite their suffering and would sing in very dark hours. When they had a piece of bread, they shared it with someone who had none. Their faces would shine as they spoke to someone whom Khamara could not see.

Day 263

But God demonstrates his own love for us in this: While we were still sinners, Christ died for us.

Romans 5:8

One day two Christians sat down with Khamara and asked him about his story. Khamara told them his sad tale and finished by saying, "I am a lost man."

One of the Christians, with a smile, asked Khamara, "If somebody loses a gold ring, what is the value of that gold ring when it is lost?"

"What a foolish question! A gold ring is a gold ring. You have lost it, but somebody else will have it."

"A very good answer," said the Christian. "Now tell me, what is the value of a lost man? A lost man, even a thief, an adulterer, or a murderer, has the whole value of a man. He is of such value that the Son of God forsook heaven for him and died on the cross to save him."

The Christian said to the robber, "You may have been lost, but God's love can find you." Hearing this, Khamara gave his life to Christ.

How is value measured? Usually by a person's investment of time, money, or emotion. That is, how a person treats a possession, an activity, or even a relationship reveals how much it is valued by that person. Consider, for example, the difference in the treatment of old work clothes and a new suit. Or the contrast between the care for a paper cup and a crystal goblet. And when a valued possession is lost or a loved one injured, oh the tears that are shed. So, how valued are people . . . are you? As the Christian told Khamara, so valuable that Jesus left heaven and died on a cross for His lost and rebellious creatures. God loves them that much. You are loved; you are valuable. Rejoice and spread this Good News to the other "loved ones" near you.

eXtreme thief-part two

Nikolai Khamara had gone into prison a thief and come out a Christian. After his release, he joined the underground church in Russia.

Sometime later, the pastor of Khamara's church was arrested. The authorities tortured him, hoping he would betray the church, but he told them nothing. Then they arrested Nikolai Khamara. They brought him before the pastor and told him, "If you do not tell the secrets, we will torture Khamara in front of you."

Day 264

The pastor could not endure someone suffering for him. But Khamara said to him, "Be faithful to Christ and do not betray him. I am happy to suffer for the name of Christ." Then they gouged out Khamara's eyes.

The pastor could not bear it. He cried to Khamara, "How can I look at this? You will remain blind!"

Khamara replied, "When my eyes are taken away from me, I will see more beauty than I see with these eyes. I will see the Savior. You must remain faithful to Christ to the end."

When the interrogators told the pastor that they would cut out Khamara's tongue, Khamara said, "Praise the Lord Jesus Christ. There, I have said the highest words that can be said. And if you wish, you can now cut out my tongue." The former thief stole from the officers a chance to rob his faith. He died a martyr's death.

The thief comes only to steal and kill and destroy; I have come that they may have life, and have it to the full.

John 10:10

Khamara's story is a lesson in contrasts between the kingdom of God and the kingdom of the devil. The Bible teaches us how to recognize those who steal, kill, and destroy as members in the kingdom of the devil. In Khamara's case, the enemy stole his eyesight, destroyed his speech, and eventually killed him. In contrast, Jesus' kingdom is about life—life to the extreme. As such, Jesus gave Khamara a new life and restored a former thief to righteousness. The two kingdoms are in conflict, and our lives are the spoils. Khamara "defected" to the other side when two believers showed him how to join God's kingdom. What are you doing to bring others into God's kingdom?

eXtreme possession

ENGLAND: A CHRISTIAN WIDOW

Six men and one widow were taken before the court for committing an extreme crime against the Church of England. They had taught their children the Lord's Prayer and the Ten Commandments in the English language.

Day 265

Latin was the only language allowed for biblical instruction in England in 1519. However, the common people spoke English. The believers secretly translated parts of Scripture into English and carefully passed the translations from home to home. But now they had been caught, and they were to be tied to stakes and publicly burned.

The mercy of the court had smiled solely on the widow out of the seven prisoners, and she was allowed to go free. No one protested, for she was alone and had children to care for at home.

A guard named Simon Mourton generously offered to walk the pardoned widow home. As Simon was leading her by the arm, he heard a rustle within her coat sleeve. He pulled from her coat the English translations, the same materials they had been teaching their children. Even though she had just escaped a death sentence, she subsequently refused to part with the translations, believing her children still needed to know the truth of God's Word. Her fate was now sealed.

Shortly after, the six men and the courageous widow were secured to three wooden poles and were burned alive.

The law from your mouth is more precious to me than thousands of pieces of silver and gold.

Psalm 119:72

We live in a digital age of home alarm systems that rival the complexity of most banks. What we value is clear—our homes and our belongings are too precious to risk being lost. Yet, to Christians living in the sixteenth century, Scripture was their most prized possession. Like the tenacious widow in this story, they considered mere pieces of the Bible worth the cost of their lives. While the times may have changed, the value of God's Word has not. Our lives must still demonstrate to others that God's Word is precious, though we are unlikely to die in doing so. Do others know how much or little you treasure Scripture? Can they tell the personal value God's Word has in your life?

Day 266

Christian missionaries must be reported
and ferreted out without fail because
they are cunning wolves that serve
as a tool of imperialism.

AN OPEN WARNING ISSUED BY THE
NORTH KOREAN GOVERNMENT TO ITS PEOPLE

eXtreme translation

ENGLAND: WILLIAM TYNDALE

"But, Master Tyndale, you must admit," scoffed the learned doctor of theology, "that men are better with the laws of the church that they can understand than God's own law in the Bible!"

Day 267

For I endure scorn for your sake.

Psalm 69:7

William Tyndale fumed at this. "I defy the priests and their laws! If God sees fit to let me live, then it won't be long before any boy who drives a plough will know the Scriptures better than they do!" His remark caused a division between Tyndale and the established church. He soon fled England for the mainland, where he produced his outlawed version of the New Testament in English.

For years, Tyndale's small New Testaments were smuggled into bales of cotton, aboard German ships, and any other place where they could secretly enter England. However, Tyndale was then betrayed by a "friend," Henry Philips, and tried for heresy.

While William Tyndale remained in prison more than a year awaiting execution, it is believed that he finished the Old Testament translation in English. His last words before being burned at the stake in October 1536 were, "Lord, open the king of England's eyes!"

God did. A few years after Tyndale's martyrdom, the monarchy allowed the first English Bible to be legally printed. The King James Authorized Version appeared seventy-five years later. Today's King James Version of the Bible matches an estimated ninety percent of Tyndale's work word-for-word.

Opposition does not equal failure. Sometimes it means just the opposite. The most well-meaning colleagues may sometimes oppose our vision for ministry. We may be taken aback by their criticism and begin to question our calling. When God gives us a vision for ministry, as He gave Tyndale, we must be faithful to the task despite the odds. Criticism should not squelch our enthusiasm—it should make us all the more committed to improve our vision. Has God given you a vision for ministry? Like Tyndale, you may not see the results of your labor for some time, if at all. And you may be reproved in the meantime. Still, stay true to the task, and God will take care of the criticism.

eXtreme kids of courage

NORTH KOREA: CHENG LEE AND HONG JUN

Communists tell North Korean children that they will suffer a horrific fate if they are ever caught in China. But the children also know that if they are fortunate enough to escape, they should look for a building with the shape of a cross on it to find help. Two North Korean children who managed to arrive at a Chinese church relayed their stories to the pastor.

Day 268

When they saw the courage of Peter and John...they were astonished and they took note that these men had been with Jesus.

Acts 4:13

"My name is Cheng Lee. My sister and I watched our parents starve to death. We managed to walk across the Yalu River while it was still frozen. Once on the other side, my older sister said, 'You stay here. I have to go on a little farther by myself.' She never returned." Cheng is only six.

Hong Jun, an eleven-year-old boy, said, "I want to return to North Korea and tell others about Christ." Then he cried as he sang:

Oh, Lord, give us the voice of the gospel,
For our beloved brothers the Lord so loved before.
Where are all these gone? The Lord is looking upon them.

Oh, Lord, send us to them, to our beloved Korean brothers,
Oh, Lord, send us to them, to our beloved Korean brothers.
Wherever they are, let them bloom as flowers.

A few months later, Hong Jun was kidnapped from the village and forcibly returned to North Korea. Perhaps he is witnessing to his captors even now.

Courage is one of those things people don't know they have until a situation requires it. At the crucial moment when it is needed, they either have it or they don't. The same can be said of character; certain situations will definitely reveal whether we have it or we don't. As a result, character and courage are two things that are difficult to fake. Fortunately, Jesus Christ gives us irrevocable courage and unquestionable character for the times we need it most. We may put on a brave front, but only Jesus can make us courageous. We may have a sterling public reputation, but only Jesus can give us character for those times when no one is looking. Where do you see character and courage at work in your life?

eXtreme reversal

PAKISTAN: ZAHID

Zahid was a Pakistani Muslim priest who ambushed Christians and burned their Bibles. Once he kept one of the Bibles and started studying it to prove that Christianity was a lie.

Day 269

Jesus answered, "I am the way and the truth and the life. No one comes to the Father except through me."

John 14:6

"I read the Bible, looking for contradictions I could use against the Christian faith," Zahid shared. "All of a sudden, a great light appeared in my room and I heard a voice call my name. The light illuminated the entire room.

"'Zahid, why do you persecute Me?' the voice asked.

"I was scared. I didn't know what to do. I asked, 'Who are You?'

"'I am the way, the truth, and the life.' For the next three nights, the light and the voice returned. On the fourth night, I knelt down and trusted Jesus as my Savior."

Having converted to Christianity, Zahid was arrested and imprisoned as a traitor to Islam. He was tortured in prison for two years and eventually sentenced to death. As the noose was placed around his neck, Zahid told his executioners that Jesus was "the way, the truth, and the life." He wanted his last breath to be used to save his countrymen.

Then suddenly, guards rushed in and said that there had been a stay of execution and Zahid was released. No one knows why Zahid's sentence was reversed, but today Zahid continues to travel Pakistan as an evangelist.

People who have been through a near-death experience usually say the same thing. They conclude that God must have had a purpose for extending their lives. Unfortunately, television interviews rarely go back to see what that purpose turned out to be! Did they discover God's purpose for their lives or not? Actually, God has the same purpose for each one of our lives. He wants us to know Him and to make Him known to others. Some, like Zahid, may go through unique experiences to come to those particular places where they are to make God known. However, our mission remains basically the same. Ever feel like God has you on this earth for a specific reason? He does. It's to know Him—and to make Him known.

eXtreme power

ROME: VINCENT

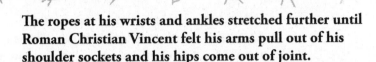

The ropes at his wrists and ankles stretched further until Roman Christian Vincent felt his arms pull out of his shoulder sockets and his hips come out of joint.

Decius, the Roman emperor, stood by the rack where Vincent was tied. "You will die in terrible pain," he told the young Christian.

Day 270

"No death is more honorable than that of a martyr," Vincent said to the king with conviction. "I see heaven, and I abhor your idols."

Furious, the king called for the now-crippled Christian to be tortured even more. Yet they could not rid Vincent of his smile. He told the emperor through his pain, "You destroy only my body, which has to perish anyway. Inside of me lives another Vincent, and over him you have no power. That Vincent cannot be put on a rack and cannot be killed." Vincent welcomed death with a smile.

Being strengthened with all power according to his glorious might so that you may have great endurance and patience.

Colossians 1:11

Finally, the Roman soldiers pulled him from the rack, but his torments were not over. They stripped him of his clothes and threw him into a cell, the floor of which was covered with shattered glass. Unable to stand, Vincent was forced to lie on the ragged glass. Even there, God's peace was with him. Guards later reported to the emperor that he rested on the shattered glass "as on a bed of flowers."

In modern culture, the idea of power is tied to authority and office. Power is reserved for the outwardly important, the cultured, and the refined. History, however, shows that people with the mere position of power are ineffective without the inner strength to carry out their duties. In contrast, God targets our inner strength through the presence of the Holy Spirit. Suffering is His classroom, where He teaches us what it is like to be strong. We are able to endure more than we imagined. We are bold beyond our means. You may feel as though your sufferings have made you weak. Ask God to show you how they can, in fact, make you stronger. Flex your muscles. You will see you are stronger than you think.

eXtreme soldiers

Emperor Constantine legalized Christianity in the Roman Empire in AD 320. However, Licinius, who controlled the Eastern half of the empire, broke allegiance with the West and continued to suppress Christianity.

Day 271

Endure hardship with us like a good soldier of Christ Jesus.

2 Timothy 2:3

When Licinius demanded that every soldier under his command sacrifice to the Roman gods, the forty Christian men of the "Thundering Legion" refused. Their general, Lysias, had them whipped, torn with hooks, and then imprisoned in chains. When they still refused to bow down and give up their worship of God, he ordered them stripped of their clothing and left in the middle of a frozen lake until they relented.

A warm bath was poured for any who would give up their convictions. The men prayed together that their number would not be broken. However, as it grew dark, one could not bear the cold any longer and ran to the warm bath.

One of the guards who had watched the forty brave soldiers sing to Christ became angry that one would give in to Lysias's orders. His anger turned to conviction, and then his conviction turned to faith. He tore off his clothes and ran out on the icy lake, fulfilling their promise to be "forty brave soldiers for Christ!"

The forty died together that day. The one who gave up his faith for a warm bath also died.

Christian community is made up of several committed individuals who act in one accord. Whether it is a Christian campus, a Christian ministry, a church, or a family, the band of sisterhood and brotherhood is a force with which to be reckoned. We always stand stronger whenever we stand together. Throughout Scripture, God exhorts us to come together in a community of commitment—a family of faith. More than the principle of strength in numbers, a Christian community encourages its members' faith. Like this story, the strong compensate for those who are weak. Have you identified your Christian community? Have you assured your church or family or other group of your love and allegiance despite all costs?

eXtreme beauty

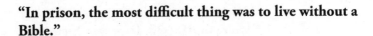

"In prison, the most difficult thing was to live without a Bible."

Aida Skripnikova was a beautiful young woman. In her early twenties, she stood on a corner in the streets of Leningrad and handed out poems declaring her love for Jesus and her joy in knowing Him as Lord and Savior. She was soon arrested, but she proved to be resolute in her convictions, even though she was sentenced to a year in prison.

By the time Aida was twenty-seven years old, she faced her fourth prison term for her determination to defend the gospel. She had remained outspoken, saying in one publication, "We cannot be silent about what constitutes the whole meaning of our life—Christ."

Her fourth stay in prison proved her most difficult. The guards constantly tried to corrupt her faith with everything from abuse to offers of chocolate. But the hardest thing for her was living without God's Word. Her copy of the Scriptures was confiscated. As a punishment, she spent ten days in solitary confinement. Later she received a New Testament and guarded it as more precious than life.

When she was finally released, Aida was hardly recognizable —her dazzling beauty was gone, and she looked decades older. But the love of God shone through her smile, revealing her unparalleled beauty from within.

Day 272

Your beauty... should be that of your inner self, the unfading beauty of a gentle and quiet spirit, which is of great worth in God's sight.

1 Peter 3:3,4

In many grocery stores, beauty creams outnumber canned vegetables. The cosmetics aisle is crammed with formulas promising to renew and restore our outward appeal. If only we were as concerned about our inner character as we are our outward appearance. Martyrs teach us to value the renewal of who we really are on the inside. The inner self. This is the person that no amount of torture can dismay. This is who is being transformed into the image of Christ. You may wish to impress others according to worldly standards. However, God thinks your inner self is far more striking. Are you as focused on your inner character as on your outward appearance? In what ways is your inner self growing more beautiful as you age?

Day 273

I asked for strength—
and God gave me difficulties to make me strong.

I asked for wisdom—
and God gave me problems to solve.

I asked for prosperity—
and God gave me brain and brawn to work.

I asked for courage—
and God gave me dangers to overcome.

I asked for love—
and God gave me opportunities.

I received nothing I wanted—
I received everything I needed.

My prayer has been answered.

FROM THE FAMILY OF MICHAEL JOB,
AN INDIAN CHRISTIAN MEDICAL STUDENT
WHO WAS KILLED IN JUNE 1999 BECAUSE OF HIS
FATHER'S EVANGELISTIC ACTIVITIES

eXtreme teaching—part one

The people of Hadley begged Dr. Rowland Taylor not to go see the bishop of Winchester and Lord Chancellor. They knew the bishop was furious at the teachings of Dr. Taylor.

Day 274

Jesus replied, "If anyone loves me, he will obey my teaching."

John 14:23

For nearly twenty years, the English Bible had been legally distributed in England. Dr. Taylor had simply taught all those in his church to read the Bible for themselves and to follow its teachings. In contrast, religious leaders under the brutal rule of Queen Mary I called for strict adherence to the customs of the Roman Catholic church.

After being insulted and accused by the bishop, Rowland replied, "I am a Christian man. I have not blasphemed against the church. In fact, by your own charge, you are the heretic. Christ died once and for all for the sins of mankind. It is sufficient. You and your traditions can offer nothing more."

For the next two years, Dr. Taylor was a prisoner. When he learned that he would be burned at the stake outside Hadley, he leaped for joy. He was not concerned for his safety. Instead, he rejoiced at the thought of traveling through Hadley and once again seeing his brothers and sisters in the faith.

Dr. Rowland Taylor was martyred in the winter of 1555.

Love is spoken in many different languages. People need to hear love in their own language in order to recognize it. Some husbands serve their wives breakfast in bed to demonstrate their love. Still other spouses need a thoughtful gift in order to hear "I love you" loud and clear. Greeting card companies hope we'll say it with words. Jesus, however, says that His love language is obedience. That is how we express our love to Him. When we obey Him, we show that we love Him. Taylor was martyred for teaching his followers to speak Jesus' love language. He taught them to read the Bible and obey its teaching. Show Jesus you love Him, and honor Dr. Taylor's memory today.

eXtreme teaching—part two

ENGLAND: DR. ROWLAND TAYLOR

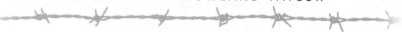

Before being burned at the stake for teaching the Bible, Dr. Rowland Taylor wrote these beautiful words:

"I say to my wife and to my children, the Lord gave you to me, and the Lord has taken me from you and you from me: Blessed be the name of the Lord! I have ever found him more faithful and favorable than is any husband or father. Trust in Him by means of our dear Savior's merits: Believe, love, fear, and obey Him. Pray to Him, for He has promised to help. Count me not dead, for I shall eternally live and never die. I go before, and you shall follow after, to our eternal home.

"I say to you my dear friends of Hadley, and to all those who have heard me preach, that I depart from here with a quiet conscience concerning my teaching, for which I pray you thank God with me. For I have, in keeping with my little talent, declared to others those lessons that I gathered out of God's book, the blessed Bible. Therefore, if I, or an angel from heaven, should preach to you another gospel than that which you have received, God's great curse be upon that preacher!

"Departing from here with sure hope, without any doubting of eternal salvation, I thank God my heavenly Father, through Jesus Christ my certain Savior."

Rowland Taylor

Day 275

Keep my commands and you will live; guard my teachings as the apple of your eye.

Proverbs 7:2

Can you recall your most memorable childhood teacher? Perhaps it was a certain perfume she wore. Maybe it was the peculiar way he smoothed his bald spot. Something about the person remains in your mind. However, when we grow older, we value teachers for different reasons. We recall what they taught us—lessons we'll never forget. We'll always remember the one who first taught us God's Word. We cannot afford to forget the basic truths our teachers shared with us about God's love and His salvation. When someone else comes along in the name of enlightenment or academia, God's truths will protect you and help you recognize falsehood. They are more than mere memories. They are your most valuable possession.

eXtreme family

In the Cambodian jungle, Haim and his family were given shovels and told to dig their own graves. They were hostages of the Khmer Rouge who considered Christians "enemies of the glorious revolution."

Day 276

Whoever does God's will is my brother and sister and mother.

Mark 3:35

The soldiers allowed Haim and his family to kneel, hold hands, and pray. Haim then urged the soldiers to repent and trust Jesus as their Lord and Savior. The soldiers were puzzled by the compassion in his voice in the face of death.

As he spoke, one of his sons jumped up and fled into the woods. The soldiers started after him, but Haim stopped them. His calmness convinced the Communists to see what the boy would do.

While his family knelt with the soldiers' guns trained on them, Haim stepped to the edge of the forest. "Son, can stealing a few more days of life as a fugitive in that forest compare to joining your family here around a grave, but soon free forever in paradise with Christ?" After a moment, there was a rustling of some brush as Haim's son tearfully walked out and knelt down with his father.

Haim looked at the soldiers, "Now we are ready to go."

But none of the soldiers could pull their triggers. Soon, however, an officer came by who had not witnessed the boy's return, scolded the soldiers as cowards, and killed the Christians.

Some families are known for being extremely close-knit. Others pride themselves on being extremely wealthy. Still other families point to their extreme busyness for significance. While God can use these other things, His idea of influence is very different. What makes a family useful in God's kingdom? Extreme obedience. It's not the size of a family's minivan that counts; it is their commitment to Christ. God designed family as a place where parents lead by example in order for children to learn how to obey Christ. While Haim's scenario is unique, we can be just as obedient in our own situations. How would you characterize your own family's commitment? Whose family is an example of an extreme family?

eXtreme exchange

RUSSIA: A UNIVERSITY STUDENT

The godless professor smiled at the photo of Lenin hanging next to the door and then stepped up to the pitcher of water sitting on a table. He pulled out a packet of powder, and as he slowly poured it in, the water turned red.

Day 277

They exchanged the truth of God for a lie.

Romans 1:25

"This is the whole miracle," he began his lesson. "Jesus had hidden in his sleeves a powder like this and then pretended to have changed the water into wine in a wonderful manner. But I can do even better than Jesus; I can change the wine into water again."

He pulled out another packet of powder and put it in the red liquid. It became clear. With another packet, it became red again.

One of the students sat at his desk, shaking his head, unimpressed. Finally, he challenged the professor: "You have amazed us, Comrade Professor. We ask of you just one more thing—*drink your wine!*"

The professor chuckled and said, "This I cannot do. The powder is poison."

The Christian replied, "This is the whole difference between you and Jesus. He, with His wine, has given us joy, whereas you poison us with your wine." The professor angrily stomped out of his room and had the student arrested and thrown in prison. But news of the incident spread very far and strengthened many in their faith.

The enemy's promise of an easy exchange is a lie. Most department stores have a user-friendly return policy that allows customers to exchange their purchases in order to be satisfied. People stand in line to swap a smaller size for a larger one or one color for another in hopes that it will make them look thinner or prettier or just plain happier. Likewise, many people in life are standing in line, God's truth in hand. They are told to swap God's truth for anything, and it will make them satisfied customers. We always end up disappointed in the end. God wants you to see through the enemy's lies. Hold on to God's truth—at any cost.

eXtreme plea

INDONESIA: DELORES

Day 278

Delores's aging body was weary from running, and she wept, "God, please have mercy on us, your children!" Delores was fleeing for her life, along with other believers, as attackers showered artillery on her village. Using her crude walking stick, she climbed, step by step, over a steep mountain range until she reached a safe location. She settled in a makeshift refugee camp among hundreds of others who had been displaced by the violence.

They called out in a loud voice, "How long, Sovereign Lord, holy and true, until you judge the inhabitants of the earth and avenge our blood?"

Revelation 6:10

Delores is one of millions of Christians living in Indonesia—a nation comprised of more than thirteen thousand islands. Indonesia is also the most populous Muslim country in the world. Yet the Muslims and Christians have shared the same space for years, living together in peace for generations. However, they face a new enemy: fanatical Muslim groups have recently incited many *jihads* (holy wars) on the islands.

Today, there is no peace between the Muslims and Christians. In one city, Christians gathered and sang "I Surrender All" at the governor's office in a peaceful demonstration of the cause of Christ. They pleaded for the government to acknowledge how many Christians have been slaughtered at the hands of militant Muslims. Even while the calm body of believers continued to sing, Muslim forces attacked another village and ravaged it. Many communities that used to thrive are now just piles of ash and rubble.

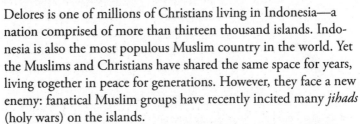

Delores is just one of a multitude of persecuted believers in Indonesia who cry out to God for deliverance. The book of Revelation speaks of a multitude of martyrs who long for God's judgment and justice. However, they must not cry out alone. We who are living must join our voices along with their earnest pleas. Even though we may be a world away in our own comfortable homes, our sincere support is merely a prayer away. When we offer our prayers for safety and deliverance, we join our hearts with those who are suffering. Will you pray today for Delores and other believers in Indonesia? Will you ask God to protect them on their journey and to hear our prayers for deliverance?

eXtreme prayer

SWITZERLAND: MICHAEL SATTLER

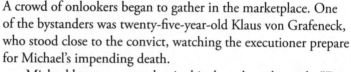

Michael Sattler was not surprised by his sentence—to have his tongue cut out and then to be burned as a heretic. It was the sixteenth century, and Michael was Anabaptist, a movement of believers who wanted to return to a New Testament form of church. However, Europe's religious and social institutions saw the Anabaptists as a threat.

Day 279

And pray in the Spirit on all occasions with all kinds of prayers and requests.

Ephesians 6:18

A crowd of onlookers began to gather in the marketplace. One of the bystanders was twenty-five-year-old Klaus von Grafeneck, who stood close to the convict, watching the executioner prepare for Michael's impending death.

Michael began to pray despite his then-slurred speech, "Dear Lord, open the eyes of this young man..."

Klaus suddenly jumped back, in shock that this criminal was praying for him!

As the executioner bound Michael, the prisoner turned to the crowd and in garbled speech said, "Be ye converted!" Then he closed his eyes and prayed: "Almighty, eternal God...I will...on this day testify to the truth and seal it with my blood."

With that, the executioner threw Michael into the fire. When the ropes on his hands were burned through, he raised them into the air and prayed, "Father, I commend my spirit into thy hands."

Klaus was so touched by the condemned man's prayer for him that he recorded Sattler's death as a tribute. He concluded it by writing: "May God grant us also to testify of Him so bravely and patiently."

Prayer is a Christian's secret weapon. It makes a silent statement or an open overture about one's faith in Christ. When Klaus heard a condemned man pray, it made him stop and think. Likewise, when others in a restaurant see us bless our meals before we eat, we may also cause them to stop and consider God. Even if we capture people's thoughts for a mere moment and turn their minds toward Christ, we have done our duty. As Michael proved with Klaus, prayer changes lives and inspires commitment. However, God can't use the prayers you don't offer. Take some time to offer a silent prayer for the benefit of someone you meet today. You never know what will happen as a result.

Day 280

The word "missionary"
is not in the Bible—
the word "witness" is.

JIM ELLIOTT, MISSIONARY TO ECUADOR WHO WAS MARTYRED
WHILE TRYING TO BRING THE GOSPEL TO THE AUCA INDIAN TRIBE—
QUOTED BY ELISABETH ELLIOTT IN *MY SAVAGE, MY KINSMEN*

eXtreme manuscript

ITALY: EUSEBIUS

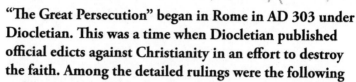

"The Great Persecution" began in Rome in AD 303 under Diocletian. This was a time when Diocletian published official edicts against Christianity in an effort to destroy the faith. Among the detailed rulings were the following orders:

Day 281

They will proclaim his righteousness to a people yet unborn.

Psalm 22:31

Christians holding public office were to be put out of office;

All accusations against Christians were to be welcomed and received;

Christians were to be tortured for their faith;

Scriptures were to be confiscated and burned immediately;

Church buildings were to be destroyed;

A Christian's civil rights were to be forcefully denied; and

Presidents, bishops, and leaders of churches were to be arrested in order to sacrifice to the gods.

During this time, a young writer named Eusebius documented the atrocities committed against the early church. A church leader and theologian named Pamphilus greatly inspired him. Pamphilus was arrested and tortured in AD 308, but not before he made a significant impact on Eusebius's life.

Eusebius wrote, "We saw with our very eyes the houses of prayer cast down to their foundations...and the inspired and sacred Scriptures committed to the flames...and the pastors of the churches, some shamefully hiding themselves here and there."

Pamphilus's execution in AD 309 did not deter Eusebius from writing the manuscript *History of the Church*.

Eusebius was later arrested for his contribution to the Christian cause. However, his life was spared. God protected him so he could continue to write his message to the future church. His writings opened the eyes of future generations to the tribulations the early church faced. His record of the life and death of a legacy of Christian leaders reminds us of the great heritage of Christian heroes. If we can learn today from the courageous faith and undying love of our forefathers who were persecuted, the writings are not in vain. And neither are their sufferings. What are you doing today that might inspire the next generation toward greater commitment? Ask God to help you leave your own legacy.

eXtreme cover-up

SAUDI ARABIA: A HUSBAND AND WIFE

A man and his wife arrived in the oil-rich nation of Saudi Arabia from another country.

Day 282

For there is nothing hidden that will not be disclosed, and nothing concealed that will not be known or brought out into the open.

Luke 8:17

They lived and worked in this Muslim nation that they called their new home. Eventually, they met and worshiped with other foreign workers who shared their faith—Christianity. However, practicing Christianity in the spiritual capitol of Mohammed is not only unpopular; it is also illegal. Even so, the couple accepted the risks of imprisonment, deportation, and possible death in order to faithfully continue their worship.

They lived for many years in peace. However, one day members of the Saudi police raided their home. They were taken to the police station for questioning concerning their religious beliefs. Their computer, which by this time contained contact information for many other local Christians, was confiscated. They feared others would soon suffer their same fate.

The husband remained in prison, but his wife was cleared of the charges and released. She made several appeals to outside governments to help clear her husband's name and release him from prison. She relied on those who stood for freedom. Yet other countries were unwilling to intervene in her situation. Her spouse was left wondering if he would ever see her again. Their case is one of many secret persecutions against Christians in the Muslim nation of Saudi Arabia. Yet the truth will one day be known.

Saudi Arabia is a country that reportedly has one of the highest rates of execution in the world. In 1999, Saudi Arabia spent more than $1,000,000 on public relations firms to ensure secrecy about their human rights abuses. Yet they cannot keep their secret forever. We must pray that the voices of Christians in Saudi prisons will be heard and answered in our lifetime. We know that when Christ returns, no public relations firms will be able to protect persecutors from His judgment. But what about today? Prayer is the first step toward making a difference. It's no secret—the opposition is powerful. However, God is more powerful. What are you doing to summon His power on behalf of those in prison?

eXtreme insubordination

THE ROMAN EMPIRE: THE THEBAN LEGION

In AD 286, the 6,666 men of the Theban Legion were ordered by Emperor Maximus to march to Gaul and to assist him against the rebels of Burgundy. Every member of this division was a devout Christian.

Day 283

But Peter and John replied, "Judge for yourselves whether it is right in God's sight to obey you rather than God."

Acts 4:19

After traveling a difficult trail through the Alps, Maximus demanded a general sacrifice before going into battle. Every man of the Theban Legion refused to dishonor God. The emperor was angered by their insubordination, so he sought to persuade them by having every tenth man slain with the sword. Yet the legionnaires were no less resolute in their stand. The emperor tried to change their position by having his soldiers go back through the ranks a second time, again killing every tenth. These men died with great dignity and poise as if in battle. But this second massacre was no more effective than the first.

If anything, the remaining soldiers were more determined than ever to resist after the slaughter of their companions. Not desiring to die, and at the direction of their officers, they drew up an article of allegiance to the emperor. They declared that their faith and dedication to God only made them more loyal to the emperor. They had hoped this would appease the emperor, but it had the opposite effect. Enraged, he ordered the rest of the Theban Legion slain.

Insubordination is the highest military offense. Yet, the Theban Legion had no other choice, for to disobey God would have been an even greater crime. Humans rule with authority. However, only God grants authority. The Bible gives examples of how God's people chose to overrule human authority when it conflicted with God's command. Consider the Hebrew midwives and also Moses' parents who disobeyed Pharaoh's orders. Consider Daniel and his companions who refused to serve foreign gods. Their examples and the examples of these brave soldiers remind us we have a duty to recognize human authority. Yet we must respect God's authority most of all. When human orders are in direct conflict with God's commands, you must consider the risk of insubordination.

eXtreme restraint

ROME: SEBASTIAN

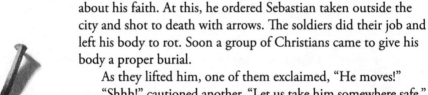

Sebastian walked through the halls of the palace daily. He had worked hard to get to this position in the royal guard, but once he had gotten to Rome, he restrained himself from the idolatrous lifestyle of imperial Rome. He only wanted to serve Christ wholeheartedly.

Day 284

When Emperor Diocletian heard of his restraint, he had little interest in his service record. He confronted him and found out about his faith. At this, he ordered Sebastian taken outside the city and shot to death with arrows. The soldiers did their job and left his body to rot. Soon a group of Christians came to give his body a proper burial.

As they lifted him, one of them exclaimed, "He moves!"

"Shhh!" cautioned another. "Let us take him somewhere safe."

Sebastian was taken to one of their homes where he was treated and recovered from his injuries. As soon as he was well enough, he placed himself before the emperor again. Once he had tasted the hope of heaven, the pleasures of this world had even less appeal for him.

I have kept my feet from every evil path so that I might obey your word.

Psalm 119:101

The emperor was of course shocked to see Sebastian seemingly back from the dead. He ordered Sebastian seized and beaten to death and his body thrown into the sewer. His body was recovered again by Christians and buried in the catacombs.

Sexual immorality. Unbecoming language. Stealing. Lying. Cheating. Too many Christians define themselves exclusively by what they do not do. Certainly, there is a whole host of activities that God forbids His people to practice. However, restraint is not profitable in and of itself. Sebastian was not martyred merely for his restraint—otherwise he would have been killed for simply being a good person. He was martyred for his forthright faith. Likewise, we must restrain or hold back from evil in order to fully embrace God's commands. Obey. Worship. Love. Serve. Define your faith by what you do, not simply by what you do not do. Are you known for merely being a good person or for being a good person with an outspoken faith?

eXtreme freedom

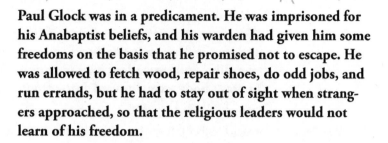

Paul Glock was in a predicament. He was imprisoned for his Anabaptist beliefs, and his warden had given him some freedoms on the basis that he promised not to escape. He was allowed to fetch wood, repair shoes, do odd jobs, and run errands, but he had to stay out of sight when strangers approached, so that the religious leaders would not learn of his freedom.

Day 285

The jailer brought [Paul and Silas] into his house and set a meal before them; he was filled with joy because he had come to believe in God— he and his whole family.

Acts 16:34

Paul was puzzled by his freedom. His warden, Klaus von Grafeneck, had witnessed the martyrdom of fellow Anabaptist Michael Sattler in 1527. A mere bystander, Klaus was overcome when Sattler prayed for him just before he was executed. That had been twenty-five years before, and perhaps Klaus had a soft place in his heart toward the unjustly persecuted Anabaptists.

Paul had nothing to lose. His wife and child were already dead; he had only his fellow brethren in Moravia. But Paul would not yield to the temptation to flee. If he escaped, Klaus, who had been so good to him, would be in tremendous legal trouble, and future Anabaptists imprisoned in that area would be scrutinized. Paul resolved to be a person of his word.

God later honored Paul's decision. In 1576, a fire broke out in the castle where he was held. He and a fellow prisoner helped put out the flames and so won their freedom before the religious leaders, who staunchly opposed Paul, could revoke it.

Martyrs' imprisonment stories are not the stuff of Hollywood movies, where ingenious characters dig tunnels and make secret escape hatches. The plot does not hinge on how the prisoner will escape peril. In fact, like Paul Glock, martyrs did not escape, even when they had the chance to do so. Their stories are about reckoning every situation for God's glory, regardless of their circumstances. Consider how Paul and Silas led their jailer and his family to Christ because they chose not to escape from jail. Are you preoccupied with finding a way out of your troubles? What if you are exactly where God wants you to be? Maybe God wants you to endure instead of escape.

eXtreme witness

PAKISTAN: SHERAZ

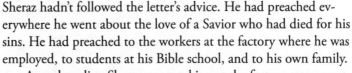

The letter's power didn't come from its one line of words: "Stop preaching to Muslims." Its delivery method made the greater impact; it was attached to the bloody body of a Bible college student named Sheraz. The letter and Sheraz's body were dumped at the front gate of his church near Lahore, Pakistan.

Day 286

For we cannot help speaking about what we have seen and heard.

Acts 4:20

Sheraz hadn't followed the letter's advice. He had preached everywhere he went about the love of a Savior who had died for his sins. He had preached to the workers at the factory where he was employed, to students at his Bible school, and to his own family.

A week earlier, Sheraz was working at the factory to support his parents and three sisters when he got into a discussion with some Muslim coworkers. They became angry, and other workers reported a heated argument.

That was the last time anyone saw Sheraz alive.

Sheraz had known the risk. Many others in Pakistan had been killed for sharing their faith. Others had been accused of blasphemy and locked away in prison. But the gospel message was too good, and Sheraz just couldn't keep it to himself.

The members of his church wouldn't take the letter's advice either. They continued to preach to Muslims, offering Jesus' love to those enslaved by the hatred and fear of Islam. They, too, knew the risks, but they have continued and will continue, even if they must follow Sheraz's example.

The most effective witness is a sincere one. We don't have to memorize the theological significance of the atonement to tell others that Jesus makes a difference in our lives. All Jesus asks is that we testify to what we have seen and heard with our own eyes and ears. Our personal experience is the most powerful argument for faith in Jesus Christ. No one can dispute it, because it happened to us. Are you hesitant to share your faith? Are you afraid you will say the wrong thing or be stumped by someone's questions? Just say what you know to be true. Your personal experience makes you an expert witness in the case for Christianity.

Day 287

Jesus told me to go.
He never said I would come back.
Isn't this the life of a Christian?

CELSO, A COLOMBIAN EVANGELIST

eXtreme crackdown

"Is my name on the list?" The question was on the mind of every Christian in Jeddah, Saudi Arabia, after religious police raided a fellow believer's home and confiscated a computer with information about Christians in the area. "Will they knock on my door next?"

Day 288

I will never blot out his name from the book of life, but will acknowledge his name before my Father and his angels.

Revelation 3:5

Prabhu Isaac was the first to receive a visit from the *mutawa*, or religious police. Isaac was a citizen of India, but in Saudi Arabia it is illegal to promote any faith except Islam. Even the display of a cross is a crime. The mutawa was concerned that Saudi citizens were reportedly interacting with the Christians. They refused to allow Isaac to access his nation's consulate, despite the requirements of international law. The police also questioned his wife and warned her not to have outside contact.

Then another believer, Eskinder Menghis, was arrested after his name was found on Isaac's computer. Wilfredo Caliuag was next. Shortly after his arrest, Caliuag was sent to the hospital, reportedly for treatment of "heat stroke." However, visitors said Caliuag's body was bruised and battered, as if the police had mistreated him.

Saudi Arabia is closed to the gospel, but brave Christians who have taken jobs in the Muslim nation have begun planting seeds of faith in friends and coworkers. The work is difficult, and the risks are great. But the Good News is advancing God's kingdom.

The Christians in Saudi Arabia fear that their names will be on the crackdown list of the religious police. Yet before their computers were confiscated and before their names were listed as targets, their names appeared on a different, more important list. The Bible teaches that there is a "Book of Life" in heaven that lists name after name of believers. Those whose names are written in the Book of Life will be saved. Those whose names are not found will be lost for eternity. If you have trusted in Jesus Christ as Savior, let your name be marked down by every form of opposition without fear. Are you listed with Christ first and foremost?

eXtreme punishment

AFGHANISTAN: FOREIGN-AID WORKERS

Day 289

The punishment that
brought us peace
was upon him.

Isaiah 53:5

The Taliban. The name of the radical Islamic government of Afghanistan is now known throughout the world. Practicing Christianity has always been a crime in this oppressive nation run by the Taliban.

The children were allegedly taught about Christianity and were subsequently arrested by the Afghan government. Foreign groups who were allowed into the nation to distribute humanitarian aid had also brought in Christian books and materials. In many nations, humanitarian aid is the only open door to the gospel. However, the government quickly seized the materials.

The government decided that the children weren't to blame for being exposed to the teaching. Their parents had failed to guide and care for them. "The arrests should be a lesson to parents that they should watch their children and know what they are doing," said the Taliban's deputy minister for the promotion of virtue and the prevention of vice.

The official's remarks came after eight foreign-aid workers were arrested in August 2001 along with numerous Afghans who had worked for Christian organizations. As of November 2001, the foreigners are being tried for preaching Jesus Christ to Muslims, a charge that could bring a death sentence. The Afghan workers face a chance to return to Islam. Yet they will be tried as apostates if they refuse. They also could face the death sentence.

At least two of the workers are American Christians, whose story of unjust punishment seems like a disaster in the making. However, what seems like a tragedy can actually turn out for God's greater purposes. Just look at Jesus' life. On the surface, Christ's death seemed to be the worst thing that could happen. His ministry appeared to be over. However, God used His unjust punishment in order to bring us salvation. In the same way, the fact that these workers are willing to endure capital punishment in order to bring others the Good News has been heard around the world, bringing many to faith in Christ and inspiring other believers. Are you suffering under unjust circumstances? That's God's specialty.

eXtreme trial

ROMANIA: SHENIA KOMAROV

The dog came forward, pulling on its leash, its wicked teeth bared. "Attack!" screamed its master, prison guard Captain Nudnii.

"Lord, have mercy!" cried out Shenia Komarov, the Christian prisoner. He knew the vicious guard dogs had killed many prisoners, and he prayed God would save him.

Day 290

The large German shepherd rushed toward him but suddenly stopped. It cowered in fear, refusing to bite the Christian. Nudnii ordered the dog forward and even beat it, but it would not attack Komarov.

The prisoners were given almost nothing to eat, and when Komarov had humbly asked for a little more food, his request had earned him Nudnii's wrath.

Days later, Komarov prayed. "Lord, I am at the end of my rope with hunger, scorn, and sorrow. Please, end everything. May I die and find rest, or else do a miracle as you did for Elijah."

Immediately, Nudnii approached rapidly—although this time without his dog. Komarov thought God had answered his prayer and that he would soon die. Instead, the leader of the guards took the Christian to the kitchen where he gave him soup and bread to eat. He also provided food to other Christian prisoners.

"Forgive me for sending the dog to attack you," Nudnii said to the Christian. "This torments me now."

Komarov forgave the guard and thanked God for His miracle.

My God sent his angel, and he shut the mouths of the lions. They have not hurt me, because I was found innocent in his sight.

Daniel 6:22

Many people can relate to the story of Daniel and the lions' den. Their roughest circumstances resemble the tortuous fate Daniel was supposed to suffer at the hands of evil. Daniel's story was a victorious one. He rose above his dire circumstances because he trusted God to save him. In the same way, we may be placed in circumstances—some even life-threatening—that are beyond our control. God can rescue us from our frightening reality and give us His peace. We must simply trust Him to deal with our "den" of problems. What intimidating situation do you face? Ask God to give you a sense of His protective presence. Trust Him to deliver you safely through your trials.

eXtreme change

INDONESIA: YOUNG CHRISTIAN GIRL

The cold water sprayed over the crowd in front of the Indonesian village mosque. Gun-toting, white-clad *jihad* warriors surrounded the place. The ritual washing was a forced preparation for the group to convert to Islam. The crowd knew that they would be ordered to convert or be shot or beheaded on the spot.

Day 291

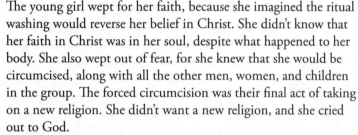

And he said: "I tell you the truth, unless you change . . . you will never enter the kingdom of heaven."

Matthew 18:3

The young girl wept for her faith, because she imagined the ritual washing would reverse her belief in Christ. She didn't know that her faith in Christ was in her soul, despite what happened to her body. She also wept out of fear, for she knew that she would be circumcised, along with all the other men, women, and children in the group. The forced circumcision was their final act of taking on a new religion. She didn't want a new religion, and she cried out to God.

Indonesia used to be a haven of tolerance. Though the nation is home to more Muslims than any other nation in the world, there was little trouble. Muslims, Christians, and Buddhists lived side-by-side, working together with little animosity.

That has changed. Radical Muslims have dragged the nation into jihad, or holy war, and every Christian is a target. Many recite the Muslim creed just to save their lives; yet in their hearts, they cry out to God, knowing only He can offer salvation.

People attempt to change us from the outside in. But only God can truly change us—from the inside out. Before we come to Christ, we often try to fit into the world's standards for our lives and lose sight of our real selves. We are forced to become people we were never meant to be. However, once God changes people from the inside out, they are changed forever. We cannot be moved. We cannot be changed back into our old selves. Like this young girl discovered, others can influence us and exercise some degree of control over us. But they cannot change us like Christ has already done. Have you experienced the "change" that the Bible teaches?

eXtreme politeness

On the road to Emmaus, the resurrected Savior walked with two disciples, talking with them about the recent events in Jerusalem. Though they did not recognize Him, He talked with them about God's plan for the Messiah. When they arrived at their town, Jesus acted as if He had to go further. Why? Didn't He want to stay and continue the conversation?

Day 292

But grow in the grace and knowledge of our Lord and Savior Jesus Christ.

2 Peter 3:18

To Piott, a Russian believer, Jesus' actions showed politeness. He didn't want to stay unless He was truly wanted. Piott had seen the Communists overrun his country. The police burst into people's homes anytime they chose. Finally, a Christian shared with Piott the story of a Savior who knocked gently at his heart, waiting to be allowed in. Piott was impressed with this gentle Jesus and willingly opened the door. Jesus became Piott's Savior and Lord.

Piott knew the meaning of conversion. He was changed. God sent him as a worker in the underground church. Here, he learned from the example of others. Growing Christians showed him how to develop his witness and exercise his faith. Soon, Piott made countless trips smuggling Christian literature into Russia. He grew more and more bold. He was driven to be not just a disciple, but a disciple maker, bringing others to Christ.

Finally, he was arrested and imprisoned. No one knows what happened to him.

Romanian pastor Richard Wurmbrand once said: "We should never stop at having won a soul for Christ. By this we have done only half the work. Every soul won for Christ must be made to be a soul winner. The Russians were not only converted, but they became 'missionaries' in the underground church. They were reckless and daring for Christ..." How does a person like Piott grow from being saved to saving others? Just as someone showed Piott how to become a Christian, someone showed him how to grow in his faith. People must be shown how to be more like Christ. Is your growing faith an example to others? God calls you to be a disciple as well as a disciple maker.

eXtreme forgiveness

TURKEY: MARTYRS' WIDOWS

It wasn't the message that the gathered reporters, with their tape recorders and video cameras, expected to hear. Three Christian men had been killed in the offices of a Christian publishing house in Malatya, Turkey. The five young men arrested for the crime said they were protecting their nation and their religion (Islam). And now, here were the two widows of the men who had been slain, standing in front of the cameras and journalists.

Day 293

But if you do not forgive men their trespasses, neither will your Father forgive your trespasses.

Matthew 6:15

The women's message wasn't one of anger or vengeance. Instead it was forgiveness. "We forgive the killers," they told the assembled press, even echoing the words of Christ on the cross: "Father, forgive them, for they do not know what they are doing."

It was broadcast on national television throughout this Muslim country, beaming a living, breathing example of the power of the gospel into countless Turkish homes. And it was effective.

A Turkish journalist—a Muslim—wrote of the widows' example: "The murderers wanted to hinder the activities of missionaries. But what these women have facilitated in a few days by their statements [of forgiveness] is something that a thousand missionaries could not have done in a thousand years."

In the face of persecution, suffering, and loss, there is no human explanation for forgiveness. It is a supernatural act that God empowers His children to accomplish. Because of that, it is an incredible witness for Christ. It makes people question themselves, their beliefs, and their god. "What would I do in that situation? Would I be able to forgive?" If the answer is no, then seek the Lord, asking Him to remind you of the great debt He paid for you on the cross. Is there someone you need to forgive today? Ask God to give you His strength to do so.

Day 294

More persecution—more growing!

FAVORITE QUOTE OF PASTOR SAMUEL LAMB,
A CHINESE HOUSE-CHURCH LEADER WHO HAS SPENT
TWENTY YEARS IN PRISON FOR HIS FAITH

eXtreme wounds

On October 24, 1931, Amy Carmichael prayed, "God, please do with me whatever You want. Do anything that will help me to serve You better." As a missionary to India and a "mother" to the many Indian children she had rescued from prostitution at pagan temples, Amy was accustomed to praying and trusting God for the outcome.

Day 295

Later that same day, she fell, dislocating an ankle and breaking her leg. Because of complications, Amy was hopelessly crippled and spent most of the next twenty years confined to her room.

But Amy didn't waste time brooding over her condition. She refocused her energies toward writing and encouraging the saints around the world. She sent thousands of letters from her bed, authored thirteen books, and wrote beautiful poetry.

> But those who suffer he delivers in their suffering; he speaks to them in their affliction.
>
> **Job 36:15**

Hast thou no wound?
No wound? No scar?
Yet, as the Master shall the servant be,
And pierced are the feet that follow Me;
But thine are whole: can he have followed far
Who has nor wound nor scar?

(From *Mountain Breezes* by Amy Carmichael.)

Amy became crippled, yet her wounds brought her closer to God. She walked in sweet fellowship with a Savior she had come to understand better because of her scar. People who have gone through a particular tragedy relate to one another and feel an instant bond. Those who come from a divorced family relate to each other in a way others cannot. The same is true of Christ. When we suffer, we begin to relate to Jesus on a whole different level. We feel He knows our hurts, and we somehow have a greater sense of His. What are your wounds teaching you about Jesus? Are you allowing them to draw you into a more intimate relationship?

eXtreme code

Alone in his underground cell, the pastor complained to God, "You say you give the sun and the rain to the good and the bad. So which is it? Am I good or bad?"

God said this to his heart: "You are something else entirely—a child of God. A child of God does not wait for sun or rain. He should be a giver of sun. You are the light in a dark world, so give light. Instead of complaining about what you don't have, why don't you give? There are so many souls around you in the other cells."

Pastor Wurmbrand prayed, "How am I supposed to bring someone to salvation when I sit alone in a cell?"

"Think it through for yourself."

Richard Wurmbrand then had an idea and tapped on the walls. Sure enough he heard return taps. He then proceeded to teach the prisoners on each side Morse code. Eventually they were able to communicate effectively, and Richard began preaching the gospel. Others in turn did the same to those next to their cells.

His new attitude allowed God to turn a seemingly hopeless situation into an effective method of spreading the gospel throughout the prison.

Years later, Richard heard someone testify that in a Romanian prison, a prisoner adjacent to his cell had won him to Christ by tapping on the wall.

Day 296

Therefore, since Christ suffered in his body, arm yourselves also with the same attitude.

1 Peter 4:1

Facing facts can be a difficult task. When Pastor Wurmbrand evaluated his situation, the facts did not look good. However, his sufferings actually led him to a new discovery. He realized that a person's attitude is more important than facts. Armed with an attitude of renewed hope, he began to reevaluate his situation. He could not speak to others. Yet he could tap in Morse code. He could even share the gospel—his true love. When we find our circumstances stacked against us, we must pay attention to our attitudes. We should be prepared for suffering, as was Christ. Yet we must determine that it will not defeat us. We will survive it. Do you pay more attention to facts? Or are you a person of faith?

eXtreme labor

Day 297

Brother Da was a faithful Communist Party member in North Vietnam when he first heard the Christian programs on his shortwave radio. At first he rejected the ideas as stupid superstition, but after two months of listening, he could no longer resist Christ. He was excited about his love for God, and it seemed to overwhelm his heart. He soon won many of his neighbors to Christ.

We continually remember before our God and Father your work produced by faith, your labor prompted by love, and your endurance inspired by hope in our Lord Jesus Christ.

1 Thessalonians 1:3

But his excitement was short-lived. On December 29, 1998, Vietnamese police, angered by Da's evangelistic activities, raided his house and led him out at gunpoint. His wife and four children could only watch as he was taken away to a prison camp.

In the crudely constructed labor camp, Da was forced to work in the brick factory. Every day meant carrying another two thousand bricks. If Da did not meet his quota, he was brutally beaten. Just when he thought he could not take the labor anymore, he was released on October 15, 2000.

Still under house arrest, Da was again ordered to stop sharing his faith. He was told, "You have just returned from labor camp. Do you want to go back? Think carefully."

But Da was committed to a "labor of love" for God, and he continued his work of sharing Christ with those around him. No physical labor—even carrying two thousand bricks a day—could deter him.

Few people would admit they love going to work every day. For some, work is a necessary evil. However, those who labor while being God's witnesses have a completely different mindset. God's work is never drudgery. Yet we are always on the clock, constantly laboring to advance the gospel everywhere. He gives us energy for the task at hand and endurance when times get tough. Why do Christians labor so hard? Is it the paycheck? Is it the bonuses, perks, or other benefits? No, love motivates us to give our all in God's service. If you love Christ, you will gladly work for Him. What has He called you to do today in His service?

eXtreme request

Day 298

When the boy in the hotel finally spotted the visiting "businessman," he ran to him and grabbed his hand. The startled visitor tried to pull away but soon realized that the boy was making the sign of the cross on his palm silently with his finger. The man, a missionary who had prayed to make contact with the church, looked down into the face of the rail-thin boy and immediately understood the message: "The church is alive in North Korea!"

And my God will meet all your needs according to his glorious riches in Christ Jesus.

Philippians 4:19

The next day, the missionary met secretly with the boy. He learned that his father was a Christian who had been imprisoned years before. The boy's family had greatly suffered under the brutal government and had to beg for food just to survive. Now because of drought, people everywhere were dying from severe malnutrition.

When the missionary asked what he could do, he thought surely the boy would request food for his family. But the boy asked him for only four things: to take his tithe that he had saved over many years, to baptize him, to give him Holy Communion, and to give him a better Bible.

The man was moved to tears as he realized the boy's wisdom. Physical help would only serve him for a day or two, and then he would be back in the same predicament. Spiritual help would prepare him for eternity.

Wanting something and needing something are two entirely different things for most people. What they want is not what they need. Yet what they need most is not what they want. This is why so many people are frustrated. The boy in this story teaches us what happens when all our wants are lined up with all our needs. He got it right. He wanted the very thing he needed most: Jesus Christ. When all you want is all you need, you will find great satisfaction. You may say you want money, but you'll soon find that money meets only so many needs. You may say you need money, but soon you'll want other things as well. Only Jesus can satisfy your wants and needs at the same time.

eXtreme stand

"I will not run away. I am ready to take a stand."

Saratu Turundu was thiry-five and unmarried. She loved kids so much and desperately wanted her own, but God had not answered her prayer.

Day 299

And he will stand, for the Lord is able to make him stand.

Romans 14:4

Saratu chose to devote herself to God and the church. She embraced her church family with her whole heart and especially loved teaching Sunday school. Her interaction with the kids and her opportunity to show them the way to Christ filled Saratu with incredible joy. She knew she could never be happy without Christ.

But the fanatical Muslims who dominated her town of Kaduna, Nigeria, started persecuting Christians. She had heard stories of Christians being persecuted in other villages, their homes and possessions burned. Some were even beaten and killed.

So when mobs came to attack the Christians in Kaduna, Saratu had already decided to stay and take a stand for Christ. Saratu's brothers begged her to flee into the woods with them. But even as she watched the angry mob burn her beloved church building to the ground, she wouldn't leave. She knelt and prayed on the floor of her apartment as Muslims doused the building with gasoline and set it on fire.

She is remembered by her family and friends as a kind, compassionate person who showed love to everyone. She died loving her Savior.

Tales of super-human strength are as inspiring as they are incredible. We are awed by stories of mothers lifting burning cars off their children in terrible accidents. Driven by adrenaline, the human body is capable of amazing feats. In the same way that adrenaline affects the human muscles, our faith can enable our spiritual muscles to accomplish what we never thought possible. Saratu flexed her spiritual muscles when she decided to take a stand for Christ in her community. She likely never realized she had the strength to do so before that moment. Yet God enabled her to do it. Have you ever done something you thought you could never do? Thank God today for His faithfulness to make you stand strong.

eXtreme revenge

"I beg you to take revenge..."

The readers of the letter from Spanish martyr Bartolome Marquez were shocked to see a call for revenge in his final letter. Then they saw that his call was not for human bloodshed to avenge him, but for more people to come under the blood of Jesus.

Day 300

"I beg you to take Christian revenge by trying to do good to those who do me evil," Marquez challenged other believers. "I hope to see you where I will be soon, in heaven."

The Spanish Communists killed Marquez, along with many other pastors, in 1939. His final letter was an epistle of joy to his wife and Christian brothers and sisters.

"In a few hours, I will know the inexpressible joys of the blessed. How easy is the death of those persecuted for Christ's sake! God gives me an undeserved privilege: to die enjoying His grace.

The God of peace will soon crush Satan under your feet.

Romans 16:20

"As long as my heart still beats," he wrote to his bride, "it will beat with love for you. When I was sentenced for defending the high ideals of religion, fatherland, and family, the doors of heaven were opened for me. In remembrance of our love, even more intense now, please consider the salvation of your soul as your supreme duty. Thus we will be united for eternity in heaven. There, nobody will separate us."

Those who suffer for Christ must have the ability to see the bigger picture. The Bible is filled with stories that teach us about individual lives. Those lives, however, fit into a greater scheme—the battle between God and evil. The bigger picture enables us to see how Satan is behind oppression and suffering; therefore, we need not take revenge upon our oppressors. They are merely pawns in Satan's plan. Christian martyrs like Marquez remind us that there is no greater revenge for Satan's attacks on Christians than when the attackers are led to Christ. Pray for leaders of oppressive governments and regimes. Support those missionaries and others who are in a position to share the gospel with them.

Day 301

The church has been and always will be persecuted. Everyone watches us. If we die in faith, hope, and love, it can change the history of nations. If we fail to stand in love and hope for our faith, nations often can reject Christ.

FROM A MISSIONARY WHO WORKS IN CHINA AND NORTH KOREA

eXtreme intervention

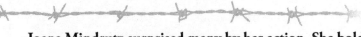

Joana Mindrutz surprised many by her action. She boldly walked up to a police officer and stated, "Six disciples of Christ from God's chosen people suffer here. I want to suffer with them." Soon she was singing with the accused who had been arrested earlier that day—a Jewish Christian pastor, his wife, and the four other imprisoned Christians.

Day 302

You gave me life and showed me kindness, and in your providence watched over my spirit.

Job 10:12

The Romanian government, since allying with Nazi Germany, had persecuted and murdered Jews at an alarming rate. But this particular Jewish Christian couple was widely known and loved throughout Romania: Pastor Richard Wurmbrand and his wife, Sabina.

The day of the trial, several renowned religious leaders came to the defense of the Wurmbrands, hoping that their intervention would free them. But suddenly the skies filled with Soviet warplanes and everyone, including the prisoners, was escorted quickly to the bomb shelters. There, Pastor Wurmbrand was able to pray aloud for the group, even the judges. His prayer was really a disguised call to faith and repentance, and when the danger passed and the trial resumed, a miracle took place. God had moved in the hearts of the judges during that crisis, and the Wurmbrands were acquitted! One judge added, "The police arrested six people, but there are seven standing before me. There is obviously a mixup. Case dismissed!"

It was, in fact, the only case at that time in which accused Jews were acquitted.

It's inexplicable. It's unbelievable. Whenever God steps into our reality, His footsteps are unmistakable. Sometimes things happen in such a way that even those who are unbelieving observers admit someone or something is watching over us. They may refer to "the Man Upstairs" looking out for us or our "guardian angel." As Christians, however, we know our heavenly Father is powerful and caring enough to do a miracle for us when we need one. Have you been privileged to witness God's intervention in your life or the life of a loved one? Spend some time today thanking God for intervening in your life.

eXtreme protection

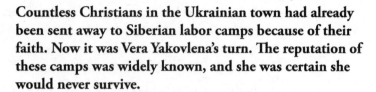

Countless Christians in the Ukrainian town had already been sent away to Siberian labor camps because of their faith. Now it was Vera Yakovlena's turn. The reputation of these camps was widely known, and she was certain she would never survive.

Day 303

For he guards the course of the just and protects the way of his faithful ones.

Proverbs 2:8

When a guard found her witnessing for Christ, her punishment was to stand barefoot for hours on the ice. When she failed to meet her work quota, she was beaten and denied the watery broth they called the evening meal.

One evening, depressed and crying, Vera walked out into the prison yard to be alone. In her misery she didn't notice that she had crossed into the forbidden zone, where prisoners are shot on sight.

Suddenly a harsh voice yelled, "Hey, is your mother a Christian?"

The stunned and frightened Vera, who had actually been thinking of her mother at the time, answered, "Why do you ask?"

The guard said, "Because I've been watching you for ten minutes, but I haven't been able to shoot you. I can't move my arm. It's a healthy arm—I have been moving it all day. So I figured you must have a mother who is praying for you. Run back—I'll look the other way."

Vera saw the guard later that day. He smiled at her and raised his arm saying, "Now I can move it again."

We like to play it safe. We like security over adventure. We prefer comfort to challenge. When it comes down to it, we want to safeguard our lives from as much doubt and fear as possible. Yet we have forgotten that God offers His protection at times when we are on the front lines in His service. God's protection is more like a shield in battle than a security blanket for our comfort at home. When is the last time you stepped out in faith so much that you simply had to rely on God's protection? Are you so busy safeguarding your life that you have forgotten how to trust God? Are you so cautious that you never take risks for God? Regardless of the outcome, witnessing is not simply a "risk." It is faith in action.

eXtreme decision

ROMANIA: RICHARD AND SABINA WURMBRAND

It wasn't too late to flee the country; thousands were still able to buy their way out. The pastor and his wife struggled with the decision to go or stay. "If we go to prison, it could be for years. What about our son?"

Day 304

For whoever wants to save his life will lose it, but whoever loses his life for me and for the gospel will save it.

Mark 8:35

But they did not want to leave their church. The members looked to them for strength and support, and the couple felt guilty for being tempted to leave. A friend reminded them of the angel's words to Lot, "Escape for thy life; look not behind thee."

The pastor wondered, "Was that a message from God? Should we escape for our lives?"

His wife read another verse. "For whoever wants to save his life will lose it, but whoever loses his life for me and for the gospel will save it" (Mark 8:35).

So the debate continued until one night at a secret house-church meeting, where fifty believers had gathered for an all-night vigil. Around midnight, a woman kneeling with the rest cried out, "And you, the one who is thinking of leaving—remember that the Good Shepherd did not desert his flock. He stayed to the end."

This dear woman knew nothing about the struggle of the pastor and his wife, but to them the message was clear. They stayed and chose to serve their flock, and later suffered with them in prison.

Like the Wurmbrands, we must pray about our decisions, search the Bible, and listen to others' counsel. And, like the Wurmbrands, we must be committed to obeying God's answer before we receive it. That is the key. It is as if we begin our prayers with a firm "Yes" before we even ask what we should do. We must be willing to let go of our own lives and lose all sense of ownership. Only then can we find our true life and accept God's full will for our lives. Do you often keep such a tight grip on your life that if God wanted to change your mind about a certain decision, you wouldn't allow Him to do it anyway?

eXtreme birthday parties

RUSSIA: BELIEVERS

"Is it my birthday today, or yours?" the young Christian asked, a twinkle in her eye.

Day 305

And the God of all grace, who called you to his eternal glory in Christ, after you have suffered a little while, will himself restore you and make you strong, firm and steadfast.

1 Peter 5:10

"Yours today," said her father. "Mine was last week." For Christians in Communist nations, birthdays were a great excuse to get together with other believers. Some families would gather each week for a birthday party that was really an underground church service.

Young people used these "parties" to strengthen their commitment to the gospel. In 1966 in Russia, three young boys and four girls were arrested for singing a hymn on a train.

In court, the seven young people fell to their knees. "We surrender ourselves into the hands of God," they said in front of the judge and the gathered witnesses. "We thank You, Lord, that You have allowed us to suffer for this faith."

After their confession, other Christians in the courtroom began to sing the very hymn for which the kids had been arrested. They said, "Let us dedicate our youth to Christ."

The Communists couldn't stop the church from meeting and growing. One Russian newspaper told of a pastor who had been sent to prison three times. Each time he was released, he immediately went and held Sunday school meetings.

These believers used whatever means possible to express their loyalty to God. They risked their lives and suffered the condemnation of their country in service to God's church.

In order for our physical muscles to get stronger, they must first be broken down and stretched through exercise and hard work. Likewise, faith is a muscle that grows only when it is flexed. Suffering flexes the muscle of our faith. We are stretched and "broken" before God during times of trials. Yet we grow stronger as a result. Churches in restricted nations exhibit enormous strength because of their sufferings. Can the same be said of our faith in America? Exercise wears us out—we don't want to do it. Similarly, the thought of suffering may disturb you. However, you cannot grow if you don't flex your faith.

eXtreme manifestation

RUSSIA: AN UNNAMED PRISONER

Day 306

Be imitators of God.

Ephesians 5:1

The widow stood near the body of her martyred husband, holding the hands of two of her four children. Her husband had died in prison, and the marks on his body made it clear that death had come slowly and painfully.

The other believers knew this could be their fate too, yet hundreds came to his funeral. He had died for his faith only three months after his conversion, and now they mourned him.

The people crowded around the house where the funeral was being held, and many were inspired by his example. Eighty individuals publicly confessed their faith in Christ that day, including many young people who had been part of the Communist Youth Organization.

The Christians walked the length of the city to the river, where they baptized the new believers. The crowd had now grown to over fifteen hundred people.

Soon, carloads of police arrived. They set out to arrest the leaders of the service, since they couldn't arrest everyone there. The Christians immediately knelt in prayer, asking God to allow them to finish the service. Then they stood, shoulder to shoulder, blocking the police from coming forward as the baptism service went on. The crowd dispersed only after all the new believers had been baptized, allowing the police to come forward.

One thousand people were inspired by the sacrificial example of one new believer.

manifestation *n. plainness, visibility; demonstration; display, prominence. The meaning of the word is clear. Yet is the manifestation of our faith just as obvious? The man in this story imitated Jesus. Plain and simple. As a result of his clear example, a host of others were compelled to follow suit in their own manifestation of faith. So, too, our lives ought to plainly display our own faith in Christ for all to see. Would others know how to follow Christ simply by watching your example? Better yet, would they be compelled to imitate your faith? Be careful that you do not muddle the manifestation of your faith with confusing rhetoric or other religious distractions. Simply be like Jesus, and others will follow.*

eXtreme verses

"Bible verses remain true, even if the devil quotes them."

Day 307

How sweet are your words to my taste, sweeter than honey to my mouth!

Psalm 119:103

Originally, the idea was to ridicule the Christian Bible, to make such a mockery of it that no self-respecting person would believe it. To carry out the plan, millions of books were printed, including *The Comical Bible* and *The Bible for Believers and Unbelievers*.

The books made fun of Jesus, called into question His miracles, and ridiculed other aspects of the Christian faith. But the criticisms were so outrageous that no one took them seriously. Countless verses of Scripture were inserted into the text as "proof" in the Communists' minds of the fallacy of the book.

Members of the underground church snatched up copies of these "comic" books as fast as they were printed. The verses that were quoted in the books were a smorgasbord of delights to those who were spiritually famished. And all of it was legal, printed by their own God-hating government. Just as the ravens fed Elijah when he was hungry, so God used government printing houses to feed His starving children in Communist nations.

The publishers were delighted to receive thousands of letters asking for reprints of the books. They quickly rolled the presses to print more copies. Little did they know those letters came from believers who wished to distribute the precious books full of God's words to other underground church members.

Is it that important to send Bibles into restricted nations? Read the stories of the martyrs and decide. In a nation where Bibles are sold at garage sales for a quarter, we cannot really appreciate the experience of those in a spiritual famine. While we might stack Bibles on the coffee table for display, other believers clamor for a single copy to share among an entire church. Is it fair for the over-churched nations to have multiple Bibles in nearly every household while a restricted nation has none? God, revive our own hunger for Scripture and for getting the Word out to those who are already starving! Consider how you might help support Bible distribution in restricted nations today.

Day 308

Friendship with Jesus is costly.
Faith alone saves, but saving faith is never
alone. It is always accompanied by
great sacrifices for Christ's sake.

PASTOR RICHARD WURMBRAND

eXtreme testimony

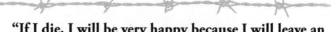

"If I die, I will be very happy because I will leave an example for other Christians to follow in my wake."

Kuwa Bashir, a Sudanese youth pastor, was busy studying for the next Bible class when he heard the terrible but not unexpected news. The year was 1987, and the government of Sudan Muslim forces had just captured the area of the Blue Nile in Sudan.

Day 309

However, if you suffer as a Christian, do not be ashamed, but praise God that you bear that name.

1 Peter 4:16

Muslim forces soon arrested Bashir, determined to convert everyone to Islam. Bashir was beaten and tortured for seven days before being released, but he refused to convert. They told him never to organize youth activities or attend church again, but Bashir refused to be intimidated. He knew the Islamic forces were unable to touch his soul.

When he was arrested for the second time, Bashir testified, "I will gladly die without fear like Jesus did on the cross." He continued to speak to his captors about God, and the officer in charge threatened to have him shot. Instead, they decided to pour acid on Bashir's hands as a constant reminder of his refusal to convert to Islam.

But Bashir's faith has remained strong, and today his burned, useless hands have become a living testimony to the youth in the Bonga refugee camp, where he works along the Sudanese-Ethiopian border.

The message that the martyrs speak through their dramatic deaths is one we must share through our everyday lives. We must be a living testimony of the grace of God. We may never join the ranks of the martyrs, dying for our faith in Christ. However, we have daily opportunities to live for Him. It has been said, "That which does not kill us makes us stronger." We survive sufferings so that we can live on to tell others about God's grace. Has your life been scarred by sufferings? Don't be ashamed. Let your scars be your testimony. Let them tell your story to all who see your unwavering faith.

eXtreme opportunity

Though the Soviet invaders were terrorizing their country, the Romanian children walked steadily toward the Russian soldiers with warm, confident smiles on their faces.

The soldiers greeted them kindly, patting them on the head. Each soldier was thinking of his own children, whom they had been forced to leave behind in Russia.

Day 310

"Have some candy," said one of the officers, holding out a handful of chocolate to the youngsters, who eagerly grabbed the hard-to-find treats.

"Thank you, sir," the boys said. "We have gifts for you as well." They dug into their pockets, pulling out gospel tracts and New Testaments in Russian.

"What is this?" the soldiers asked.

"It is a book of Good News," the boys said through mouths full of chocolate. The soldiers thumbed through the tracts. One officer recognized the booklets as being religious and knew the dangers. He looked down at the children with deep concern in his eyes. If adults had handed out the material, he would have to arrest them. *But what harm could these children do?* he thought.

Ask and it will be given to you; seek and you will find; knock and the door will be opened to you.

Matthew 7:7

What the officer didn't know was that these children had passed out hundreds of tracts and New Testaments, helping many in the Russian army to find God. These children were enlisted into another "army" with an eternal "battle."

Where adults could not safely minister, children walked through a wide-open door with the gospel.

The difference between a pessimist and an optimist is the difference between "can't" and "can." Certainly, believers in both religiously restricted nations and countries with religious freedom encounter closed doors. In some countries, possessing a Bible means a jail sentence. In America, the "separation of church and state" is often taken to extremes. Sometimes our focus on what we are not supposed to do as Christians makes us miss God's opportunities. We see the closed doors more readily than we see the open ones. For example, while missionaries cannot enter restricted nations as such, "professional" workers are recruited. We can also support national Christian workers who live there. The door is open. Walk through it.

eXtreme commitment

SUDAN: SCHOOL CHILDREN

Seated on logs under the shade of a tree, the 230 Christian students were just beginning their English lesson when they heard the terrifying sounds overhead. A plane roared across the sky above the schoolyard. Within minutes, the Islamic army had dropped five bombs from a large Russian-made bomber.

Day 311

Simon Peter answered him, "Lord, to whom shall we go? You have the words of eternal life."

John 6:68

Terrified and screaming, the children immediately started running. Two of the bombs landed in dry trenches around the village, and another failed to detonate.

Unfortunately, the other two nail-studded bombs landed squarely among the frightened students. The explosion was tremendous. The damage, unthinkable.

By 9:15 a.m. the bomber was gone, and the horrible reality began to set in. Students wandered dazed around the schoolyard, crying and bleeding. Twelve of their classmates, ranging in age from nine to sixteen, had not survived the blast. Their beloved young teacher, Roda Ismail, also lay dead among the rubble.

Another seven students lost their battle for survival in the days following the attack, and three had to have limbs amputated.

The very next day, children showed up for school as usual. The exhausted and despondent schoolmaster told them to go home. "I cannot tell you when or if we will resume classes."

A ten-year-old boy approached him and said, "Please let us continue. We want to learn, and if it is God's will, then today we won't die."

Life at the crossroads. We've all been there, wavering between giving up and going on. Like the schoolboy, the crowds who were following Jesus one day realized the path they were on was fraught with danger. Like the despondent schoolmaster, many in the crowd headed for home, not able to say if or when they would continue to follow Christ. Yet Peter and the other disciples remained. The schoolboy's solemn request echoes Peter's response: let us continue. When we are tempted to give up, let us continue. When it seems like following Christ is too difficult, let us continue. Are you facing the crossroads of commitment? Ask God to give you the strength to go on instead of give up.

eXtreme survivor

As he slowly came around, his eyes adjusted to the smoke. He cried out for his pastor, but no one answered. Horrified, he quickly began digging his way out of the pile of flesh and rubble.

Day 312

Here is a trustworthy saying that deserves full acceptance: Christ Jesus came into the world to save sinners.

1 Timothy 1:15

That morning, he had been among a group of 190 North Korean believers when the police stormed in, rounded them up, and harshly marched them to the town center.

Their nation's leader, Kim Il Sung, stood before them. The heartless dictator walked to the center of the square and drew a line in the dirt, ordering those who wanted to live to deny Christ and cross the line.

Not one stepped forward. Infuriated, Kim Il Sung ordered the group thrown into a mining tunnel with sticks of dynamite.

The last thing the surviving believer remembered was his pastor, consoling and encouraging the group. Realizing he was the lone survivor, he cried, "Why God? Why didn't You let me die with the others?"

God immediately filled his heart with peace, and he knew that someone must remain and be a witness to their faith. This was the first of many brutal attacks by Kim Il Sung's form of communism and worship, called *Juche*. News of the heroic event spread rapidly among the Christians and is still told today in North Korea.

Like the believer in this story, the firefighters who survived the terrorist attack on the World Trade Center are not silent witnesses. Though they cannot explain why they survived and their comrades did not, they are outspoken patriots who know that someone must remain to tell the stories of those who died saving others so that they could live. As a Christian, you have an even greater survivor story to tell. Jesus did not survive the cross. He conquered it. He did not merely survive His ordeal; He triumphed. He returned in His resurrected body to deliver the news to His disciples who would soon tell the world. Jesus died saving others so that they could live. Yet He is now alive, back from the dead, offering salvation to the world.

eXtreme daughter

"Munira, you have five minutes before I kill you. Whom do you choose: your family or Jesus?"

For months, Munira had tried to keep her faith a secret; she loved her family so much and had no desire to hurt them. But when her father made arrangements for Munira to marry, she told them of her love for Christ.

Day 313

Munira was down to her last ounce of faith. She answered her father, "I must choose Jesus." He was so enraged that his beautiful daughter would turn against the family by denying her Islamic upbringing in Tajikistan that he beat her for another two hours.

But God intervened. A Christian friend took her to safety for a period of time. Munira said, "During my time away, God revealed His faithfulness to me, and after much prayer, I knew it was time to reconcile with my beloved family."

Therefore do not worry about tomorrow, for tomorrow will worry about itself. Each day has enough trouble of its own.

Matthew 6:34

When she returned home, everyone was happy except her father. His first words were, "I hate you! Get out! My daughter died three months ago!"

Devastated, Munira wept at her father's feet saying, "My God told me to come back to you. I will never leave you, even if you beat and kill me."

Her father broke down and hugged Munira. He soon resigned himself to her new faith and even agreed to let her attend Bible College.

Some readers get so caught up in a story that they read ahead to see what will happen. They skip one chapter ahead or maybe turn to the back of the book. They simply must know if the hero wins out in the end. They need to see if everything will work out as planned. Unfortunately, you can't read ahead in your life's story. Like Munira, you must take it one chapter, one day at a time. Like her, you will not be disappointed in the results. Are you anxious to see where your obedience will lead? Do you want to find out what God has planned for you next? The best you can do is obey today and leave tomorrow to God.

eXtreme companion

EGYPT: ORIGEN

"They have burned our possessions, but they cannot burn Jesus from our hearts."

Origen was not the typical eighteen-year-old. He was a teacher in second-century Egypt. As the church of his day suffered severe persecution, Origen did not spend his time chasing girls or trying to impress his peers.

Day 314

I, John, your brother and companion in the suffering and kingdom and patient endurance that are ours in Jesus.

Revelation 1:9

Instead of running from the horror that had killed even his own father, Origen chose to become a companion with the persecuted church. He spent his time encouraging Christians who had been brought before the court. When they were led to death, he walked up to kiss them. He even visited the prisons to comfort the believers.

But Origen soon found himself in grave danger for his compassion toward the condemned believers. Soon soldiers were posted around his house because of his influence on the church. He had many enemies, and the anger toward him grew hotter each day.

He was eventually forced to leave the city. He moved from house to house because of the many threats against his life. But spurred on by the examples of faith in Hebrews, he continued being a companion to those who were persecuted. He even employed several people to handwrite additional copies of the Scriptures.

Eventually, his amazing attitude drew some of his enemies to Christ. However, he was eventually imprisoned, tortured, and killed for this same attitude.

What does it mean to be a companion to those who are persecuted? People are not necessarily companions because they are going through the exact same sufferings. We may be in entirely different situations from our brothers and sisters in restricted nations, yet we can still be their companions. Physical distance does not make us soul mates. Personal devotion does. Unwavering support, prayer, and concern link our hearts and lives together. Like Origen, are we willing to align ourselves with those who are suffering for the gospel? We can neither be ashamed of our friendships nor ignorant of the ensuing risks. When we hear the voice of the martyrs calling to us in our prayers, will we heed their cries as true companions?

Day 315

With Him, my beloved Master, it is good everywhere. With Him I have light in the dark dungeon. I had asked Him to be where I am needed, not where it is better for the outward man, but where I can bear fruit. This is my calling.

RUSSIAN PASTOR P. RUMATCHIK, FROM A LETTER WRITTEN WHEN HE WAS IMPRISONED FOR THE FIFTH TIME

eXtreme advocate

GERMANY: DIETRICH BONHOEFFER

When fourteen-year-old Dietrich Bonhoeffer announced his desire to be a minister, his wealthy family criticized the church. Dietrich told them that he would reform it.

At the age of twenty-one, his dissertation, *The Communion of Saints*, was praised as a "theological miracle." As an ordained minister, theology professor, and author, Bonhoeffer spent his life probing the issues of the church.

Day 316

All men will hate you because of me. But not a hair of your head will perish. By standing firm you will gain life.

Luke 21:17–19

When Adolf Hitler rose to power in Germany in 1933, the church adopted one of Hitler's clauses denying the right of the church to ordain ministers of Jewish heritage. Only Bonhoeffer openly spoke out against the decision and pledged to get it repealed.

Through lectures and published articles, Bonhoeffer opposed the evil Nazis and reproved the church for not having "raised its voice on behalf of the victims and . . . found ways to hasten to their aid."

In April 1943, Bonhoeffer was arrested in Berlin for "subversion of the armed forces." But while in prison, he continued to write. "The church was silent when it should have cried out."

In 1945, Bonhoeffer was moved to the Flossenburg concentration camp where he was hung with six others on April 9. The camp doctor who had watched him kneel and pray before being led to the gallows stated that he had "hardly ever seen a man die so entirely submissive to the will of God."

It has been said that if we do not stand for something, we are sure to fall for anything. Such was the case in Nazi Germany. The church in a Christian nation remained silent while wave upon wave of evil crashed against history's shore, deafening Bonhoeffer's lone cry. Can we say we are advocates for the truth if we remain silent on these kinds of issues? Does our silence on these issues signal our consent to the atrocities in restricted nations? An advocate for the truth must be straightforward in the faith. Like Bonhoeffer, we must be willing to endure the consequences of our stance. Otherwise, we risk the danger of "falling for anything" while we are busy deciding whether or not to stand up for Christ.

eXtreme weapon

ROMANIA: SABINA WURMBRAND

At 5:00 a.m. they heard pounding on the door and immediately knew it was a police raid. Sabina's husband was already in prison, and she worried about the fate of her young son if she were taken away, too. So when the Romanian police burst in early that morning, shouting and intimidating her houseguests, Sabina quietly prayed and committed herself and her family to God's care.

Day 317

Take the helmet of salvation and the sword of the Spirit, which is the word of God.

Ephesians 6:17

They demanded, "Sabina Wurmbrand? We know you are hiding weapons in here. Tell us where they are!" Before she could argue, they were throwing open trunks and closets, and emptying drawers on the floor. They kept shouting, "So, you won't show us where the weapons are hidden? We'll tear this place apart!"

Sabina, struggling to remain calm, said simply, "The only weapon we have in this house is here," and picked up the Bible from under their feet.

The officer replied, "If you don't tell me the truth, you will have to come with us to make a full statement about those weapons."

Sabina laid the Bible on the table and responded, "Please allow us a few minutes to pray, and then I will go with you."

As Sabina was led away, she mourned the loss of her "weapon," her Bible, but gained strength from knowing that she had hidden its words in her heart, where they could not be confiscated.

There is only one offensive weapon listed in the description of what is commonly referred to as the armor of God. In Ephesians, Paul lists defensive measures in a Christian's faith, represented by a helmet, a breastplate, a belt, a shield, and protective shoes. However, he lists only one offensive weapon: the Word of God. It is the weapon of choice. As an ancient soldier would depend on his sword, so we must depend on the sharp edge of Scripture to clear a path for our safety. Sadly, too many Christians are left defenseless in a spiritual struggle. They have not memorized the Bible like Sabina; they are unable to draw upon its strength. Don't be another spiritual casualty. Take up your sword today.

eXtreme forgiveness

ROMANIA: DIANA AND FLOAREA

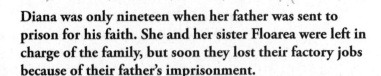

Diana was only nineteen when her father was sent to prison for his faith. She and her sister Floarea were left in charge of the family, but soon they lost their factory jobs because of their father's imprisonment.

Day 318

Godly sorrow brings repentance that leads to salvation and leaves no regret, but worldly sorrow brings death.

2 Corinthians 7:10

With a sick mother and four younger siblings at home, Diana and Floarea were desperate. So when a young man called them and said he could get Diana a work permit, they were ecstatic. She met him for dinner, where he gave her plenty of wine and then seduced her. Afterward, he gave her some money, and this became a pattern. Nothing more was said about a work permit, and Diana accepted the money because she was so desperate.

Diana continued to prostitute herself in order to support the family, although she was filled with guilt. Soon her sister became involved, and together they hid their shame.

Now, as they looked into the face of their mother and confessed what they had done, they said, "How can you forgive us? We thought you would be disgusted."

She offered them words of love and comfort: "You feel shame over what you have done, and so you should. But this sense of shame and guilt will lead you to a shining righteousness. Remember, the soldiers not so much pierced Christ's side as 'opened' it, that sinners might easily enter His heart and find forgiveness."

Being sorry for our sin and feeling sorry for ourselves are two different things. Many people who go through suffering feel sorry for themselves. They are all too eager to blame others for their misfortune. How tempting it would have been for the girls in this story to blame their mistakes on their father. "If he was not a Christian, then he would not have been arrested, and we would not be in this mess." Yet they came to their mother with true shame and repentance for their willful disobedience. And they found forgiveness—not just from their mother but also from God. Godly sorrow leads to repentance, which leads to forgiveness. Are you feeling sorry for yourself in your sufferings? Watch out! It can quickly lead you to disobedience.

eXtreme lift

He was the most wanted criminal in all of Saudi Arabia. He was not wanted for robbery, or murder, or rape. He was wanted for being a Christian pastor and for leading a large secret church in the Saudi Arabian capital city.

Day 319

For he will command his angels . . . they will lift you up in their hands, so that you will not strike your foot against a stone.

Psalm 91:11,12

Without being charged, Pastor Wally, a Filipino worker, was taken from his home and brought to a room with three men. There he was slapped, kicked, and punched. The most painful abuse was the lashes on the bottoms of his feet. When the lashing was done, his hands and feet were as purple as eggplant.

In the midst of that pain, the torturers ordered Wally to stand. "I cannot," he told them. Every square inch of his feet hurt, and there was no way to support his weight. "Please just allow me to kneel." The torturers refused.

While the three men beat him, Pastor Wally prayed for them. His prayers reminded him of a verse. "For he will command his angels . . . they will lift you up in their hands, so that you will not strike your foot against a stone" (Psalm 91:11,12). In spite of his feet, Wally stood straight up among the men. They were shocked that he could stand after such a beating.

"I was standing on the hands of God's angels," Pastor Wally later said. "They could not see angels, but I felt that they were there to help me stand."

Some people seem to send their guardian angels into overtime. Like Pastor Wally, they are constantly on the edge for Christ with a prayerful witness and a daring spirit. Still, we might imagine that some guardian angels have time on their hands, assigned to Christians who do nothing to further the kingdom. While Pastor Wally's situation was unique, his prayer should not be. Sometimes we must stand on the hands of God's angels in order to be faithful to Christ. Do we exude that type of fervent desire in our workplace? Our homes? Our school? Wherever you find it difficult to take a stand for Christ today, ask God to send His angels to give you a lift.

eXtreme guidance

**"He said to me, 'Come over to Macedonia and help us,'"
Paul said.**

Silas asked, "You believe it was a godly dream then?"

"I do."

Silas smiled and replied, "Then we are going to Macedonia with godspeed!"

Day 320

Guide me in your truth and teach me, for you are God my Savior, and my hope is in you all day long.

Psalm 25:5

When they got to Philippi, an important merchant woman was converted, and a young girl was delivered of a demon. Surely the men had heard God correctly, and they were following His lead.

"There they are!" the man at the head of the mob screamed. Before Paul and Silas knew what was happening, they were dragged before the city judges and accused of disturbing the peace with their gospel message. The chief magistrate tore their robes from them and ordered them to be beaten with rods and thrown into prison.

That night, bloodied and bruised, with their feet in stocks, Paul and Silas had every right to feel as though God had misled them. But the question, "How could God let this happen to us?" never came up. Instead, at midnight, they were still singing and praising God. They trusted God's guidance. They knew He had not abandoned them, as their miraculous rescue would soon attest.

Silas and Paul continued to follow God's guidance in their travels together. Eventually, Silas became the head of the church in Corinth. Both men followed God's lead, and both men became martyrs for the faith.

If only God's will for our lives would come to us in a dream! If only His plans were clearly laid out before us like a billboard. Better yet, to have a voice telling us exactly what to do! However nice that would seem, such direct methods would rule out the element of faith altogether. God wants us to rely on Him as a map when we are determining our life's direction. Paul and Silas didn't know what would happen to them in Philippi. They only knew that God had said to go. You may not know where God is taking you, but are you willing to follow anyway? You will not go unless you trust Him completely.

eXtreme healing

"Lord, anything can happen here tonight," Pastor Wally prayed. "But please, don't allow them to take my life."

Day 321

For we are the temple of the living God.

2 Corinthians 6:16

As he was being beaten, Pastor Wally prayed for his Saudi torturers. In the midst of his prayers, he was reminded of verses that say that our bodies are the temple of the Holy Spirit.

"Thank You for allowing me to be Your temple," Wally prayed. "I believe that You don't want a temple that is ruined and abused by the enemy, God. You want a temple that is glorified and full of Your splendor. I am claiming a complete restoration of my body, Lord. No matter what these torturers do, I pray that You will be glorified all the more when I am completely healed. People will not see a trace of what these torturers did to my body."

Pastor Wally's back and legs were beaten with a cane, and his hands and feet were bruised almost beyond use. Finally, they returned him to his cell when they were too tired to continue torturing this Christian.

Wally prayed for hours and then fell into a fitful sleep during which he sensed God's presence and healing touch. When he awoke, his hands and feet were healed. He felt no pain from the beatings. Wally was overwhelmed, for God had healed him.

Did Pastor Wally go too far when he prayed in faith for his healing? Did he take advantage of Scripture in his brazen request? The evidence would seem to suggest that Wally did none of these things. In fact, Pastor Wally simply took God at His Word. Many Christians would benefit by doing more of the same. Yet we cannot take God at His Word if we do not know it. Pastor Wally was able to recall encouraging verses in the time of need because he had spent time in Scripture. Many faithful Christians who are beaten are not instantly healed, but God uses our testimonies whether we are healed or not. Are you able to recall God's Word when necessary? Do you know more about Scripture than you know of the actual Scriptures? Tell God that you are ready to take him at His Word.

I meditate here on the words of Jesus: "that whoever believes in him shall ... have eternal life." (John 3:16)

Day 322

I am among criminals. It is an understatement that men can become like animals. Animals are without sin. But the men surrounding me in jail reach depths of devilish darkness unreachable for animals.

It would be easier to live in a stable than among these criminals. Every word of theirs is filthy, every gesture repugnant. "Their throats are open graves ... Their mouths are full of cursing and bitterness."
(Romans 3:13,14)

But against this background shines the extraordinary love of God. For it is true that whosoever believes—even men like these—can have eternal life. God sent me to prison to bring them this Good News.

A LETTER FROM A RUSSIAN CHRISTIAN PRISONER

eXtreme vacation

IRAN: A PASTOR'S WIFE

"Now, we are on vacation, honey," the Iranian pastor said to his wife. "Please, don't do anything that will make the police question us. Let's not ruin this time together."

The pastor's wife was a walking witness for Jesus Christ. She had handed out thousands of Bibles to Muslims in Iran and over five thousand copies of the *JESUS* film.

Day 323

Preach the Word; be prepared in season and out of season.

2 Timothy 4:2

At the seaside city where they were vacationing, they went to the mall. They separated to look for the different things they wanted, and when the pastor returned, he found his wife telling a large group of people in the store about Jesus Christ.

Looking around for secret police, he quickly ushered his wife out of the store and into their car. "Honey, we are on *vacation*. I thought we weren't going to do that here."

She looked him in the eye. "There are many people back in that store who don't know Jesus," she said seriously. "If they die and go to hell, you are responsible."

The chastened pastor turned the car around and drove back to the mall. Quickly his wife went back inside, handing out copies of Scripture and the *JESUS* film.

One lady came forward. "Oh, thank you so much," she said tearfully. "For five years I have been praying for a Bible, and now the Lord has answered my prayer."

Vacations make great memories. Walks on the beach. Shopping in the city. Reading by the fire. Yet as much as we need a break from our everyday routine, we are never really entitled to take a break from our witness. In fact, our witness ought to be so much a part of our personalities that we can't separate the two. The apostle Paul never went anywhere as a "tourist." For people like the pastor's wife in this story, it's not something they can turn off and on like a light switch. Their bold witness is simply who they are, and it comes out naturally in season and out of season. The unnatural thing is a compartmental-ized faith—it comes across as fake. Instead, let your faith grow freely in your everyday experiences.

eXtreme answer

NORTH AFRICA: A NEW BELIEVER

"Why do you continue these meetings?" the secret police-man asked the Christian. "Do you think your neighbors wouldn't report you to us?"

The young man was a new Christian, but already he had led twenty others to Christ. They were praying that God would provide them a place to gather and worship together.

Day 324

For three weeks, the North African Christians met in an apartment—an illegal gathering that could lead to their arrest. Their praise and singing alerted the neighbors, who reported them to the secret police. Three times the young Christian had been hauled in for questioning.

"Do you speak against Islam?" demanded the officer during the third interrogation.

"No," the Christian answered. "We have nothing to do with Islam. We worship Jesus."

"Do you speak against our leaders?"

"No, sir. We pray for our leaders, just as Jesus told us to."

"Why don't you find another place to meet? Then your neighbors will stop reporting you."

"How can we, sir? We don't have the proper permission."

The officer reached into his desk and took out a form. He wrote for several minutes and handed the form to the Christian. It granted the Christians the right to meet together in a church building that was no longer being used. A beautiful building and government permission to meet there—it was an answer to their prayers.

I call on you, O God, for you will answer me.

Psalm 17:6

There is no such thing as an unanswered prayer. God always answers each of our prayers. Yet He may not answer in the way we prayed He would. Sometimes the answer is "slow." We must wait on His timing in order to move ahead. Sometimes His answer is for us to "grow." Our request is right on target, but we still have some growing to do in order to move ahead. Other times we are disappointed to hear His answer is "no." Our request is not in line with His will, or the timing is not right. And still other times, the answer is "go." Our request is on target. We are spiritually prepared, and the timing is right. What is God's answer to your prayer right now?

eXtreme worth

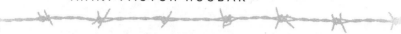

It was after midnight, and the prisoner was tired. He was in the midst of twenty-eight days in solitary confinement in the Iranian prison, praying that God would help him endure. When the knock came on his cell door, he was tired and irritated.

Day 325

Those who oppose him he must gently instruct, in the hope that God will grant them repentance leading them to a knowledge of the truth.

2 Timothy 2:25

"Pastor," said the guard, "I want to talk with you about Jesus."

"Go away," groaned the pastor. "I don't want to speak with you."

"But you have to speak to me," said the guard. "You are a pastor."

The young Iranian guard had many questions. He wanted to know the difference between Christianity and Islam, between the burdensome demands of Allah and the loving call of a heavenly Father.

For four hours the two men talked, and the pastor explained the Christian faith, salvation from sin through Jesus' death on the cross, and how he could receive Christ into his life.

At 4:30 the next morning, the two men prayed together. With tears streaming down his cheeks, the guard placed his trust in Christ. With tears in his own eyes, the pastor welcomed him into God's kingdom.

As the guard entered into a new life, the pastor felt a change in his own heart. "For the first time," he said later, "all the bitterness was gone." He felt only love for his captors and for the Muslims in his homeland. His ministry increased greatly after that moment.

Furniture that is passed down from generation to generation makes up in sentiment what it lacks in beauty. A particular chair that belonged to your grandparents carries special memories that blind you to the stains and spots and other signs of wear and tear. A scuffed and scarred cedar wardrobe once kept by a beloved relative is a treasure of immeasurable worth. In the same way, God can give us a special love for the unlovely. He can help us see worth in the worthless. His love can overshadow another person's faults—just as it does with your own sins. Try it and see. Ask God to help you love the unlovable by seeing others through His eyes.

eXtreme missionary

One by one the arrows struck his flesh, and one by one Stanley Albert Dale pulled them out and broke the cane shafts over his knee. The blood flowed from his many wounds and onto the riverbank. The screaming Yali warriors feared that the white man, or *duong*, was immortal.

Day 326

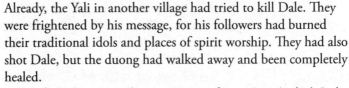

He has also set
eternity in the hearts
of men.

Ecclesiastes 3:11

Already, the Yali in another village had tried to kill Dale. They were frightened by his message, for his followers had burned their traditional idols and places of spirit worship. They had also shot Dale, but the duong had walked away and been completely healed.

Dale had come to the mountains of Irian Jaya (today's Indonesia) in the 1960s to share Christ's love. Now facing hundreds of screaming warriors, he pulled arrows out of his body as fast as they pierced his skin.

These Yali had been warned that the Spirit inside him was very powerful. Finally, Dale and the other missionary fell. More than sixty broken arrows were piled at Dale's feet. The warriors then dismembered his body parts for fear that he would rise again.

The Yali thought that would be the end of the gospel message in their valley, but it was not. Other Christians came, and many of the same warriors who had fired arrows into Dale's body became believers. The duong who would not die now celebrates Jesus alongside his own converted murderers.

Although the Yali thought Dale's earthly body was immortal, it was actually his soul that would not die. The missionaries who followed in Dale's wake helped the Yali understand eternity. They shared God with the Yali. Think for a moment about what events, people, and tasks took the bulk of your time this past week. Certainly, the practicalities of life call us to deal with things that are hardly eternal issues: dirty diapers, ringing phones, dry cleaning, and soccer practice. However, Dale's story reminds us to prioritize things that matter for eternity. What part of your daily life does have eternal significance? If you don't make time for it, who will?

eXtreme poem

RUSSIA: ALEXANDER ZATSEPA

When Alexander Zatsepa, a Russian soldier in the Communist army, was killed in action, this poem was found in his clothing:

Hear me, O God; never in the whole of my lifetime have I spoken to You.

But just now I feel like sending You my greetings.

You know from childhood on they've always told me You are not.

I, like a fool, believed them.

I've never contemplated Your creation. And yet, tonight, gazing up out of my shell hole, I marveled at the shimmering stars above me and suddenly knew the cruelty of the lie.

Will You, my God, reach Your hand out to me, I wonder?

But I will tell You and You will understand.

Is it not strange that light should come upon me and I see You amid this night of hell? . . .

Although I have not been a friend to You before,

Still, will You let me enter now, when I do come?

Why, I am crying! O God, my Lord, You see what happens to me.

Tonight my eyes were opened.

Farewell, my God. I'm going and not likely to come back.

Strange, is it not? But death I fear no longer.

Day 327

He is patient with you, not wanting anyone to perish, but everyone to come to repentance.

2 Peter 3:9

Martyrs teach us about God's faithfulness, His peace, His love, and His protection. However, the stories of the martyrs are not only about the martyrs themselves, but also about their enemies. Those who converted from communism to Christianity tell another side of the story. They reveal God's patience, His grace, His willingness to forgive even the worst sinner who asks for His forgiveness. Alexander's poem gives voice to the plea of any repentant sinner whose "eyes are opened" to the truth. His story reminds us that we serve a loving God who longs for us to realize who Jesus is and to come to Him for salvation. This is the mighty message of the martyrs. Is it yours?

eXtreme danger

People came many miles, seeking help and medicine from Eve Barendsen and her husband, Erick. Their meager home in Kabul, Afghanistan, became a place of hope for thousands of Afghans—Muslims and Christians alike. They told any who asked that they were there serving Jesus Christ. However, their mission made them a target for the opposition.

Day 328

We have come to share in Christ if we hold firmly till the end the confidence we had at first.

Hebrews 3:14

Erick and Eve took a brief furlough in 1980 but quickly returned to the war-torn nation that had become their home. "How can you go back?" some asked. "Don't you worry? Won't it be dangerous?"

The couple didn't see danger; they saw opportunity. They didn't see potential killers; they saw potential Christians. "I know only one great danger," said Eve. "The only danger is not to be found in the center of God's will."

They returned to Afghanistan, along with their children, ages five and three. Soon after their return, they were attacked in their home, which also served as the meeting place for their Christian converts. They were killed with switchblades, leaving their children orphaned. Yet, they had peace even in those final moments.

Days before the murders, Eve's mother had a vision of Erick and Eve in heaven, with angels putting golden crowns on their head. The vision gave her strength, even in her grief when she later learned of their murders.

In a Muslim nation, being an active Christian is one of the most dangerous propositions possible. However, Eve and Erick put a new spin on the idea of danger. While their friends said they could not afford to be in Kabul, Erick and Eve felt they could not afford to be anywhere else. They saw it as their calling. They saw it as God's will. It has been said that if we step outside of God's provision, we risk losing God's protection. If the only danger is being out of the center of God's will, it is the only danger you cannot afford. How often do you actually put yourself in more danger by sidestepping God in the name of self-preservation? Extreme obedience puts danger in perspective.

Day 329

Where there is no cross, there is no crown.
This lesson cannot be learned from books, and
men do not usually taste this sweetness. This
rich life does not exist in a comfortable environ-
ment. If the spices are not refined to become oil,
the fragrance of the perfume cannot flow forth;
and if the grapes are not crushed in the vat,
they will not become wine.

FROM A CHINESE CHRISTIAN

eXtreme grasp

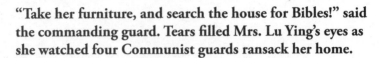

"Take her furniture, and search the house for Bibles!" said the commanding guard. Tears filled Mrs. Lu Ying's eyes as she watched four Communist guards ransack her home.

"I found it!" yelled the guard. But just as the guard held out the Bible to give it to his commanding officer, Mrs. Lu Ying bravely grabbed it back from him.

Day 330

"This book contains all I need to know about my dear Lord and Savior Jesus Christ, and I do not want to part with it," she said passionately while holding her Bible close to her chest.

"Take her outside," yelled the commander. "We'll see how long she wants to hold on to her book about Jesus."

The four Communist guards took Mrs. Ling into the street, mocked her, spat on her, and beat her until she could no longer stand. "Do you still believe in your book of myths?" laughed the guards.

And the words of the LORD are flawless.

Psalm 12:6

Through a swollen, bleeding mouth, still holding her Bible, Lu Ying repeated her statement of faith.

The guards grabbed an iron bar and smashed the bones in her hands, causing her now crippled hands to lose their grip. The Bible fell to the street and was confiscated.

Nearly twenty years later, a mission courier delivered Mrs. Ling a Bible. Her eyes filled with tears. She clutched it with her deformed hands and whispered, "This time I'm not letting go."

Many people have a full grasp on a half-truth. Whether they are atheists or agnostics, Buddhists or Hindus, all the dedication they can muster cannot transform their false beliefs into facts. Their sincerity is no substitute for the lack of substance. In contrast, Christians have the unchanging certainty of God's Word to back up their beliefs, and they know that God's Word is truth. We cannot afford to handle the Bible carelessly, though others come against us with all their might. Are you as tenacious in holding to God's Word as you hold to other valuable possessions in your life, such as money or your reputation? Let all else slip from your grip; yet hold onto God's Word at all costs.

eXtreme recovery

Conditions at the Chinese labor camp were brutal. With the food rations down to almost nothing and the subfreezing winter temperatures, an epidemic broke out in the camp. When winter began, there were thirteen hundred prisoners. When spring came, only two hundred fifty had survived.

Day 331

They came to Philip ... with a request. "Sir," they said, " we would like to see Jesus."

John 12:21

Mizhong Miao was sent to the camp for preaching the gospel and for refusing to deny his faith. His five-year sentence was tripled when he refused to stop preaching to fellow prisoners.

During that harsh winter, guards thought Mizhong Miao was dead. The life seemed to have left his nearly frozen body, but Miao's spirit was alive, and he was praying. Left alone in the morgue, he saw a visitor—an angel dressed in white and with a shining face. The angel came and blew upon Miao. As the angel blew, he felt the sickness leave his body and warmth enter him. He immediately knelt and said a prayer of thanksgiving.

He walked out of the morgue to the prison doctor. The doctor stared with a look of horror on his face; he thought he was seeing a ghost.

"Don't be afraid. I am Mizhong Miao," said the Christian. "God restored me to health. He sent me to show you the way of God."

Bowing reverently, the doctor said, "Your God is real." That night he trusted in Christ as his Savior.

Seeing is believing. We can talk about God. We can learn about Jesus. Yet we must experience Him by faith in order to confess with the doctor, "God is real." The chances of a doctor in the Chinese labor camp coming to Christ were slim to none. However, when confronted with a living miracle, he chose to believe in Mizhong Miao's God. Sometimes we may feel like our loved ones face similar odds. We must pray for them to experience God. They may encounter Him through creation. They may see Him at work through a love relationship. While miracles like Mizhong Miao's are few and far between, pray for your lost loved ones to have a life-changing encounter with the living, loving Lord.

eXtreme "deal"

EASTERN EUROPE: PRISON INMATES

The preacher was only making his first point when the prison guards burst into the cell, grabbing him and shoving everyone else to the floor.

Day 332

You have persevered and have endured hardships for my name, and have not grown weary.

Revelation 2:3

"You know this preaching is forbidden," one of them growled. "Now you will face the punishment." The husky guards dragged him out of the cell and down the hall. The other prisoners knew that the Eastern European Communist guards were taking their friend to the "beating room." They heard the door of that terrible room slam and then the muffled shouts and cries as the guards ruthlessly beat their friend.

Almost an hour had passed before the guards threw open the cell door and shoved in the man who had been preaching. The other prisoners saw that his clothes were now bloody and his face bore the marks of the beating.

He looked around at his cellmates almost as if taking attendance. "Now, my brothers," he said, "where did I leave off when we were so rudely interrupted?" And the sermon continued. Christians in prison knew the price they would pay to deliver a sermon, and yet many preached. Some, with no theological training or ministry experience, would preach passionately and eloquently in prison.

"It was a deal," wrote one prisoner later. "We preached, and they beat. We were happy preaching, and they were happy beating—so everyone was happy."

In a world where a contract is no longer binding, a family is dissoluble, and divorces outnumber marriages, Christians must reinstate the meaning of commitment—at all costs. What is the value of a promise if it does not mean anything? However, the consequences of our commitment to Christ are not cheap. It may cost us a chance at being very successful according to the world's standards. It may cost us friends and popularity. It may cost us our family, our security, and for some, even our lives. Commitment must have a price. The prisoners understood that full well. Yet Christ's reward is also part of the bargain. Are you holding up your end of the deal?

eXtreme calling

ROMANIA: CAPTAIN RECK

For days, the Communist guards would beat the imprisoned pastor, help him gain strength with good food, and then beat him again. He was to be systematically beaten to death, but not a quick death. They wanted him to suffer.

Day 333

Now to him who is able to do immeasurably more than all we ask or imagine, according to his power that is at work within us.

Ephesians 3:20

Captain Reck said one day as he beat the pastor, "I am God. I have the power of life and death over you. The one who is in heaven cannot decide to keep you in life. Everything depends upon me. If I wish, you live or die. *I am God!*"

The pastor responded calmly. "You don't know what a deep thing you have said. You were not created to be a torturer, a man who kills. You were created to become like God, with His life in your heart. Many who have been persecutors like you have come to realize, as the apostle Paul did, that it is shameful for a man to commit atrocities. They can do much better things. Believe me, Captain Reck, your real calling is to be Godlike, not to be God. You can have the character of God, not a torturer."

Reck pretended not to hear the Christian's words, and he continued beating the pastor for his faith. However, he couldn't stop thinking about his calling. Eventually, on bended knee, Reck surrendered his life to Christ.

Every caterpillar is really a butterfly, if it develops correctly. If not, it may continue to live, though it is something it was not intended to be. Likewise, our true calling as humans is to enter into a personal relationship with Jesus Christ and develop Christlike character. Without Christ, we may still be very accomplished with several credits to our names. We may become lots of admirable things—a successful businessperson, a loving mother, a devoted dad. Yet if we miss our true calling, we never become the person we were originally created to be. A caterpillar is interesting. But a butterfly far surpasses it in beauty and ability. Have you had a life of worldly success, yet missed your true calling?

eXtreme presence

Day 334

"We do not need to defend ourselves before you in this matter. If we are thrown into the blazing furnace, the God we serve is able to save us from it, and he will rescue us from your hand, O king. But even if he does not, we want you to know, O king, that we will not serve your gods or worship the image of gold you have set up" (Daniel 3:16–18).

For no other god can save in this way.

Daniel 3:29

The king's rage grew toward the three young men. They had refused to bow to the idol he had built for his nation, a crime punishable by death in the fire. "Stoke the furnace!" he commanded. "I want it seven times hotter than normal." He had the strongest men from his army come forward and bind the hands of the three young men. The furnace roared, and its walls glowed red as if ready to melt. "Throw them in," the king commanded.

As they did so, the heat proved too much, and the soldiers burst into flames. The prisoners disappeared from view in an instant as the flames flashed too bright to gaze into the furnace.

Then as he was watching, King Nebuchadnezzar suddenly jumped up in amazement. He said, "Look! I see four men walking around in the fire, unbound and unharmed, and the fourth looks like a son of the gods" (Daniel 3:25).

Suddenly Nebuchadnezzar knew his limitations before the presence of the one true God.

When it comes to the battle between good and evil, it is not a fair fight. The enemy is powerful. But God is more powerful. Satan is strong. Yet God is stronger. Satan must send his demons throughout the world to do his evil bidding. In contrast, God alone is omnipresent—fully present in all places at all times. Even so, the enemy's limitations are not always so obvious when we are under pressure from the opposition. At the time, the enemy seems scary. Intimidating. Consuming. We temporarily forget God's unlimited power. Do you have your eye on the thermostat when you are in the enemy's furnace? Or do you focus on God's presence and find strength to take the heat?

eXtreme clapping

ENGLAND: THOMAS HAUKER

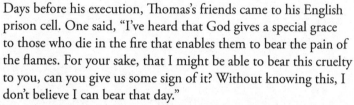

Thomas Hauker, a bright, well-favored, good-looking young gentleman, would not deny his personal relationship with Jesus Christ. For this he was sentenced to die at the stake.

Day 335

So we fix our eyes not on what is seen, but on what is unseen.

2 Corinthians 4:18

Days before his execution, Thomas's friends came to his English prison cell. One said, "I've heard that God gives a special grace to those who die in the fire that enables them to bear the pain of the flames. For your sake, that I might be able to bear this cruelty to you, can you give us some sign of it? Without knowing this, I don't believe I can bear that day."

Thomas thought for a moment. "If the rage of pain can be tolerated, before I die I will lift up my hands to heaven as an indication."

On the day of execution, the crowd was abuzz with Thomas's promise. As he was chained to the stake, he spoke quietly and with great grace to the men who laid the wood. Then he closed his eyes and the fire was kindled.

Thomas continued to preach to those around him, but soon, for the roar of the flames, he could not. All were sure he had died. Suddenly, his hands rose above his head to his God and, with praise and thanksgiving, clapped together three times. A shout arose in the crowd, and Thomas sank into the fire and gave up his spirit.

"I can't take it anymore." How often we catch ourselves expressing frustration at the least little trial. A crying child. A stuck doorknob. A late-night project deadline. However, the story of the martyrs haunts our petty thoughts when we are tempted to give up under pressure. We often overstate our problems and underestimate our ability to bear up under them. In fact, God promises He will not allow anything into our lives that will be more than we can endure. Thomas, hands upraised in worship, signaling his triumph over the flames, is evidence enough. When you think you can't take much more of a certain situation, remember Thomas. And remember God's faithfulness. He knows exactly what you can and cannot take.

Day 336

O God, accept all my sufferings, my
tiredness, my humiliations, my tears, my
nostalgia, my being hungry, my suffering of cold,
all the bitterness accumulated in my soul.
Dear Lord, have pity also on those who
persecute and torture us day and night.
Grant them, too, the divine grace of knowing
the sweetness and happiness of your love.

FROM A CHRISTIAN WOMAN WHO WAS SERVING TIME
IN THE SIBERIAN LABOR CAMP VORKUTA

eXtreme reformer

On October 31, 1517, Martin Luther nailed ninety-five statements of biblical faith to the door of a church in Wittenberg, Germany, and then spent the rest of his days only one step away from execution. Despite this danger, Luther never shied away from an opportunity to argue the validity of scriptural doctrine versus the doctrine of works that had taken over the church in his time.

Day 337

Preach the Word; . . . correct, rebuke and encourage—with great patience and careful instruction.

2 Timothy 4:2

Though he had been warned repeatedly not to attend the gathering in Worms, he said, "Since I am sent for, I am resolved and determined to attend, in the name of our Lord Jesus Christ; even though I know there are as many devils to resist me as there are tiles to cover the houses in Worms."

When he was ordered to revoke his doctrines, Luther answered, "My conscience is so bound and captured by Scripture and the Word of God, that I will not, nor may I, revoke anything; I do not consider it godly or lawful to go against my conscience. On this I stand and rest: I have nothing else to say. God have mercy upon me!"

He escaped those who wanted him dead, and—in hiding—he translated the Scriptures into German. Though he was constantly in danger, he lived to the age of sixty-three and died of natural causes.

People are quick to criticize the church for one thing or another. Like writing a critique for a Broadway play, church members are all too eager to rate a worship service as if it were a performance. The music's too loud. The sermon's too short. The facility is freezing. The pews are uncomfortable. However, Luther was not a critic, though he did not support the established church. He rebuked it. A rebuke is different from a critique in that a rebuke calls a church that has strayed from Scripture back to God's Word. In contrast, a critique is merely a call to human opinion or preference. Are you carefully ministering to the body of Christ like Luther, or merely criticizing God's church?

eXtreme bearer

"The life of man is a continual death, unless it be that Christ lives in him."

Ignatius was a disciple of the apostle John and had publicly reproved Emperor Trajan Antioch for worshiping idols. However, Trajan swore to take public revenge on Ignatius in return for his embarrassing rebuke.

Day 338

For I bear your name, O LORD God Almighty.

Jeremiah 15:16

Ignatius was arrested and brought to Rome. As he was led away to the pit of lions, he told another believer, "My dear Jesus, my Savior, is so deeply written in my heart, that I feel confident, that if my heart were to be cut open and chopped into pieces, the name Jesus would be found on every piece."

When the multitude of people was assembled to witness his death, Ignatius boldly addressed the cheering crowd. "I am the grain of God. I am ground by the teeth of the beast, that I may be found a pure bread of Christ, who is to me the Bread of Life."

As soon as he had spoken these words, two hungry lions devoured him.

He lived up to his surname, Theophorus, "the bearer of God." To the very end, he bore the name of God and his Savior on his lips. He had often said, "The crucified Christ is my only and entire love." And to the end he found solace in this simple truth: "As the world hates the Christians, so God loves them."

Marriage tradition holds that a wife should bear her husband's name as a symbol of their union. They are no longer two people, but one. As a couple grows old together, they begin to share more than just the same last name. They share the same friends and interests. They begin to finish each other's sentences. And some begin to even strangely resemble one another... such is their long-standing intimacy. In the same way, those who bear the name "Christian" or "little Christ" develop the same intimacy—a oneness with the Savior. Are you wearing well the name of Christ? Like Ignatius, does sharing Jesus' name inspire you to share in His sufferings, His ministry, and His life?

eXtreme question

"We cannot ask that question. We don't know the answer!"

The scriptwriters were working on a children's video called *Stephen's Test of Faith*, in which a young boy travels through time to learn the history of persecution. They were working on a scene where Christians were thrown to hungry lions after being accused of setting Rome on fire.

Day 339

"We can't have Stephen ask, 'If God protected Daniel in the lion's den, why didn't He protect the Christians in the Coliseum?'"

Why would God protect one of His children and allow thousands of others to perish? The lead scriptwriter thought and replied, "It is not the answer that's the problem; it's the question. We should not ask, 'Why?' We should ask, 'Are we willing?' Daniel was willing to perish before the hungry lions. Believers were also willing to die in the days of Nero. The fact that one escaped and the others didn't does not change the condition of their hearts. It is our obedience that creates the witness, not the act of suffering."

And the peace of God, which transcends all understanding, will guard your hearts and your minds in Christ Jesus.

Philippians 4:7

When Shadrach, Meshach, and Abednego were to be thrown into the furnace by King Nebuchadnezzar, they said, "The God we serve is able to save us from it . . . But even if he does not, we want you to know, O king, that we will not serve your gods" (Daniel 3:17,18).

Many people today are asking why. We have entered a new era of unanswered questions regarding unexplained tragedy. The world is crying out for answers to its questions, yet we all know that no answer would be sufficient to heal the pain. Even if we knew the reason tragedy occurred on every specific occasion for every individual, it would do little to ease our heartache. Instead, we need the faith of Daniel's companions who said that even if God chooses not to move in the way we prayed He would, we can remain confident that He is working all things together for our good. Instead of asking why, pleading for understanding, we must pray for peace that surpasses it.

eXtreme heritage

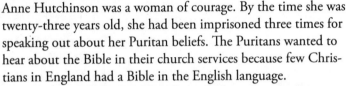

"Children get down!" Anne Hutchinson screamed as she heard the arrow sharply strike her door. Then they heard the harrowing screams of the Indians who surrounded her home. More arrows seemed to come from everywhere, and she could hear footsteps near the window. "I will see you today, Lord!" Anne said.

Day 340

One generation will commend your works to another; they will tell of your mighty acts.

Psalm 145:4

Anne Hutchinson was a woman of courage. By the time she was twenty-three years old, she had been imprisoned three times for speaking out about her Puritan beliefs. The Puritans wanted to hear about the Bible in their church services because few Christians in England had a Bible in the English language.

Anne and her husband, William, had come to America in 1634 seeking religious freedom, but even in America, they had been met with persecution for holding religious meetings in their home. People who supported their ministry had been arrested and had even lost their right to vote.

At forty-six years of age and pregnant with her eighteenth child, Anne was convicted and imprisoned for four months. After being banished from the colony, her family and friends started a new town and home church in Rhode Island.

With her pioneering spirit, Anne Hutchinson helped make the idea of freedom in worship an American ideal. She and five children died at the hands of her Indian attackers. She met her Savior with courage and faith, just as she had lived her life.

Freedom is never free. It always comes with a cost. Jesus Christ was the first to pay the ultimate price for religious freedom—giving us access to God through His death on the cross. He was the only one who could pay the price for our liberty from sin. His death and resurrection established true liberty, and many believers have since sacrificed to uphold everyone's right to experience freedom in Christ. Believers like Anne have made the dream of religious freedom a reality in America. Our heritage of sacrifice is huge. What price are you willing to pay for the next generation to experience the religious freedoms that you enjoy? Ask God to show you how to pass it on to the next generation.

eXtreme cross

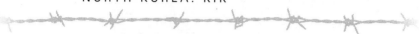

"Look for the cross," the young Korean man named Kik heard a villager say.

Word spread to those who escaped from North Korea into China that they should look for a building with a cross. He finally found one, and with it, food and clothing. He also found a new relationship with Jesus Christ.

Day 341

The church members discipled Kik for three months. But Kik knew he must return to North Korea to tell others about Jesus.

Kik and another young believer were given five Bibles and food for their journey. However, border guards captured them just after they made it across the river back into North Korea.

The guards discovered the Bibles that Kik's friend was carrying. The guard then beat Kik's friend to death with an iron rod. Then they turned on Kik, but he managed to escape. After several months, he began to share Christ with others and started an underground church in North Korea.

For, as I have often told you before and now say again even with tears, many live as enemies of the cross of Christ.

Philippians 3:18

Before long, Kik realized he needed more Bibles for the rapidly growing number of believers. He remembered how his friend had given up his life trying to bring the Word of God back to their homeland. When Kik decided to return to China for more Bibles, the believers were very anxious for his safety.

Kik remembered the advice given to him some time ago. He simply replied, "Just look to the cross."

The cross is controversial. Many people will talk about religion, but the cross makes them uncomfortable and even offends them. Kik was told to look to the cross for security. However, Kik did not realize his enemies were looking for the same sign and with good reason. They knew that Christians rally under the sign of the cross. Since they opposed Christianity, the cross became their enemy. Our spiritual enemy looks upon the cross with fervent disgust, fear, and hatred. Are you looking to the cross with the same intensity expressed in joy, hope, and gratitude? Your enemy is squarely fixed on the cross—as an opponent planning an attack. Are you equally focused on honoring, serving, and loving the cross?

eXtreme unity

"When I saw the airplanes fly into the World Trade Center on September 11, it brought back painful memories for me," said Nus Reimas, the general secretary of the Indonesia Evangelical Fellowship.

Day 342

How good and pleasant it is when brothers live together in unity!

Psalm 133:1

"More than a year ago, hundreds of well-armed Muslims who were said to be tied to Osama bin Laden attacked our islands of Maluku. Their mission was to get rid of all the Christians." It is estimated that over six thousand people were killed, and five hundred thousand additional residents were chased from their homes due to nonstop shooting and arson. "The Muslims murdered thirty-eight members of my extended family," Reimas said somberly.

In an interview in the October 22, 2001 *Christianity Today*, Reimas relayed how difficult it was for him to apply 1 Thessalonians 5:18, "Give thanks in all circumstances, for this is God's will for you in Christ Jesus." The pain was so great, and the recovery seemed like it would never come. However, by God's grace, Reimas determined that he would live what God's Word taught.

"Only [then] could I stand up and face the situation. No one expects things like this, but they happen." Reimas now organizes meetings between many Christian leaders from different denominations. Just as people in America have drawn together from all walks of life for support and prayer, many Christian leaders are coming together to pray and fellowship in Indonesia. Reimas smiles as he reflects, "It has never happened before."

We'd never come this way before. A collapsed sense of human decency. Crumbling Twin Towers. Anthrax. The American flag draped over the wounds of the Pentagon. We believed the pain and scars of September 11 would serve as permanent reminders of the past and motivate us to a better future. But the "narrow road" is hard to follow. The "wide gate" and "broad road" is an easier way and entices us to return to the familiar. After all has been said and done, we know one thing: one point doesn't mark a trail or set a direction. Only by starting from where we are and keeping our eyes on Christ can we follow the "narrow road that leads to life" (Matthew 7:14).

Day 343

The craziness, anxieties about my family, the constant tension all destroy me. But if they drive me mad or if I remain sane, I accept everything God sends, as a child accepts everything from the hand of his father. Cowardice is unreasonable. In the asylum, I have often thought that the will of God keeps intact the freedom of man.

FROM BROTHER SHIMANOV, CONFINED TO A RUSSIAN PSYCHIATRIC ASYLUM FOR HIS FAITH

eXtreme "loss"

CZECHOSLOVAKIA: BROTHER ZAVARSKY

Day 344

Finally, the frustration was too much. "All my time is spent in slave labor!" complained Brother Zavarsky, a Czech prisoner. "Ten hours a day I weave baskets, which the Communists sell for good money. Why did I study so much to be a pastor? Those miserable ones in the service of communism have high positions at the church now. They preach, they advise, they feed the flock. And I suffer."

What is more, I consider everything a loss compared to the surpassing greatness of knowing Christ Jesus my Lord, for whose sake I have lost all things.

Philippians 3:8

"Why do you complain?" said another Christian at the prison. "God doesn't need your sermons or your theology. The puppets of communism do this work. But they cannot share the sufferings of the Savior. This is the main promise that one should give at ordination. Did you never preach about enduring sorrows for Christ? Thank God He has given you now the opportunity to fulfill what is the most valuable part of any sermon."

Chastened, Zavarsky no longer complained about being in prison or the long days of labor. After leaving prison, Zavarsky could not continue his work as a pastor because his imprisonment had left him very ill. But visitors to his bedside did not find a beaten and ruined man. They saw a man whose face shone with love for the Savior. He confessed his life had not been lost or stolen from him. He gave it up willingly to help Jesus carry His cross.

What will cause people to willingly take a loss on a business deal so that they can give generously? What will cause people to leave their Christian homeland for a pagan foreign nation? What will cause someone to die rather than give in to temptation? It's extreme commitment to the person of Christ. They see an opportunity for spiritual gain in every personal loss. They are willing to take a personal hit to their wallet, schedule, plans, comforts, and conveniences in order to advance the kingdom of God. How do you express your extreme devotion? Do others think you're crazy for the level of your commitment? "Losing it" for Jesus means heaven's gain.

extreme revolutionary

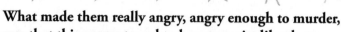

What made them really angry, angry enough to murder, was that this convert used to be a terrorist like them.

Maria Elena Moyano had screamed with them for revolution in Peru. She had pleaded for feeding the peasants by the power of the gun. Then she met Jesus Christ and found a different kind of revolution—a revolution of love in her heart.

Day 345

She became the vice-mayor of Lima's largest shantytown. She organized far-reaching relief efforts among the poorest of the poor, feeding the hungry, caring for the sick, and tending to the orphans.

"They call us Christians 'firefighters of the revolution,'" she said, "because they say we extinguish the fires they set. They want the population to have absolutely nothing to eat, hoping that then the people will resort to arms. But we must not fear terror. We must oppose injustice and savagery to help those in need."

So the Pharisees said to one another, "See, this is getting us nowhere. Look how the whole world has gone after him!"

John 12:19

Maria knew she would suffer, but she also knew that she must share Christ's sorrows before sharing His glory. Maoist terrorists attacked with a violent rage, blowing up the building where the food for the poor was housed. "Sometimes I fear," said Maria, "but I insist we should never resort to violence. It is difficult to defeat terrorism, but not impossible."

Angry at the effectiveness of Maria's work and unable to stop her, the guerrillas killed Maria on February 1, 1992.

The Pharisees were not exactly tactical experts. Like the terrorists in Lima, their strategy for discouraging people from following Christ brought unintended results. Both the Pharisees and the terrorists worked hard for the people's allegiance. The Pharisees tried starving the people's souls while the terrorists tried starving the people's stomachs. However, the people in Jerusalem and the people in Peru followed the revolutionary teachings of Jesus all the same. The harder the opposition works against Jesus, the more it works to advance His cause. The opposition can work against you and your efforts, but it will never defeat you when you work for God's kingdom. In fact, the opposition may unwittingly work in your favor.

eXtreme proof

RUSSIA: PASTOR "GEORGE"

Day 346

Pacing around the small room of the church, the Russian captain nodded toward the cross on the wall. "That is a lie, you know," he said. "It's just a piece of trickery you ministers use to delude the poor and make it easier for the rich to give you money. Come on now—we're alone. Admit to me that you've never really believed Jesus Christ was the Son of God."

Pastor "George" looked at the cross and then smiled. "Of course, I believe it. It's true."

"I won't have you play tricks on me!" cried the captain. He drew the revolver from the holster at his side and held it close to the minister's body. "Unless you admit that it's a lie, I will shoot you."

"I cannot admit that, for it would be a lie," said George. "Our Lord is really the true Son of God. Shooting me will not change that."

The captain flung the revolver to the floor. The pastor was surprised when the soldier grabbed him by the arms with tears in his eyes.

"It's true!" cried the captain. "It is true. I believe, too. I could not be sure men would die for this belief until I found it out for myself. Oh, thank you! You have strengthened my faith. Now I, too, can die for Christ. You showed me how."

We accept man's testimony, but God's testimony is greater because it is the testimony of God, which he has given about his Son.

1 John 5:9

Martyrs are found in any religion. We say we are willing to die for our faith. They say they are willing to die for theirs. How do Christian martyrs prove their faith any more so than Muslim extremists? We don't. That Muslims are willing to die for their faith does not prove the reliability of their religion any more than our own willingness proves Christianity. God alone proves He is the true God. We testify to the truth. But God is the truth. His testimony about His Son far outweighs your own. Others can show you how to die for Jesus. But only God can give you complete assurance that it is worth it.

eXtreme gratitude

THE NETHERLANDS: HANS

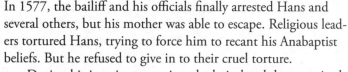

Hans had distinguished himself in Antwerp, a city in the Netherlands, as a serious student of the Bible. He even spent his Sundays instructing new converts. But Hans and his mother were considered a threat. They were Anabaptists, and their beliefs caused them to be considered heretics in the eyes of religious leaders.

Day 347

In 1577, the bailiff and his officials finally arrested Hans and several others, but his mother was able to escape. Religious leaders tortured Hans, trying to force him to recant his Anabaptist beliefs. But he refused to give in to their cruel torture.

During his imprisonment in a dank, isolated dungeon in the castle of Antwerp, he wrote letters of encouragement to his family and friends. Hans wrote the following letter:

"Most dearly beloved mother, I am glad to tell you that I am well according to the flesh. But according to the spirit, I thank the Lord that He gives me strength by His Holy Spirit, so that my mind is unchanged. For from Him alone we expect our strength to withstand these cruel wolves, so that they can have no power over our souls."

Hans was soon brought before a court where he boldly proclaimed his faith. He was then sentenced to be burned at the stake. His letter testified to his solid gratitude to Christ for protecting and saving his soul.

> But thanks be to God! He gives us the victory through our Lord Jesus Christ.
>
> **1 Corinthians 15:57**

"God is great. God is good. Let us thank Him for our... sufferings?" That's not the childhood prayer of blessing we are used to hearing. The phrase itself is dissonant to our ears, yet it reminds us how dissonant the principle is to our hearts. We would much rather thank Him for our food than for our trials. In the same way, Hans penned his gratitude for his sufferings in an odd thank-you note. However, it is the sincere prayer of a martyr whose sufferings made him the man he always wanted to be. Are you exactly who you want to be for Christ? Are you willing to thank God for allowing whatever it takes, even intense sufferings, to bring you that victory?

eXtreme calling

PAPUA, NEW GUINEA: JAMES CHALMERS

"I wonder if there is a boy here who will ... bring the gospel to the cannibals?" challenged a missionary in a letter to young James Chalmers's church. James resolved to be that boy.

Day 348

In 1866, Chalmers and his young wife sailed for the Southern Seas and were shipwrecked on Rarotonga, where they settled. Eleven years later, they left for Papua New Guinea, and were warmly received into a cannibal village called Suau.

Chalmers began journeying up and down the coast. At one of his stops, the natives surrounded him and demanded tomahawks and knives. Otherwise, they would kill him and his wife. Chalmers stood his ground, and the natives respected his tenacity. They even apologized the following day and soon became friends.

In 1879, his wife died. James was devastated and told a friend, "Let me bury my sorrow in work for Christ."

I ask you, therefore, not to be discouraged because of my sufferings for you, which are your glory.

Ephesians 3:13

Chalmers returned to England twice on furlough, only to be further convinced of his calling. "I cannot rest with so many thousands of savages without knowledge of God near us."

On April 7, 1901, Chalmers, Oliver Tompkins, and a group of assistants sailed to the island of Goaribari. The following morning he and Tompkins went ashore and were escorted to a large building. Once inside, the natives killed the men and cooked them that same day.

How depressing. Understandably, when we read the stories of martyrs like James Chalmers, our natural reaction may be one of sympathy, and sorrow, and even shame. What a waste. But, we must take a closer look at their stories. Chalmers gave his single earthly life in order to share eternal life with many others. Chalmers did not consider his martyrdom a foolish mistake. Why should we be discouraged? When our earthly sufferings bring the glory and honor of heaven one step closer to the lost, nothing is in vain. Suffering becomes an inextricable part of God's plan ... for you and for others. Are you willing to endure earthly pain in order to bring heaven's opportunity to others?

eXtreme resistance

INDONESIA: SUTARSI SELONG

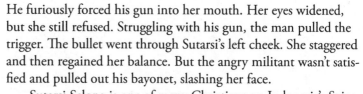

The man grabbed the Indonesian woman and shouted in her face: "Say, 'Allah-u-Akbar' (God is great)! Just say it!" But young Sutarsi Selong refused to submit and so dishonor her true God.

Day 349

My heart is steadfast, O God, my heart is steadfast.

Psalm 57:7

He furiously forced his gun into her mouth. Her eyes widened, but she still refused. Struggling with his gun, the man pulled the trigger. The bullet went through Sutarsi's left cheek. She staggered and then regained her balance. But the angry militant wasn't satisfied and pulled out his bayonet, slashing her face.

Sutarsi Selong is one of many Christians on Indonesia's Spice Islands who were attacked by a fanatical group of Muslims called the Laskar Jihad, or holy warriors. Selong and fellow believers knew the fanatics who dress themselves in white robes and camouflage would soon attack them. They gathered together at Nita Church, which is surrounded by a seven-foot wall, and several took turns keeping watch.

When the Islamic warriors came, the Christians tried to surrender peacefully. However, their white flag was cut down with a sword, and within minutes, violence erupted. This scene has become more and more common on Indonesia's islands as fanatical Islamic factions incite violence, burn churches, and kill believers.

Thankfully, many Christians in Indonesia, like Sutarsi Selong, refuse to surrender. They resist the jihad warriors' demands to embrace Islam and deny Christ.

Won't we give in just a tiny bit? One little inch? What's the harm? The enemy can taunt us like the fanatical Muslims did with Sutarsi. Yet she refused to surrender in the slightest. Likewise, we do not have the luxury of cafeteria-style commitment—giving in here and there whenever the temptation gets unbearable. We cannot pick and choose when it is okay to give in to the enemy and when it is not. We must remain steadfast. Being steadfast does not mean you are less likely to give in to the enemy. It does not mean you try harder. God gives you a steadfast heart so that you will not give in. Period. Ask God for a steadfast heart today.

Day 350

I didn't come here to sit silently with my hands folded on my lap. I came to speak about Christ.

GALINA VILCHINSKAYA, A TWENTY-THREE-YEAR-OLD
IMPRISONED IN RUSSIA IN THE 1980S FOR
TEACHING CHILDREN IN A CHRISTIAN SUMMER CAMP

eXtreme bounty

Day 351

In northern Nigeria, Muslims have instituted Sharia law— the strictest Islamic legal code. Christians dominate the Nigerian population, so the Islamic leaders insist that the law applies only to domestic matters for Muslims. However, the Christians know better. Hundreds of their churches have already been destroyed. If they are rebuilt, they are burned down again. Many Christians are being martyred.

Love your enemies, do good to those who hate you, bless those who curse you, pray for those who mistreat you.

Luke 6:27,28

In the city of Kaduna in northern Nigeria, one church leader claims that Muslim extremists have placed a bounty on the heads of all Christian leaders, offering one hundred thousand *naira* (about one thousand US dollars) for each one killed. Likewise, there was also a bounty on Christ's head, and He was betrayed for just thirty pieces of silver.

With the continued threat, some believers are contemplating fighting back. But one Christian leader recently challenged believers in Kaduna: "In the midst of this we need to remember our Lord's teaching about turning evil to good and patiently suffering in the face of what is happening. And because Nigeria is a proclaimed democracy, there is a responsibility for Christians to make sure everyone is treated justly and fairly."

Christ delivered a similar challenge almost two thousand years ago: "'Love the Lord your God . . .' This is the first and greatest commandment. And the second is like it: 'Love your neighbor as yourself'" (Matthew 22:37–39).

Following Christ's command to love our neighbors as ourselves is hard enough. It's even harder to follow Christ's command to love our neighbors when they have it out for us. We all know the feeling. You may have a colleague who is bent on sabotaging your work. You may have a teacher who rides your case for no apparent reason. Or you may be blessed with a so-called friend who seems strangely pleased when things are going wrong in your life. Jesus knows the feeling of having others celebrate your sufferings. How can you love those who would pay to see you suffer? Others may treasure seeing you put to shame. However, your obedience to God in this area is priceless.

eXtreme servants

It was midnight when officers burst into their home and abruptly awakened Eskinder Menghis and his wife and three children. The family walked out to find agents with Saudi Arabia's Ministry of Interior ransacking their home.

"What are you doing? You have no right to destroy our home like this."

Day 352

For we are God's workmanship, created in Christ Jesus to do good works, which God prepared in advance for us to do.

Ephesians 2:10

"And you have no right to practice your religion in the land of Mohammed! You were warned before you came to leave your religion behind." The officer pushed Eskinder out the door as the others gathered up the Bibles, hymnals, photos albums, audiotapes, and anything else they could use as evidence.

Eskinder was brought to the police headquarters for interrogation, leaving behind his frightened wife and children. Eskinder and his family are Ethiopian Christians. They are among the many foreigners who make up one-third of Saudi Arabia's population, working in the oil-rich nation. Many of these foreigners are Christians who face a terrible predicament when it comes to expressing their faith.

Some Christians are hestitant to practice their faith when they go to work in a Muslim nation. But once under the dark cloud of Islam, they begin to look toward heaven and find fellowship with other believers around them. Many even start to witness to their Muslim employers. In Saudi Arabia, converting a Muslim to Christianity carries a death penalty for both parties.

Where no career missionaries can tread, full-time Christian servants enter the scene. They bring a unique and powerful witness to one of the most restricted nations in the world. They are committed Christians cleverly disguised as ordinary engineers on the oil fields of Saudi Arabia. Their mission is clear, though their methods are covert. Their witness is strong, yet secretive. Their task is to present the gospel by being a servant: a selfless and hardworking colleague at work and an unselfish neighbor at home. Our task is to support them through prayer. We are all servants, doing our part, to bring the world to faith in Christ. Those like Eskinder in Saudi Arabia are doing their job. Are you doing yours?

eXtreme witness

ROME: ZOE

"Kill her! Long live Diocletian!" echoed in Zoe's ears as she stood in the middle of the Coliseum before the angry crowd.

Day 353

We proclaim to you what we have seen and heard, so that you also may have fellowship with us.

1 John 1:3

Zoe thought about why she was there and smiled. She remembered the day she visited her husband at the jail where he worked, guarding the Christians imprisoned for refusing to sacrifice to the gods. Zoe grew up hearing that Christians were misguided and followed a deadly superstition. They set fire to Rome during Emperor Nero's reign and got the punishment they deserved—they were nailed to crosses and thrown to lions.

But that day in the prison, Zoe witnessed a Christian family praying together: "Dear Lord, help our death bring glory to your name. We forgive those who imprisoned us." Zoe left the jail puzzled. Why did these Christians have so much peace, knowing that they would soon face the lions?

Zoe began to secretly meet with this family and ask them about their faith. Soon, she gave her heart to Jesus.

Word quickly spread of Zoe's newfound faith, and guards were sent to her home to give her a chance to recant and sacrifice to the god Mars. She refused. The guards put her in chains and hauled her to the very prison where her husband stood watch.

When Zoe continued to refuse to recant her faith, she was hanged, burned, and thrown into a river.

Who is the extreme witness in this story? Is it the family who prayed before they were tossed to the lions? Or is it Zoe who would not recant her newfound faith before the guards? The answer is, yes. The family, on their way out of this world, brought another person into heaven. Both became extreme witnesses for Christ who left an indelible mark on the pages of history. Zoe would have otherwise been forgotten as a pagan wife of a pagan prison guard. History would have paid the family no mind as one of thousands killed. Yet an ordinary person with extraordinary faith is worth remembering. Will your life pen you into history as an extreme witness for Jesus Christ?

eXtreme prisoner

"You are saying it wrong," the exasperated guard instructed the elderly Chinese believer. "You are supposed to say 'Prison is good,' not 'Jesus is good.'"

Al Ling smiled. "But prison is not good. That's the point. Am I supposed to lie?"

"Then give me fifty push-ups!" the frustrated Communist guard commanded. "Just like yesterday."

Seventy-year-old Al Ling did her push-ups and returned to her camp. Ling's husband had been arrested for spreading the gospel, and he had passed away. Now she was in prison for telling her fellow Chinese people about the love of Christ.

"Food is good, prison is good!" the prisoners were forced to shout as instructed after a hard day's labor in the field. "Jesus is better!" Her strong voice stuck out from the crowd.

"Al Ling, do you want more push-ups today?" the guard asked.

"I want you to know how much Jesus loves you," she smiled in response. She was thrilled at the opportunity to tell the Communist guards and other prisoners how good Jesus was, even if it meant doing daily push-ups. Upon her release, the guards decided to interrogate her one last time. "Where does your husband work?" the young guard asked.

"Oh, he is doing underground work," she answered. The interested guard took out a notepad. Al Ling smiled, "He passed away years ago."

Day 354

But make up your mind not to worry beforehand how you will defend yourselves. For I will give you words and wisdom that none of your adversaries will be able to resist or contradict.

Luke 21:14,15

Al Ling was no theologian. She was not a practiced orator. Yet with her innocent, steadfast, and even humorous replies, she was able to confound the Communist enemies. We may play mind games, wondering what we would say or do if we were in the same situation. Could we think on our feet? Jesus reminds us that we ought not worry about what we will say when we are asked to defend our faith. We are not asked to give a prepared speech. We are asked to rely on Him for words of wisdom—at the moment we need them most. When that moment arrives, God will give you the words to say to be an effective witness for His sake.

eXtreme suffering-part one

SUDAN: KAMERINO

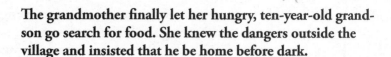

The grandmother finally let her hungry, ten-year-old grandson go search for food. She knew the dangers outside the village and insisted that he be home before dark.

Kamerino and his friends had walked several miles picking berries when they suddenly heard soldiers yelling at them. Frightened, the boys ran into a field with tall grass and ducked down. The soldiers lit the field on fire and waited for the boys to run out.

Day 355

Christians in Sudan have been displaced within their own country for their religious beliefs. Many have fled the cruel Islamic assaults with barely the clothing on their backs.

The flames quickly reached the boys, and they had no choice but to run for their lives. Only three boys made it out of the fields; Kamerino remained.

Devote yourselves to prayer.

Colossians 4:2

When the fire burned down, the soldiers, having caught the other three, walked to where Kamerino was lying. Scorching pain caused his body to curl up in the fetal position. The boy's burned body was motionless, and he was left for dead—another Christian casualty. Or so they thought.

By some miracle, Kamerino crawled out of the field and was discovered by fellow villagers, who brought him back to his grandmother's home. Large portions of his body were grossly burned. There was nothing they could do for Kamerino but pray for his sufferings.

The Christians in Sudan put the power of prayer in perspective. Their sufferings and daily dangers have reduced their reliance upon themselves and increased their dependence upon God. Prayer is all that remains for many Christian families in Sudan. It's a scary proposition—and a wonderful place to be. We are not likely to say that God is all we need until and unless God is all we have. Otherwise, we are quick to rely on our own abilities. Prayer—what can do the most, we are apt to do the least. God is calling you to extreme prayer in these extreme times. How often do you rely on prayer as if there were nothing else you could do but pray?

eXtreme suffering–part two

SUDAN: KAMERINO

An American missionary team was traveling through Sudan delivering food, blankets, and Bibles and showing the *JESUS* video. Everything was on schedule until their truck got stuck in a river and they lost a day's work.

Day 356

He will wipe every tear from their eyes. There will be no more death or mourning or crying or pain, for the old order of things has passed away.

Revelation 21:4

The missionaries committed the events to God and asked Him to guide their path. Knowing they would have to cut their travels short to make their deadline, they decided to visit a closer village. Shortly after arriving, a number of women came running up to the foreign visitors. In broken English they cried, "Come quickly ...our boy...you must help...come quickly!"

The team followed the women into a small, dark building. On the floor they found a small boy lying motionless, wrapped in a ragged blanket. When the blanket was lifted off, they discovered the severe burns covering Kamerino's body.

They quickly and carefully loaded Kamerino into their truck and drove to the hospital fifty miles away. There, the boy immediately received the treatment he badly needed. Today Kamerino's eyes fill with tears when he remembers how prayer and providence rescued him. He knows the love of Christ and His power to heal, and for the first time in many months, he smiles.

The missionaries also thank God that after being surrounded by so much death and suffering in Sudan, He allowed them to save the life of a brave, ten-year-old boy.

Kamerino brings new meaning to the phrase "to be continued." His life seemed destined for unending suffering, living out his life wrapped in a ragged blanket. However, part two proved to be a happy ending and a reminder of God's grace. However, his story does not end even there. Part three is yet to be written. One day, Kamerino will experience the ultimate healing—a heavenly home where there is no suffering or pain. Earth will get worse before it gets better. Yet God will step into the worst situation imaginable and call for an end to all suffering. Then we will all head for home. If you are going through unimaginable pain right now, remember where you are ultimately headed.

Day 357

Religion is nothing else than
doing the will of God and not our own.
Heaven or hell depends on this alone.

Susanna Wesley, mother of John and Charles Wesley

eXtreme pastor–part one

NORTH KOREA: PASTOR IM

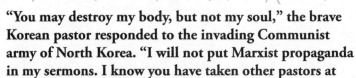

"You may destroy my body, but not my soul," the brave Korean pastor responded to the invading Communist army of North Korea. **"I will not put Marxist propaganda in my sermons. I know you have taken other pastors at night from their homes and tortured them for not obeying your orders, but I do not care what you do to my body."**

Day 358

The officer's anger grew as Pastor Im spoke. Then he said with disgust, "If you do not care for yourself, then think of your family. They will be killed also."

Pastor Im hesitated. He expected to be hurt but had not considered his family. He knew the choice he must make. He calmly replied to the Communist officer, "I would rather have my wife and babies die by your gun, knowing that they and I stood faithful, than to betray my Lord and save them."

You do not realize now what I am doing, but later you will understand.

John 13:7

"Take him away," the officer commanded. Pastor Im was kept in a dark prison cell for two years where he was not allowed to shave or change clothes. He kept up his courage by reciting a Bible verse that was precious to him. Every day from his small isolated cell, others could hear Pastor Im recite in a loving, calm voice John 13:7, where Jesus promised, "You do not realize now what I am doing, but later you will understand."

"Later." In a modern society of instant coffee, cash, and convenience, "later" is almost an obsolete term. We want what we need now, not later. Headline sports, news, entertainment, and weather—even our media give us up-to-the-minute updates in every area of life. Yet the God who reigns and rules unrestrained by time still operates on the principle of "later." Are we willing to trust Him now and defer our understanding of the events to a later time, even indefinitely? If you are going through a trial right now, your most valuable asset is trust, not understanding. Ask God for a greater ability to trust that will outweigh your desire to understand.

eXtreme pastor-part two

NORTH KOREA: PASTOR IM

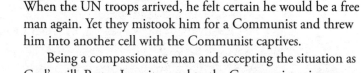

Day 359

"But I am not a Communist. You must believe me," pleaded Pastor Im when the United Nations regained the occupied territory in September 1950. The North Korean Communist soldiers had kept Im locked in an isolated prison cell for two years for preaching to others about Christ and for refusing to change his sermons into pro-Marxist propaganda.

Great are your purposes and mighty are your deeds.

Jeremiah 32:19

When the UN troops arrived, he felt certain he would be a free man again. Yet they mistook him for a Communist and threw him into another cell with the Communist captives.

Being a compassionate man and accepting the situation as God's will, Pastor Im witnessed to the Communist prisoners. Many were converted to Christ. "We keep hearing about this prison camp preacher," said an American missionary to his friend visiting Korea as a chaplain.

"Since he knows the prisoners so well, I wonder if he would help us organize an evangelistic service?" questioned the chaplain. God answered their prayers.

The American missionaries were able to get permission to have access to Pastor Im. And the "prison preacher" faithfully helped and preached at prison camps all over South Korea. Thousands of Communists accepted Christ. Within a year, twelve thousand prisoners were rising each morning for dawn prayer meetings.

Pastor Im never saw his family again, yet thousands became his brothers in Christ in the prison camps.

"What's the point?" This is the question on everyone's minds when we see unjust suffering and violence. However, we cannot always know God's purposes. We can only know they are great and they are ultimately for our good. We are like individual puzzle pieces spread out over a table. We strain our eyes from side to side and see that the pieces immediately around us do not seem to fit. We feel frustrated and frightened. Yet God is the puzzle Master—the only one who sees the whole picture. He can see all the pieces in your life at once. He knows how they fit together for His greater purpose. Will you look with trust into the eyes of the Master, content wherever He places you?

eXtreme Christmas story

"Have you ever smelled fresh hay?"

Aristar, the farming lad, began his story. "It's like someone captured the essence of spring and bundled it before it could lose its newness. Mary and Joseph must have smelled it when they arrived at the manger after their long journey."

Day 360

The other prisoners listened intently as Aristar spoke naturally of the nativity. "The horse's ears would have turned toward the Savior's cry as soon as He was born. They are great listeners, as we should be when Jesus speaks."

Outside the Romanian prison of Tirgul-Ocna, the snow was six feet deep on a bitterly cold Christmas Eve. The prisoners had few clothes, little food, and barely one blanket each. They all missed their families and turned to listen to Aristar's story of Christ's birth for comfort.

Today in the town of David a Savior has been born to you; he is Christ the Lord.

Luke 2:11

He continued, "The light of the star must have been brighter than the moon. It may have shone through the stable's doorway and made the rooster crow announcing Christ's birth." The prisoners listened and wept. After the story, someone began to sing, gradually swelling to echo in the clear, crisp air. Everyone stopped to listen to the beautiful sound.

Even in the harsh prison, the story of Christ's gift warmed the hearts of many. Because Christ is the foundation, one can never lock out the spirit of Christmas.

Sure, Christmas is an annual celebration. Christmas is much more than that, however; it happens in the hearts of all people who stop to celebrate the magic of Christ's entry into the world—regardless of the season. The Christmas spirit of warmth shines into our darkest circumstances and reminds us of our hope in Christ. Regardless of whether or not we see snow on the ground, colored lights, and a decorated tree, we can celebrate Christmas. Whatever you're going through, Christ was born to help you in your time of need. His mercy extends all year long. When was the last time you felt the hope of Christ alive in your soul? Take time today to celebrate the birth of Christ—into your world and into your heart.

eXtreme makeover

EASTERN EUROPE: A CHRISTIAN PRISONER

The prisoner was brought before the deputy commander, a harsh, angry, red-faced woman with broad shoulders. "So, you have been speaking to the prisoners about God again. I am here to tell you it must stop!" Her face illustrated the rage in Communist prisons in Eastern Europe.

Day 361

You were taught, with regard to your former way of life, to put off your old self ... and to put on the new self, created to be like God in true righteousness and holiness.

Ephesians 4:22,24

The prisoner stood quietly but steadfastly. She informed the commander that nothing could stop her from speaking about her Savior.

The commander raised her fist to strike the prisoner, but suddenly stopped. "What are you smiling about?" she demanded.

"I am smiling because of what I see in your eyes."

"And what is that?"

"Myself. I used to be quite impulsive, too. I was angry and used to strike out until I learned what it really means to love. Since then, my hands do not clench into fists anymore."

She continued, "If you look into my eyes, you will see yourself as only God could make you, just as He did with me." The prisoner could see how her former self might have defended her rights, returning insult for insult. However, because of her new life in Christ, she showed only kindness and gained the right to continue her witness.

The commander's hands dropped to her sides. She seemed completely stunned and said quietly, "Go away."

The prisoner continued to witness for Christ throughout the prison, with no more interference from the deputy commander.

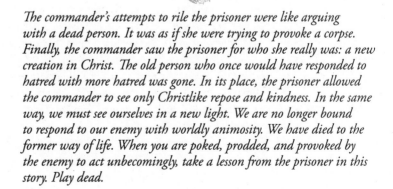

The commander's attempts to rile the prisoner were like arguing with a dead person. It was as if she were trying to provoke a corpse. Finally, the commander saw the prisoner for who she really was: a new creation in Christ. The old person who once would have responded to hatred with more hatred was gone. In its place, the prisoner allowed the commander to see only Christlike repose and kindness. In the same way, we must see ourselves in a new light. We are no longer bound to respond to our enemy with worldly animosity. We have died to the former way of life. When you are poked, prodded, and provoked by the enemy to act unbecomingly, take a lesson from the prisoner in this story. Play dead.

eXtreme river crossing

Brother Ho was sick and running a fever when he and his friend stepped into the icy waters of the Mekong River. They were Bible students in Laos before the Communist soldiers overran their college.

Day 362

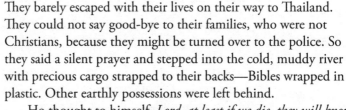

See how I love your precepts; preserve my life, O Lᴏʀᴅ, according to your love.

Psalm 119:159

They barely escaped with their lives on their way to Thailand. They could not say good-bye to their families, who were not Christians, because they might be turned over to the police. So they said a silent prayer and stepped into the cold, muddy river with precious cargo strapped to their backs—Bibles wrapped in plastic. Other earthly possessions were left behind.

Ho thought to himself, *Lord, at least if we die, they will know we are Christians and hopefully read one of these Bibles.*

About halfway across the river, Ho's friend desperately shifted the plastic bag under his chest to float on it. The sudden splashing noise alerted the guards in a nearby tower, and they shined a spotlight onto the river. The light flashed over one of the plastic bundles and the guard dismissed it as just a fish.

Relieved, Ho and his friend quietly made their way to the Thailand side of the river. They thanked God that their Bibles contained the words of eternal life and had also saved their lives that night. After arriving to safety, they dedicated themselves to ministering in the many refugee camps of Thailand.

The missionaries in this story were relying on more than paper and leather binding to save them. They relied on God. Still, their midnight river crossing gives us an accurate picture of the role the Bible should play in our lives. We are to rely on God's Word as if our very lives depended on it. We are unlikely to find ourselves in a situation where this truth becomes a literal reality. However, the illustration is valid. We must cling to the promises of Scripture to preserve our lives. When we are in trouble, we cannot swim far enough on our own to get us out of a mess. We must "float" on God's Word, or we will altogether sink.

eXtreme temptation

ROMANIA: SABINA WURMBRAND

In all the years of their marriage, Sabina Wurmbrand had never wavered in her love for her husband. But it had been many years since she had heard news of him in prison. There were even rumors that he had perished, but she felt God telling her to hold on and believe. Would they be together again someday?

Day 363

It always protects, always trusts, always hopes, always perseveres. Love never fails.

1 Corinthians 13:7,8

Sabina was still young, and, with a teenage son to raise, she often felt the temptation for love and companionship. So when a kind, handsome Christian named Paul started coming and helping her son with his studies, it was only natural that she should feel attracted. Sometimes he would take her hand as they walked together or look longingly into her eyes.

Finally, Sabina made the most difficult decision. She knew that if she were to continue believing that she would be reunited with her husband, she must avoid all temptations and focus on God's promise to her. She asked Paul not to come around anymore. He understood and graciously complied.

A short time later, God rewarded her faithfulness. One morning while she was in the church scrubbing floors, she received a postcard. It was signed "Vasile Georgescu," but her husband's handwriting was unmistakable.

Her eyes filled with tears as she read, "Time and distance quench a small love, but make a great love grow stronger."

The stories of the persecuted church are about real people with real emotions. The protagonists in these short stories are not some paper doll pinups of perfection. The Voice of the Martyrs is the unmistakable voice of reality and truth. Sabina maneuvered through temptations that came as a result of her husband's persecution. Her husband was being tested, yes. But her faith was also being examined as well. Persecution touches us at a variety of levels. Yet as we have seen, those who for a short while are gathered up in its exacting grasp end up strangely stronger as a result. Like the Wurmbrands, your capacity for love will increase through persecution—if only you will allow it to fulfill its true purpose.

Day 364

If you have vision, nothing will frighten you.
With His vision, God gives you power.
You must not be afraid.

IRANIAN PASTOR

eXtreme teenager

Tara was a seventh grader in Pakistan when she secretly enrolled in a Bible correspondence course to learn more about God. Her strict Muslim family would never answer her questions about Jesus, and she was determined to find out the truth on her own.

Day 365

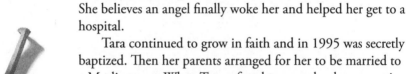

And everyone who has left houses or brothers or sisters or father or mother or children or fields for my sake will receive a hundred times as much and will inherit eternal life.

Matthew 19:29

But when her parents found her in her room reading Christian books, they became enraged. In November 1992, they beat her so severely that she lay unconscious in her room for almost a week. She believes an angel finally woke her and helped her get to a hospital.

Tara continued to grow in faith and in 1995 was secretly baptized. Then her parents arranged for her to be married to a Muslim man. When Tara refused to comply, she was again beaten. She was also made to stand for several days without sleep. During this time, Tara had three visions in which she heard a voice telling her, "I am with you. I am your Father."

After more beatings, she fell into a coma. She awoke after three days and found herself in a pool of blood. She again heard the same encouraging voice saying, "I am your Father. I will protect you."

Tara was able to escape and today lives in a safe house in another country where she serves the Lord full-time with the promise of God's protection.

Is Christianity a losing proposition? Those in restricted nations know what it is like to lose because of their faith in Christ. They know how they can lose their families in a number of ways. A Muslim family might completely reject converted family members as infidels. They are outcasts. A Christian family fares no better, though under different terms. Extremists wipe out entire Christian families because of their faith. The loss is horrendous. However, we have Christ's promise. Whatever we may lose for His sake will be recouped one hundred times over in our eternal life in heaven. It is not a gamble. It is a calculated risk based on the infallible Word of God. Either you trust it, or you do not.

Topic Index

Scripture Index

Matthew 5:43,44 (18)
Matthew 6:12 (10)
Matthew 6:15 (293)
Matthew 6:34 (313)
Matthew 7:7 (310)
Matthew 7:16,17 (230)
Matthew 9:36 (234)
Matthew 9:37,38 (232)
Matthew 10:16 (237)
Matthew 10:28 (222)
Matthew 10:32 (41)
Matthew 11:29 (69)
Matthew 11:30 (195)
Matthew 12:30 (46)
Matthew 13:23 (88)
Matthew 17:20 (94)
Matthew 18:3 (82, 291)
Matthew 19:29 (365)
Matthew 20:26 (193)
Matthew 28:18,19 (185)

Mark 3:35 (276)
Mark 4:22 (85)
Mark 8:35 (304)
Mark 10:15 (75)

Luke 1:38 (177)
Luke 2:11 (360)
Luke 6:22 (142)
Luke 6:27 (179)
Luke 6:27,28 (351)
Luke 6:35 (11, 139)
Luke 6:37 (204)
Luke 8:17 (282)
Luke 12:15 (24)
Luke 21:14,15 (354)
Luke 21:17–19 (316)
Luke 21:34 (136)

John 3:16 (99, 208)
John 3:30 (249)
John 4:35 (144)
John 6:68 (311)

John 7:17 (97)
John 8:32 (81)
John 9:4 (183)
John 10:10 (264)
John 12:19 (345)
John 12:21 (331)
John 12:32 (40)
John 13:7 (358)
John 14:6 (269)
John 14:23 (274)
John 15:13 (135)
John 16:22 (218)
John 21:19 (156)

Acts 1:8 (38, 240)
Acts 4:13 (268)
Acts 4:19 (283)
Acts 4:20 (286)
Acts 4:29 (71)
Acts 5:29 (22)
Acts 6:7 (124)
Acts 9:11 (5)
Acts 16:34 (285)
Acts 20:24 (248)

Romans 1:11,12 (48)
Romans 1:16 (93)
Romans 1:25 (277)
Romans 2:4 (74)
Romans 3:19 (250)
Romans 5:3,4 (225)
Romans 5:3–5 (53)
Romans 5:8 (263)
Romans 6:23 (235)
Romans 8:5 (87)
Romans 8:28 (244)
Romans 8:35 (15, 257)
Romans 8:37 (153)
Romans 8:38,39 (164)
Romans 10:14 (162)
Romans 10:17 (209)
Romans 12:1 (16)
Romans 12:12 (207)

Romans 13:1 (254)
Romans 14:4 (299)
Romans 14:12 (229)
Romans 15:19 (31)
Romans 16:20 (300)

1 Corinthians 1:18 (226)
1 Corinthians 2:1 (227)
1 Corinthians 3:6,7 (261)
1 Corinthians 7:23 (160)
1 Corinthians 9:22 (191)
1 Corinthians 11:1 (79)
1 Corinthians 13:7,8 (363)
1 Corinthians 13:13 (89)
1 Corinthians 15:42 (65)
1 Corinthians 15:55 (45)
1 Corinthians 15:57 (347)

2 Corinthians 1:21 (246)
2 Corinthians 3:3 (171)
2 Corinthians 3:4 (86)
2 Corinthians 4:7 (213)
2 Corinthians 4:10,11 (214)
2 Corinthians 4:17 (180)
2 Corinthians 4:18 (335)
2 Corinthians 5:13 (199)
2 Corinthians 5:17 (58)
2 Corinthians 6:4,10 (243)
2 Corinthians 6:16 (321)
2 Corinthians 7:4 (150)
2 Corinthians 7:9 (104)
2 Corinthians 7:10 (318)
2 Corinthians 11:14,15 (255)
2 Corinthians 12:9 (54, 148)

Galatians 2:20 (236)
Galatians 6:14 (114)

Ephesians 1:18 (52)
Ephesians 2:10 (352)
Ephesians 3:1 (256)
Ephesians 3:13 (348)
Ephesians 3:20 (333)

Ephesians 4:22,24 (361)
Ephesians 4:22–24 (194)
Ephesians 4:32 (121)
Ephesians 5:1 (306)
Ephesians 6:7 (130)
Ephesians 6:11 (169)
Ephesians 6:12 (129)
Ephesians 6:16 (122)
Ephesians 6:17 (317)
Ephesians 6:18 (279)
Ephesians 6:19,20 (1)

Philippians 1:3 (34, 132)
Philippians 1:6 (29, 211)
Philippians 1:12 (60)
Philippians 1:21 (27)
Philippians 2:1,2 (90)
Philippians 2:5 (67)
Philippians 2:13 (33)
Philippians 2:15 (125)
Philippians 2:17 (103)
Philippians 3:7 (96)
Philippians 3:8 (344)
Philippians 3:10 (61)
Philippians 3:18 (57, 341)
Philippians 4:7 (174, 339)
Philippians 4:11 (178, 190)
Philippians 4:19 (298)

Colossians 1:6 (145)
Colossians 1:11 (270)
Colossians 1:11,12 (262)
Colossians 1:23 (197)
Colossians 1:29 (23)
Colossians 2:2 (2)
Colossians 3:2 (115)
Colossians 3:12 (146)
Colossians 3:13 (73, 106)
Colossians 3:17 (117)
Colossians 4:2 (355)
Colossians 4:5 (123, 215)

1 Thessalonians 1:3 (151, 297)

Resources

The Voice of the Martyrs has many books, videos, brochures, and other products to help you learn more about the persecuted church. In the US, to order materials or receive our free monthly newsletter, call (800) 747-0085 or write to:

The Voice of the Martyrs
1815 SE Bison Rd.
Bartlesville, OK 74006
persecution.com
thevoice@vom.org

If you are in Canada, England, Australia, New Zealand, or South Africa, contact:

The Voice of the Martyrs
P.O. Box 608
Streetsville, Ontario L5M 2C1
Canada
Website: vomcanada.com

Release International
P.O. Box 54
Orpington BR5 4RT
United Kingdom
Website: releaseinternational.org

The Voice of the Martyrs
P.O. Box 250
Lawson NSW 2783
Australia
Website: vom.com.au

The Voice of the Martyrs
P.O. Box 5482
Papanui, Christchurch 8542
New Zealand
Website: vom.org.nz

Christian Mission International
P.O. Box 7157
1417 Primrose Hill
South Africa
Website: persecution.co.za

About The Voice of the Martyrs

Serving the persecuted church since 1967

The Voice of the Martyrs is a non-profit, interdenominational organization dedicated to assisting the persecuted church worldwide. VOM was founded by Pastor Richard Wurmbrand, who was imprisoned in Communist Romania for fourteen years for his faith in Jesus Christ. His wife, Sabina, was imprisoned for three years. In the 1960s Richard, Sabina, and their son, Mihai, were ransomed out of Romania and came to the United States. Through their travels, the Wurmbrands told the stories of the atrocities Christians face in restricted nations and established a network of offices dedicated to assisting the persecuted church. The Voice of the Martyrs continues in this mission around the world today through its five main purposes:

1. To encourage and empower Christians to fulfill the Great Commission in areas of the world where they are persecuted for sharing the gospel of Jesus Christ.

2. To provide practical relief and spiritual support to the families of Christian martyrs.

3. To equip persecuted Christians to love and win to Christ those who are opposed to the gospel in their part of the world.

4. To undertake projects of encouragement, helping believers rebuild their lives and Christian witness in countries where they have formerly suffered oppression.

5. To promote the fellowship of all believers by informing the world of the faith and courage of persecuted Christians, thereby inspiring believers to a deeper level of commitment to Christ and involvement in His Great Commission.